CONSTRUCTING THE IMAGE OF
THE MEXICAN REVOLUTION

Constructing the Image of the Mexican Revolution

CINEMA AND THE ARCHIVE

ZUZANA M. PICK

UNIVERSITY OF TEXAS PRESS
Austin

Copyright © 2010 by the University of Texas Press
All rights reserved
Printed in the United States of America
First edition, 2010

Requests for permission to reproduce material from this work should be sent to:
  Permissions
  University of Texas Press
  P.O. Box 7819
  Austin, TX 78713-7819
  www.utexas.edu/utpress/about/bpermission.html

♾ The paper used in this book meets the minimum requirements of ANSI/NISO Z39.48-1992 (R1997) (Permanence of Paper).

LIBRARY OF CONGRESS CATALOGING-IN-PUBLICATION DATA

Pick, Zuzana M.
Constructing the image of the Mexican Revolution : cinema and the archive / Zuzana M. Pick. — 1st ed.
    p. cm.
Includes bibliographical references and index.
ISBN 978-0-292-72562-1
 1. Mexico—History—Revolution, 1910–1920—Motion pictures and the revolution. 2. War films—Mexico—History and criticism. I. Title.
F1234.P55 2010
791.43′658—dc22
                                                                2009024825

*To Leutén, Simone, and Patricia
for their unconditional backing, patience, and complicity*

Contents

ACKNOWLEDGMENTS ix

INTRODUCTION. VISUALIZING AND ROMANCING
THE REVOLUTION 1

Chapter 1
THE REVOLUTION AS MEDIA EVENT:
DOCUMENTARY IMAGE AND THE ARCHIVE 11

Chapter 2
HISTORICITY AND THE ARCHIVE:
RECONSTRUCTION AND APPROPRIATION 39

Chapter 3
PANCHO VILLA ON TWO SIDES OF THE BORDER 69

Chapter 4
AVANT-GARDE GESTURES AND NATIONALIST
IMAGES OF MEXICO IN EISENSTEIN'S
UNFINISHED PROJECT 97

Chapter 5
RECONFIGURING THE REVOLUTION: CELEBRITY
AND MELODRAMA 125

Chapter 6
THE AESTHETICS OF SPECTACLE 145

Chapter 7
COMPETING NARRATIVES AND
CONVERGING VISIONS 176

CONCLUSION. THOUGHTS ON WORKING
WITH THE ARCHIVE   209

NOTES   219

BIBLIOGRAPHY   231

INDEX   243

Acknowledgments

Research funding and academic leave to prepare the manuscript was made possible by a grant from the Social Sciences and Humanities Research Council (SSHRC) and the Marston Lafrance Fellowship of Carleton University. SSHRC's financial support enabled me to disseminate the preliminary results of the work done on this project in Mexico, Canada, and the United States. The feedback I received at conference presentations, lectures, and seminars was extremely rewarding. During the completion stage, I received additional funding from John Osborne, dean of the Faculty of Arts and Social Sciences, Carleton University.

First and foremost, I want to thank Gary Cristall. Without his knowledge and magnificent library, this project would not have been formulated. My gratitude also goes to Julianne Burton-Carvajal, Elisa Cárdenas Ayala, Valdeen Ciwko, Federico Dávalos, Aurelio de los Reyes, Michael Dorland, Chris Faulkner, Elena Feder, Alberto Fierro, Barbara Gabriel, Esperanza Garrido, Bryan Gillingham, Brenda Longfellow, Mark Langer, André Loiselle, George McKnight, Eugenia Meyer, Ángel Miquel, Enrique Ortiga, Paulo-Antonio Paranaguá, Francisco Peredo Castro, Patricia Torres San Martín, Gregorio Rocha, Paul Théberge, Eduardo de la Vega Alfaro, and Marta Vidrio, scholars, colleagues, and friends, for their generosity, encouragement during various stages of the project, and willingness to play a part in carrying it out. Most of all, I want to acknowledge the attentive and courteous response to the manuscript from my readers, Marvin d'Lugo and Sergio de la Mora.

My appreciation goes to José Sánchez Mosquera, Carmen Fernández del Rio, and Anthony de Mello, for assisting with the research; Julio Valdés, for helping me to finalize the manuscript; Peter Harcourt, for introducing me to the wonders of image technology; Barbara Stevenson, Nancy Duff, Paul Shannon, and Jessica Stewart, at the Audio-Visual Research Centre; Jack Coghill, at the School for Studies in Art and Culture, Carleton University; and Simone Rojas-Pick, for lending a hand with the illustrations. My special thanks go to Víctor Urruchúa for guiding me around Mexico

City, facilitating contacts with individuals and institutions, taking notes, keeping track of a multitude of details, and helping with securing permissions. With Margarita, Víctor made all my visits seem like holidays.

In Mexico, I received invaluable assistance from Gabriel Figueroa Flores, Iván Trujillo (director), Omar Marín (academic extension), and Antonia Rojas Ávila (photos and posters) at the Filmoteca of the Autonomous University of Mexico (UNAM); Marcela Zuñiga, Ramón Gil Olivo and Rocío Pérez at the Centro de Investigación y Estudios Cinematográficos (CIEC) of the University of Guadalajara; Alejandra Moreno Toscano (director), Silvia Manuel Signoret, and Renán Bedersky at the Archivo Toscano; Gabriela Nuñez at the Fototeca INAH in Mexico City; and Leticia Medina at the Fondo Juan Barragán, CESU-AHUNAM. I am grateful also to Olinca Fernández Ledesma Villaseñor and Clemente V. Orozco in Guadalajara for graciously granting reproduction rights. In the United States, I benefited from the services provided by Priscilla Pineda, Border Heritage Center, El Paso Public Library; Patricia H. Worthington, El Paso County Historical Society; Claudia A. Rivers, Special Collections, University of Texas at El Paso; and Valerie Coleman, Cushing Memorial Library and Archives, Texas A&M University. Last but not least, I want to acknowledge the patience, advice, and support of Jim Burr, humanities editor, and his team at the University of Texas Press, especially Lynne Chapman.

Introduction
VISUALIZING AND ROMANCING THE REVOLUTION

This book is an investigation of the ways in which the cinema participated in the visual constructions of the Mexican Revolution and the processes that shaped and contributed to the dissemination of these constructions on film since the 1930s in Mexico and internationally. It highlights the convergence between film and other visual media, including photography, painting, and graphic arts, to explain the significance of visual technologies in the twentieth century and their mediating role in the forging of the collective memories of a nation.

The basic framework of the narrative is the widespread uprising against the regime of President Porfirio Díaz that began in 1910 and the protracted struggle for power that involved the various political and military forces that initially rallied around Francisco I. Madero. While the Mexican people are the protagonists, the narrative singles out such legendary figures as Madero, Pancho Villa, and Emiliano Zapata rather than the countless anonymous men and women — peasants, workers, and Indians — who participated in the revolution. Its subject matter involves popular insurrections and mass mobilizations; anti-insurgency and pacification operations led by government and revolutionary troops under the command of such disparate leaders as Pascual Orozco, Victoriano Huerta, Venustiano Carranza, and Alvaro Obregón; and peace treaties signed between warring factions but never enforced. The battles that produced one million dead in a total population of fifteen million, the insecurity in rural areas, and the loss of property that displaced entire populations within Mexico and across the border into the United States give a social dimension to the revolutionary scenario. The implementation of revolutionary principles, hampered by the opposing agendas of a peasantry fighting for land, a middle class bent on participating in the political process, and a bourgeoisie determined to preserve past privileges, and the ultimate victory of the last two sectors, furnish this narrative with a political, mostly mystifying but sometimes critical perspective.

As the Mexican historian Enrique Florescano has written, the revolution exceeds events and personalities. In his words, "It is not just a series of historical acts that took place between 1910 and 1917, or between 1910 and 1920, or between 1910 and 1940; it is also the collection of projections, symbols, evocations, images, and myths that its participants, interpreters, and heirs forged and continue to construct around this event" (quoted in Mraz, 1997a, 93). Florescano's statement provides the critical framework for this book. It suggests the need to include visual production in the study of historical representations and cultural stereotypes and to examine the mass-mediated features and multiple uses of the imagery of the revolution. The story of the Mexican Revolution that emerged is particularly complex because it transpired on an international, as well as national, field of mass production of modernity. This overdetermined set of conditions means that I am looking at the issues of cultural exchange, translation, appropriation, and commodification, which enables me to negotiate the tensions between the cross-cultural and transnational dimensions of the imagery and its nationalist projections within the modernist and contemporary historiography of Mexico.

My objective is to map the ways in which the meanings surrounding the revolution have been historicized by films that themselves participated in a wider visual field. I draw attention to the formative and ongoing impact of the imagery produced during the revolution. The modes of representation and spectatorship generated by this imagery were invested with a wide range of meanings regarding how the revolution was experienced by those who participated in and recorded it. This imagery constitutes the visual vernacular of Mexican modernity. It articulates a modernist awareness of the role of images in documenting the dynamics of social and cultural change, constructing a collective imaginary out of multiple identities and experiences. How this awareness was preserved and reconstructed is best exemplified in *Memories of a Mexican* (Carmen Toscano de Moreno Sánchez, 1950) and *Epics of the Mexican Revolution* (Gustavo Carrera, 1963), compilation documentaries consisting primarily of footage shot and collected by Mexico's prominent film pioneers, Salvador Toscano and Jesús H. Abitía, respectively. Media awareness extended across the border into the United States by means of the photographs and weekly newsreels that supplemented journalistic dispatches from the war front, as well as the nascent picture postcard business. As the Mexican film historian Aurelio de los Reyes notes, "Between 1911 and 1920 over 80 American cameramen working either freelance or for various film companies covered the Mexican revolution from the viewpoints of different groups" (2001a, 36). Concurrently public interest and profit drove the production of fiction films in which narratives of bravery and betrayal predominate and democratic values inevitably triumph over brutality. Incidents of violence set in picturesque "Mexico"—California as a stand-in for actual locations—pit American characters against Mexican *insurrectos* who look and behave like the "greaser" bandits of the pulp fiction that emerged in the wake of the Mexican-American War of 1846–1847. The above-mentioned films, as well as *And Starring Pancho Villa as Himself* and *The Lost Reels of Pancho Villa*, corroborate to what extent the allure of this history has not subsided.

In the postrevolutionary period the vernacular constructed during the protracted military and political struggle was reintegrated with historical forms of visualizing Mexican culture and identity to consolidate an official state discourse and project a renewed nationalist and modernist image of Mexico at home and abroad. Initially the revolution vanished from the screens. Embargoes of films considered denigrating to Mexico's image and fears of losing a profitable market south of the border forced Hollywood to abandon the theme. At home, war fatigue and official concerns that films dealing with the conflict would reinforce negative views of the country led national producers in the 1920s to opt for a folkloric and sanitized representation. "Although actuality films that focused on the conflict disappeared prematurely," the British visual culture scholar Andrea Noble writes, "this did not, and indeed within the terms of reference that governed the post-revolutionary state's legitimacy, *could* not spell the disappearance of the revolution from the nation's (audio) visual imaginary altogether" (2005, 53; original emphasis). The theme returned in the early years of the sound period, first implicitly in the Soviet filmmaker Sergei M. Eisenstein's unfinished project, *Que Viva Mexico!* (1930–1931, 1979), and later in three features directed by the Mexican Fernando de Fuentes, *El prisionero trece* (The Prisoner 13) and *El compadre Mendoza* (Compadre Mendoza), both from 1933, and *¡Vámonos con Pancho Villa!* (Let's Go with Pancho Villa!), released in 1935. Whereas the distinctive trait of this trilogy was its critical approach, the majority of national and foreign films represented the revolution as a "spectacular 'folk-show'" (De la Mora, 2006, 143). *El tesoro de Pancho Villa* (The Treasure of Pancho Villa) (Arcady Boytler, Mexico, 1935), *La Adelita* (Guillermo Hernández Gómez, Mexico, 1937), and *Viva Villa!* (Jack Conway, U.S., 1933) are examples.

The genre was briefly revitalized during what is commonly known as the golden age of Mexican cinema. Melodrama, star power, and patriotic sentiment coalesced in the films of Emilio "El Indio" Fernández. Starting with *Flor silvestre* (Wildflower) (1943)—and thanks to the artful cinematography of Gabriel Figueroa—the revolutionary scenario was the catalyst for a modernist reconfiguration of the visual archive. Since didacticism, rather than history, was the impulse behind the director's work and mediocre imitations undermined the aesthetic inventiveness of the cinematographer's style, the genre reverted to picturesque stereotypes. Films such as *Pancho Villa vuelve* (Pancho Villa Returns) (Miguel Contrera Torres, 1949) and *Vino el remolino y nos alevantó* (The Whirlwind Came and Swept Us Away) (Juan Bustillo Oro, 1949) cashed in on the popularity of the legendary leader and the *corridos* (ballads) recounting the heroic deeds and tragic deaths of chieftains and common soldiers. Yet a few other films made during this decade managed, in imperfect and sometimes surprising ways, to reflect on the revolution as a disruptive and contradictory event. Notable are the literary adaptations *Los de abajo* (The Underdogs) (Chano Urueta, 1939), *Rosenda* (Julio Bracho, 1948), and *La negra Angustias* (Matilde Landeta, 1949).

Regardless of their literary and generic affiliations, commercial and political agendas, and countries of origin, these films exemplify the enduring allure of the revolution as a scenario and its diverse actors as catalysts for heroic tales of conflict, betrayal, justice, and redemption. More significantly, these films are symptomatic of the multiple ways in which the visual archive of the revolution has been appropriated, translated, and reconfigured internationally, as well as nationally, since the 1930s. Seen from this perspective, the cinematic uses of Mexico by foreign directors in the 1950s and 1960s are the result of a series of conversations across cultures that were initiated by Eisenstein's unfinished project and expanded in the next decade across a range of production practices, genres, and nationalities. The primary agent of these conversations is Figueroa, a cinematographer who managed to negotiate the avant-garde inclinations of modernism and the industrial imperatives of mainstream filmmaking. Formed in the international context of cinema, yet ideally positioned as a Mexican, he was best suited as an interlocutor for that dialogue. At the conclusion of this study, I return to the ramifications of the genealogy of that dialogue as it reinforces certain aspects of the transnational dynamics of the archive.

The formative role that autochthonous and foreign elements have played in the construction and consolidation of the imagery of the Mexican Revolution is acknowledged in this book's emphasis on the cultural mediation and translation process characteristic of modernism and globalization. Since the visual construction of the revolution was taken up by both Mexican and international agents, this book takes a cross-cultural, interdisciplinary, and comparative approach to highlight the uses to which this vast visual archive has been put. My close analysis of selected films reads Mexican iconic images and visual themes with and against their international counterparts. Of necessity, it also takes into account structural conditions of production and reception. Yet if these films and their mass media counterparts of the period produced the image repertoire of a new event, their rhetoric was anything but altogether new. In fact, it often played on existing nationalist images or alternatively on folkloric motifs designed for export. I argue, then, that the transformation of traditional images into nationalist icons in the postrevolutionary period is evidence that Mexican modernism, rather than an absolute break, involves a cultural and discursive rearrangement of the already existing visual signifiers of nation, identity, and modernity.

What makes this book different is my critical and analytical approach. The detailed study of individual films aims to overcome the limitations of reductive treatments of historical cinema. As I argue, historicity is shaped by the interrelation of aesthetic and discursive elements rather than exclusively by textual narrative. By reexamining the cultural, political, and social factors that have enabled and mediated the circulation of iconic images and visual themes, I wish to encourage alternative readings. Moreover, I incorporate spectatorship into my inquiry into the historicity of film—spectatorship understood here as enabling complex, dynamic, and open-ended interactions between audiences and spectacle and cultural identity, and the images and realities shown on the screen. The production of viewing positions (gender, class, and ethnicity) is as important to visual construction as mass-mediated technologies of vision to the making of the subject of modernity. In Mexico, spectatorship and image making are irrevocably tied to *mexicanidad*—a powerful trope designating at once a search for authenticity and a fashioning of an identity capable of accommodating the multiple, even conflicting features that make up the national imaginary. From this perspective, this book sheds light on the unstable and diverse meanings and responses elicited by iconic images and visual themes instead of reducing Mexican films to reified and totalizing reproductions of postrevolutionary discourse and foreign films to demeaning or at best patronizing representations of the other. Finally, I believe that the value of this book is its potential to intervene in current discussions on modernity, which have largely rested on European conditions and models. By reading a cataclysmic twentieth-century event against the growth of an unprecedented mass-mediated modernity, I hope to contribute to a more inclusive understanding of "other" modernities.

Questions arising from how the Mexican Revolution was visualized are examined in the early chapters, with particular emphasis on the documentary image as a record of public history and as an archival artifact to be reconstructed and appropriated. Chapter 1 deals with Mexican materials filmed in the period 1910–1917 and the challenges compilation films pose to the historicity of documentary images. It discusses *Epics of the Mexican Revolution* and *Memories of a Mexican*, whose intent, as the titles indicate, is commemorative. While these films present a photogenic version of national history and revolutionary mythology, they also offer a unique chronicle of the revolution. Their remarkable imagery is a testimony to the social violence and political chaos and their producers' and actors' awareness of being agents in the recording of actions at once newsworthy and explanatory of a historical process. Of the numerous Mexican cameramen who documented the revolution, Abitía was the only one who worked in both film and photography. Images referring to the same events integrate the observer in an organic manner, with the filmmaker-photographer determining the camera's point of view, the participant as actor or internal audience, and the viewing public as historical agent. The broad chronological scope of the footage in *Memories of a Mexican* reveals how events, places, and personalities were organized into a compelling story whose power derives from a compulsion to turn the newsworthy instant into a memorable visual archive of Mexico's modern history.

The archival value of U.S.-produced period images is discussed in chapter 2. Massively reproduced and marketed as news items and novelties, film stills, press photographs, and postcards have since become an obligatory source for fiction films on the revolution. What the contract signed in January 1914 between Villa and the Mutual Film Company has come to mean is the subject of *And Starring Pancho Villa as Himself* and *The Lost Reels of Pancho Villa*, both of which engage with the visual themes generated by the contract by using the extant archive and current historiography to tell the story of the now-lost film, *The Life of General Villa*. The American film reconstructs anecdotes of the deal, replicates early silent film practices, and points to historical models of spectatorship linking vision and identity. Even if the meanings of the deal are relocated, at the end, into current concerns on media politics and war reporting, what emerges is a multilayered representation of Villa as a mass-mediated construct.

The Lost Reels of Pancho Villa is an experimental work about the Mexican film and video maker's quest for the missing film. It investigates mainly U.S. visual materials on Villa found in European and North American archives, including those that reconfigured him as the archetypal Mexican bandit after the Columbus raid in 1916. It explores the story of *The Vengeance of Pancho Villa,* a film using different footage assembled in the 1920s by the Mexican American itinerant exhibitors Félix and Edmundo Padilla from El Paso, Texas. Characters and events are represented as cultural and social projections, their agencies unstable and contingent on the material frailty of the archive. What is more, reassemblages of extant footage point to the film's strategies of reclamation aimed at reimagining Villa's subjectivity and cinematic identity as a Mexican hero.

Awareness of the power of visual media discussed in chapters 1 and 2 extends to feature films produced in the 1930s. Yet the vast visual archive generated by the fascination with Villa reveals how the American public continued to view Mexico through the prism of a long-standing history of prejudice. By making light of the revolutionary leader's transformation into a subject of his own history, feature films during this period turned him into a commodity deprived of social agency and burdened by mythology. Whether constructed during his lifetime, with Villa as an active agent, or retrospectively by numerous others, legend is key to Villa's enduring mythology and his representations on film abroad and at home. The combined power of and inconsistencies within the legend are discussed in chapter 3. *Viva Villa!* and *¡Vámonos con Pancho Villa!* were produced one decade after Villa's assassination in 1923.

In both, the aesthetic and discursive resources of cinema are used to mediate the visual themes that turned Villa into a cinematic hero. Depictions of brutality, heroism, and victimization point to the affective and perceptual disparities of the responses elicited by Villa in both countries. Shifts between epic spectacle, comedy, and melodrama in *Viva Villa!* reinforce these disparities and reveal Hollywood's inability to overcome historical attitudes. Conversely, affective and perceptual disparities shape the critical scrutiny of the themes of bravery and loyalty in the Villa legend in *¡Vámonos con Pancho Villa!* This film draws attention to the mediated features of the revolutionary leader's cinematographic and historical persona. It capitalizes on the public familiarity with *charrería* culture and performance (the historical hacienda traditions and values that were integrated into the nationalist tableau of identity in the 1920s) to counter the reified representations of male bravery and sacrifice promoted by postrevolutionary discourse. Thus it took almost three decades for the demystifying and antiheroic perspective of the film to be fully appreciated.

Chapter 4 considers the complex and diverse ways in which images of Mexico and the revolution were constructed and negotiated in the postrevolutionary period, by Mexicans and foreigners alike. *Desastre en Oaxaca* (Disaster in Oaxaca), a short documentary filmed and edited by Eisenstein in January 1930, exemplifies his goal of turning his impressions as a traveler into an investigation of the country's contrasting realities and histories. The extant footage, production stills, photographs, and drawings relative to what is known as the "Maguey" episode of *Que Viva Mexico!* are indicative of Eisenstein's engagement with the political and artistic practices of the Mexican vanguard. Hence I consider the influence of Anita Brenner's book *Idols behind Altars* and *indigenismo* on the visual reconfiguration of the Indian in the nationalist narrative. Affinities with the visual practices and culture of the time—those that can be gleaned from the artist Isabel Villaseñor's participation and the representation of the hacienda and the *charro*—demonstrate the assimilation on the director's part of vernacular forms and his critical perspective on the national reconciliation rhetoric promoted by the state respectively.

Chapter 5 charts the convergences between the cinematic revival of the revolutionary theme and the nation-building agenda of the Mexican state. Though only a handful of the films produced during the golden age of Mexican cinema avoided the totalizing tendencies of official historiography, they played a fundamental role in integrating the visual archive of the revolution into popular culture. The aesthetic and narrative protocols of fictional filmmaking were used to reconfigure character types, landscapes, and episodes. Far from being homogenous, these fictional representations reveal both the aesthetic wealth of iconic images and visual themes and the incongruities of their overdetermined meanings. *Abandoned Women* may be the most overlooked of the Fernández-Figueroa films produced in the 1940s. Yet it is a complex and idiosyncratic work that expands the historicity and iconography of revolutionary melodrama. With the city as a backdrop to visualize the precarious place of women in the modernist scenario, the film makes the most of star identification and melodrama to represent the tension between social reality and discourse. If famed actors Dolores del Río and Pedro Armendáriz are turned into gendered models and icons of Mexico's renewed nationalism, their identities are unstable and contingent on the dual protocols of degradation and redemption in melodrama. Moreover, the urban setting and the presence of the prostitute-mother in *Abandoned Women* anticipate the decline of the revolutionary genre.

Chapter 6 addresses the relationship between spectacle and overdetermined visual icons. As the golden age was coming to a close, films dealing with the revolution aligned the representation of this momentous event and the agents who participated in it with the state's promotion of history as patrimony and the marketing of culture and identity as commodity. Historicity in *La escondida* (The Hidden One) (Roberto Galvadón, Mexico, 1956) is anchored in the affective power of modes of visualizing Mexico as at once picturesque and modern. Authenticity is repackaged by means of visual citations and pictorial embellishments that transform the revolution into a canvas of desire and abjection. The performance of nationalism and glamour of María Félix sustains the fetishism of spectacle. The tendency is to think about the use of Mexico and the revolution in *The Wild Bunch* (Sam Peckinpah, 1969) as a mere backdrop for an allegory on war and violence. Yet the film's powerful effect comes from its historicizing investment in the dynamics of looking and seeing and its reinscription of the Mexican subject into the mythological world of the western. As I argue, the vision of the revolution is closer to the fatalistic and tragic imagery of Orozco's lithographs and murals than to the heroic and utopian monumentality of the murals of Rivera and Siqueiros.

Chapter 7 deals with historicity in experimental films. The minimalist aesthetic and innovative use of sound in *Reed: Insurgent Mexico* (Paul Leduc, Mexico, 1971) demystifies the revolution, blending documentary and fictional elements in a manner that is consistent with the aesthetic and political strategies of the Cuban and New Latin American cinemas. War and death are deglamorized; desolation and loss resignify actions and landscapes. The film validates the American radical journalist John Reed's participation as a witness and narrator of the revolution and reclaims the stories, subjectivities, and sentiments concealed behind official history. Not only is Reed "Mexicanized" through actor Claudio Obregón's accent and performance; his subjectivity and agency are fused with the Mexican protagonists. *Tina in Mexico* (Brenda Longfellow, 2001) revisualizes the work and life of the Italian-born American photographer Tina Modotti. Archival footage, dramatic reenactments, and stylized citations are used to peel away the numerous layers of context inscribed in her photographs. The film reveals a subjectivity deeply affected by Mexico that responds to national myths and becomes its subject. To demonstrate how her identity merged with Mexico, the film reinscribes her into the history of Mexico City as an avant-garde center in the 1920s where the aesthetics of modernism converged with the politics of modernity.

In the conclusion I summarize the main themes and modes of representing Mexico and historicizing the revolution. I focus on the various ways in which the cinema has circulated the visual archive to document, celebrate, mythologize, and reinterpret anecdotes and characters. The deployment of period images of the revolution goes hand in hand with a reconversion of visual themes and motifs associated with picturesque modes of representing Mexico that originated in Mexico and abroad. This strategy is consistent at once with the nationalist agenda of the postrevolutionary state and the cultural politics of modernism and manifests itself through multiple mediations. As a result, the meanings that emerge from the use of the visual archive of the revolution in the films are unstable, always open to negotiation, reinterpretation, and revision.

Chapter 1

The Revolution as Media Event
DOCUMENTARY IMAGE AND THE ARCHIVE

Mexican revolutionary leaders granted access and integrated photographers and cameramen into their armies to record the campaigns. This access implied, as the advertisements for *The Fall of Ciudad Juárez and Trip of the Revolutionary Hero Francisco I. Madero* stated, that the images produced thereby "were the only authentic ones" (Miquel, 1997, 58). Whether or not these claims of authenticity were simply a publicity device, the presence of cameramen on trains carrying troops, on battlefields, and among crowds greeting the triumphant armies in cities transformed their understanding of the medium. As De los Reyes writes, "The revolution developed the visual-historical consciousness of film cameramen" ([1983] 1996, 118). Among these cameramen, most of them producers and exhibitors, were Salvador Toscano, Antonio Ocañas, Jesús H. Abitía, the Alva brothers (Salvador, Guillermo, Eduardo, and Carlos), Enrique Echáñiz Brust, Enrique Rosas, Julio Lamadrid, Guillermo Becerril, Carlos Mongard, José Cava, and Indalcio Noriega. Alongside the photographers, they put their craft at the service of the revolution, documenting it extensively and representing its epic dimensions. While their images were shaped by the chaotic conditions in which they labored, they organized incidents, landscapes, and actors into a broad narrative.

These images were disseminated in full-length films and were programmed on their own to the delight of audiences fascinated by the evolving albeit confusing political situation and the cameramen-exhibitors' intention of recouping the costs. As De los Reyes indicates, the revolution facilitated the development in Mexico of a singular mode of filmmaking whereby the "actualities" format was modified by adding a theatrical structure and arranging scenes into episodic segments ([1983] 1996, 118). This mode of filmmaking "attempted to communicate ideas and concepts with images taken from reality, to rise above the isolated scene, and later to narrate a story with those images" ([1983] 1996, 123). Favorable audience response and financial returns facilitated the release of updated and

FIGURE I.I. *"Cameramen filming a battle with artillery during the Revolution." Photograph, Casasola Archive, © CONACULTA-INAH-SINAFO-Fototeca Nacional, Mexico*

revised versions promising a complete history of the revolution that surpassed the journalistic and propaganda objectives of what became known at the time as the newsreel. Hence the documentary image was used as a tool of historiography.

The leading testimony on audience reactions to these films can be found in *The Eagle and the Serpent* (1928), a memoir written by the novelist, journalist, and occasional film critic Martín Luis Guzmán.[1] In the section titled "The Film of the Revolution," he describes the screening in October 1914 at the Teatro Morelos, where the Aguascalientes Convention was held. With the repeated appearances of Venustiano Carranza, former governor of the northern state of Coahuila, the discontent of the assembled delegates grew.

> The hisses mingled with applause that greeted him in his first appearances were turning into unalloyed hissing; and then into hissing that verged upon hooting; then into open booing; and finally into an uproar. Stage by stage, it reached its climax in the scene where Carranza was making his entry on horseback into Mexico City. At this point, it became a kind of hellish din that culminated in two shots. Both of them perforated the curtain at the height of the First Chief's breast,

and buried themselves in the wall, one half a yard above Lucio Blanco and another still closer, passing between Domínguez's head and mine. (1965, 291)

Although Guzmán fails to name the film being shown, it was most likely one of the many produced in that period showing "the achievements of the Revolution taken on location" (1965, 286). He indicates that it was presented by "one of the official photographers of the Constitutionalists," but he leaves unanswered the question of whether it was "Abitía in person, or one of his assistants or imitators" (1965, 286). With the struggle for power not yet resolved in favor of any single faction and Mexico sliding into outright anarchy, "nothing could have been more opportune at the hour of an appeal for unity than to bring before the eyes of the leaders of the dissident groups the sight of themselves, even though only on the screen, fighting together for the military and political cause whose scenes were recorded on the celluloid strip" (1965, 286). Aware of the value of cinema, the various military leaders sponsored the production and exhibition of documentaries aimed at publicizing their roles in meeting the goals of the revolution. Containing materials taken from previously released films and arranged in an anthology format, these documentaries visualized the revolution primarily as a series of political events and military parades. In addition to exalting the sponsors, the screenings served to reenergize the spectators, who identified with the mostly urban and jubilant crowds appearing on the screen, and became the occasion for acting out political allegiance or opposition.

This tendency to recycle footage had started during the early years of the revolution. It resulted in the production of updated versions intended, as their sweeping titles indicate, to give an overview of the revolution. As the Mexican film historian Ángel Miquel notes, the most notorious were produced and distributed by Toscano. In regard to *La Historia completa de la revolución mexicana de 1910 a 1912* (The Complete History of the Revolution from 1910 to 1912), he explains that the aim of these films was to "describe a historical process rather than make a news, actuality, or propaganda film" (1997, 63). Another one, titled *La Historia completa de la revolución mexicana de 1910 a 1915* (The Complete History of the Revolution from 1910 to 1915), made by Toscano in collaboration with Ocañas and Echáñiz Brust, included footage shot by other filmmakers to "complete and make more credible the process being narrated" (Miquel, 1997, 71). As Miquel indicates, this was a pro-Constitutionalist film celebrating the revolution as "glorious" and adopting the rhetorically charged label "traitor" for Victoriano Huerta and "apostle of the revolution" for Francisco I. Madero (1997, 71). Moreover, the producers were aware of the film's propaganda value. Toscano requested in a letter to Félix Palavicini, secretary of Public Instruction and Fine Arts, that military authorities facilitate its presentation to "counteract the effects produced by some of the denigrating American films as well as those produced by other factions, like the Villistas" (Miquel, 1997, 72).

Most of the films have been lost or damaged, and all that remains of what must have been a remarkable filmed record of the Mexican Revolution are fragments held in various, mostly private, archives and collections. Truncated, without intertitles or indications of provenance, these extant materials have been reedited for a variety of purposes and—in accordance with different political agendas—released as compilation films. One of these films is *Epopeyas de la revolución* (Epics of the Revolution). This documentary was produced on the fiftieth anniversary of the revolution and prior to the death of the filmmaker, photographer, and postcard maker from Chihuahua Jesús H. Abitía (1888–1960), who also made violins and other musical instruments. It was edited from footage salvaged from a fire that destroyed the Abitía studios in 1947. As De los Reyes explains, Abitía's son "contacted the widow [of Álvaro Obregón], who dusted off ten decomposing rolls of nitrate film" that were in her home and belonged "to a film most likely titled *8 mil kilómetros de campaña [8,000-Kilometer Campaign]* given as a gift to General Álvaro Obregón, a reputed film enthusiast" ([1983] 1996, 16). The finished film was sold to the Ministry of Defense. Considered too biased toward Carranza, it was reedited in 1963 by Eufemio Rivera under the direction of a career officer, Gustavo Carrero. Other materials were added, some from the Alva brothers' collection (De los Reyes [1983] 1996, 16) and others from the Abitía collection that had been rescued from the fire (Miquel, 2002, 121). Labeled a "documentary of the Constitutionalist revolution filmed in the battlefields," *Epics of the Revolution* was released on December 3, 1964, at the Cine Olimpia in Mexico City (García Riera, 1994b, 345).

The other compilation is *Memories of a Mexican* (1950) and consists primarily of footage from the collection of Salvador Toscano Barragán (1872–1947). Produced and directed by his daughter, the poet and cultural critic Carmen Toscano de Moreno Sánchez, the film took four and a half years to complete (Reyes Nevares, 1973, 43). To restore the badly damaged materials stored in her father's home, she received technical support from the CLASA Films Mundiales studios and a production advance from the

National Cinematographic Bank. The labor of selecting segments with identifiable events and characters, organizing them into a narrative form, and writing a screenplay was her responsibility. The special effects technician Javier Sierra recounted that after repairing a print of *Santa* (1917) for the former actress and director Elena Sánchez Valenzuela, Toscano de Moreno gave him several reels of nitrate negatives from her father's collection to restore (Sierra, 1976, 153-155). Encouraged by the outcome, as well as by the comments of producer Salvador Elizondo on the historical value of the footage, she agreed to have additional materials repaired and copied on an optical printer. She used frame enlargements to create a storyboard to write the screenplay and the voice-over narration. The editor, Teódulo Bustos Jr., assembled the material, adding sound effects and a score of period music and *corridos* composed by Jorge Pérez.

The production and exhibition of *Memories of a Mexican* became a tribute to Toscano, who in 1920 left the hardships and monetary uncertainties of filmmaking behind to return to the engineering profession and reestablished his public profile as a Mexican film pioneer. Anecdotes about his work had been circulated by the journalist José María García Sánchez, who in 1942, when researching the history of early Mexican cinema, contacted the filmmaker and encouraged him to write about his career (Miquel, 1997, 92-93). In the year it was released, the film received an Ariel, the Mexican film industry equivalent to the Hollywood Oscar, as a film of major national interest. During its three-week run starting at the end of August 1950 in the Cine Chapultepec, it was recognized as a valuable historical document on Mexico and the revolution. Alfonso Trueba remarked in a review published in *El Excélsior* on September 20, 1950, that *Memories of a Mexican* was "a profound history lesson from which the midcentury Mexican can draw useful lessons" (cited by Peredo Castro, 2000, 392). In Great Britain, where its exhibition appears to have been limited to private screenings, Irene Nicholson speculated that it "must be one of the most complete historical documents dating from so early a period in film history" (1953, 13). In what follows, I discuss the contributions of these important Mexican film pioneers to the visualization of the revolution. By means of specific scenes, I also comment on the paradox that lies at the heart of compilation documentaries: the tension that results from the wealth of meanings conveyed by the period imagery, the commemorative intent of *Epics of the Revolution* and *Memories of a Mexican*, and the homogenizing design of official discourse.

RECORDING THE DYNAMICS AND THE
Epics of the Revolution

Of the numerous cameramen who documented the Mexican Revolution, Abitía was the only one who worked simultaneously on film and photography while accompanying the Constitutional Army commanded by Obregón. His extensive output in the years 1913–1920 can be appreciated in the footage included in *Epics of the Revolution* and the photographs he commercialized as postcards. The visual and narrative properties of images referring to the same events, in the films and the postcards, reflect Abitía's versatile use of both media and his understanding (as well as that of his colleagues whose footage was also added) of documentary's historicizing potential. As participants and witnesses, the cameramen recorded the different aspects and experiences of the revolution, albeit influenced by the partisan dimensions dominating film production and reception after 1913. In the particular case of Abitía, the observer is integrated in an organic manner into the filmed scenes and postcards, with the participant as actor or internal audience and the viewing public as historical agent.

Epics of the Revolution consists of sequentially arranged footage of military parades and political assemblies. Its exposition is shaped by an unrelenting voice-over narration and is punctuated by period music arranged by Gustavo César Carrión and performed by the choir of the National Folkloric Ballet of Mexico. After a brief section defining its objectives and principal historical actors, the film covers events that took place from 1913 to 1917. Some famous military actions are included, such as the naval battle in Mazatlán, the air bombing by the two-engine aircraft *Sonora* piloted by Gustavo Salinas in the Bay of Topolobambo three months later (1914), and the defeat of Villa during the campaign of the Bajío (1915).[2] The film ends with the triumphal tour of Carranza and Obregón to Celaya, Querétaro, and Mexico City and the proclamation of the Constitution in 1917.

Since no complete versions of the Abitía films have been located so far, it is impossible to make a definitive identification of the materials included in the film. Research indicates that most of the materials come from documentaries made from 1913 to 1915. There is footage from *La campaña constitutionalista* (The Constitutionalist Campaign), mainly the parade of the Constitutionalist troops in Mexico City and Carranza's arrival in Veracruz (Miquel, 2004, 21).[3] There is also a long segment combining a bullfight in Guadalajara featuring Luis Abitía, the filmmaker's brother, and other public events celebrating the victories of the armies and militia corps of the Constitutionalist Army. The series of filmed portraits of revolutionary leaders, including one of Madero in the introductory section, contain footage from various sources. While most of the scenes of the parade of the troops of Pancho Villa and Emiliano Zapata in Mexico City are attributed to the Alva brothers, the segment on Zapata's death contains images from Toscano's *El funeral de Zapata* (The Funeral of Zapata) (1919; restored 1999). Abitía's authorship is acknowledged in a brief scene showing him in his senior years seated in front of an oversized portrait of Villa being joined by his wife.

As Emilio García Riera explains, the decision to present the footage at the standard silent film speed of sixteen frames per second facilitates the appreciation of its cinematic qualities, despite the added sound effects and music (1994d, 345). This choice reveals also Abitía's perspective, his skillful use of the medium to record details of the action, and the responses of protagonists and spectators. From this perspective emerges a parallel discourse that manages to fracture the position advanced by the voice-over narration, music, and editing. Although these devices refocus the meaning of the images, the detached point of view and framing reflect an awareness of film as a visual record of history that surpasses the ideological function of the compilation documentary. This detached point of view is indicative of the motivation for making the film—to document the everyday experience of war—and is found in much of the battlefield footage of the introductory section. In the scenes of an execution and a mass burial, for instance, the camera is positioned in long shot, either behind a firing squad or in front of a group of men standing around corpses in a common grave to act as witnesses. Abitía draws in these scenes on a key element in the iconography of the revolution. Through the placement of the officers and civilians observing the execution, his camera constructs an internal spectator who is not just an eyewitness, but acts as a link between the actions represented and the audience of the film. More important, this internal spectator highlights the mediated dimension of the imagery of violence. Yet the music and voice-over added to these horrific scenes are at odds with the idea of letting the images speak for themselves that is expressed in the opening voice-over. An orchestrated version of "La valentina," the revolutionary hymn to bravery in the face of death, punctuates the action that has served time and again to illustrate the myth of Mexican attitudes toward dying, a man's slow walk in front of the firing squad. As in the shots of the tangled heap of corpses and peasant soldiers shoveling dirt into an open pit, the music is a rhetorical gesture. It reiterates a nationalist fiction that contends, as the narrator says, that "the blood of 500 thousand Mexicans was spilled generously . . . as an elevated price that enabled the installation of a revolutionary and constitutional government."

That the settings remain unspecified and the actors unidentified adds only randomness to the depiction of bloodshed. To the extent that this effect results from procedures typical of the compilation documentary, these scenes acquire a purely generic function. By eliminating intertitles and contextual information, the imagery marked by the daily experience of war is altered so that its meanings are drawn exclusively from myths disseminated by popular culture and political discourse. This rearrangement of meanings can be found in another scene in this section, a three-shot segment in which a brigade of peasant soldiers is laying train rails under the watchful eye of officers that illustrates what the voice-over broadly qualifies as "the combat in the countryside." The image and sound disjunction assigns a totalizing meaning to scenes that record a remarkable exploit described by the historian Adolfo Gilly as "the train that ran without a railway" (1983, 123). After the battle of Santa María in May 1913, to solve the disruption of train traffic between Sonora and Sinaloa, troops built 500-meter sections of rails at a time over 14 kilometers to connect La Bomba and Cruz de Piedra, bypassing the Empalme station controlled by the Federal army (Grajales, 1959, LVII; Obregón, 1959, 101–102). The long-shot framing details the environment, machinery, and work method. By highlighting the audacity of the enterprise, these scenes evoke the multiple postcards produced by Abitía during the Northeast Army Corps campaign led by Obregón (Miquel, 2004, 11).

Visual Experience and Modernity: Postcard and Filmed Images

Abitía's understanding of both media can be best appreciated in the distinct features of filmed scenes and postcards of the artillery battle that ended with the sinking of the gunboat *Morelos* in the Bay of Mazatlán and the signing of the Teoloyucan treaty. As Miquel points out, Abitía commercialized his photographs as postcard series, one of more than a hundred depicting the Constitutionalist army advance in the western regions (2004, 11). "Given the particular features of this series," he writes, "its consumers would have been mainly the soldiers and commanding officers, with the images serving as a vehicle for remembering exploits, reinforcing convictions, and demonstrating power" (Miquel, 2002, 114). One postcard in this series is titled "Observing Foreign Boats from the Isla de Piedra in Front of Mazatlán, Sin." Although the image evokes Obregón's

FIGURE 1.2. Epics of the Revolution, *film still. Courtesy of the Archivo Toscano, Mexico*

account of the scouting expedition, it is not a record of combat (Obregón, 1959, 113–114). Its theme is the spectacle of the bay mediated by the group of soldiers positioned with their backs to the camera. In contrast to other postcards depicting the *Morelos* titled "The cannon that struck the *Morelos* in the Isla de Piedra" and "Sailors who boarded the *Morelos* and blew it up with dynamite," the subject matter is the landscape rather than the military equipment and actors in the battle that ended on May 11, 1914, with the sinking of the gunboat in an explosion qualified as an impressive spectacle by Obregón. Be that as it may, the historicity of the image arises from its simultaneous valorization of the landscape and the look, in other words, of a visual experience that equally implicates the observer and the consumer.

The scenes included in *Epics of the Revolution* focus on the extraordinary battle. Panning shots locate the stalled gunboat and the Federal navy vessel shooting toward the island, and stationary shots show soldiers and officers firing the cannon. The camera's placement highlights the challenges and replicates the dynamics of the battle. Like the combatants, it scrutinizes the scenery and seeks shelter behind the large rocks that give the island its name. It records the soldiers' reactions, sometimes fearless and sometimes cautious, to the cannon's recoil and the mortar fire. In addition to the obvious differences between still and moving images, what distinguishes

FIGURE 1.3. Epics of the Revolution, *film still. Courtesy of the Archivo Toscano, Mexico*

the film scenes is their narrative dimension. If the framing and the composition codify space as the object of representation in the postcards, the immediacy and duration effects endow the filmed images with historical meaning.

Temporality is equally central to the Teoloyucan sequence. The fixed position of the camera, just behind the Constitutionalist officers, reveals a full view of the Camino de Cuautitlán, where Victoriano Huerta's troops surrendered the capital to the Obregón forces. In addition to the protocol details, Abitía records spontaneous actions, as when the Federal soldier rides back toward the group of officers.[4] Duration accentuates the details of the action and endows with meaning the moments of inactivity and the attitudes of the participants, either as actors or as bystanders. In the shots of the arrival of the cars carrying the officials and the signing of the treaty, the narrative structure emerges from the coming and going of military and civilians rather than from the voice-over recounting the quarrel between Carranza and the Brazilian ambassador who assisted in the negotiations. This discrepancy between what the narration qualifies as historical and what Abitía films is indicative of the paradoxical nature of compilation documentaries. These shots demonstrate that, despite his friendship with Obregón (his cousin and school friend, later employer and sponsor) and loyalty to Carranza, the filmmaker sees cinema as capable of fixing an instant, preserving it as an experience marked by temporality. This disregard for the propaganda implications of the image is reflected as well in the postcard "Gral. Álvaro Obregón signing the rendition treaty of México City." As the caption indicates, the postcard records the moment itself, but its historicity comes from its composition. By separating Obregón and the official holding the document on the mud guard of the car from the bystanders, the narrative is fractured in favor of the man in the foreground looking directly at the camera. This reflexive gesture connects the spectator and consumer to the photographic apparatus to establish representation as a category of modernity. This expansion of the visual field reveals the complementarities of Abitía's filmed images and postcards. The treatment of space, time, point of view, and duration engages at the same time the visual apparatus, the subject, and the spectator in the representation.

FIGURE 1.4. *"Gral. Álvaro Obregón signing the rendition treaty of Mexico City," Jesús H. Abitia, postcard. Courtesy of the Archivo Toscano, Mexico*

History on Parade

The understanding of the mediating possibilities of the image is reminiscent of films and photographs of the Madero presidency (1911–1913), when visual media was used primarily to document events considered of national significance. After the counterrevolutionary plot led by Huerta (1913–1914), restrictions were placed on what audiences could see and filmmakers could record. In spite of strict media censorship, informational objectives were not entirely replaced by propaganda (De los Reyes, 1996, 132, 141). In the Constitutionalist-controlled territories, documentary production was strongly associated with the various leaders. Filmmakers were conscious of their sponsors' vanity, sided with the causes they represented, and filmed those events available to them. Even so, their films were profitable because they were chronicles of incidents that happened in faraway places and a means for the largely urban audiences to reexperience the sight of columns of soldiers marching through city streets filled with enthusiastic crowds. In this sense, the production and reception of documentaries had not changed substantially, and, as in 1911, the cinema remained a spectacular expression of the dynamics of social and political change.

The innumerable scenes of military parades marking the Constitutionalist victories in *Epics of the Revolution* illustrate the filmmakers' attempts to record the differing attitudes and responses of participants and spectators toward the revolutionary leaders and their armies. Most revealing is the footage of the two notorious military parades in Mexico City: the entrance of the armies led by Carranza on August 20, 1914, and the parade on December 6, 1914, of the troops of Villa's Northern Division and Zapata's Liberating Army of the South. In the first, filmed by Abitía, the focus is the figure of Carranza on horseback. As in the postcards published at the time, he appears generally in the foreground, his body somewhat angled, with Obregón at his side. With shots taken above street level, or slightly over the heads of the predominantly male crowd, he seems to be swallowed up by the admiring masses. A singular high-angle shot, presumably taken by a cameraman riding on a horse and from behind Carranza's head, shows him interacting with those who have come to greet him. Throughout the segment that illustrates the six-hour march from the suburbs to the National Palace, the tight framing captures the magnitude of the event, the festive mood of the city people, and the triumphant demeanor of the leaders. Except when Carranza is handed Madero's flag "in front of the Daguerre store," as the narrator explains, scenes of military

FIGURE 1.5. *"Triumphant Entrance of the Constitutionalist Army into Mexico City under the Command of Its Supreme Leader, Mr. Venustiano Carranza, August 20, 1914,"* Casa Miret, Mexico, postcard. Courtesy of the Fondo Juan Barragán, Centro de Estudios Universitarios—Archivo Histórico de la UNAM (CESU-AHUNAM), Mexico

pageantry take place in the National Palace on the Zócalo Square. Placed sideways, the camera offers an awesome view of the officer's arrival in cavalry formation. It shows Carranza, hat and flag in hand, riding through the massive doorway with other senior officers and being met in the courtyard by politicians.

The sense of spectacle is greater in the second parade, comprising mostly footage shot by the Alva brothers. In the scenes of the Villista and Zapatista armies marching in orderly formation on the Paseo de la Reforma toward Chapultepec Castle, the camera assumes the onlooker role. Like the people lining the streets, the camera keeps its distance from the cavalry columns, particularly the Zapatistas in their wide-brimmed hats carrying the banner of the Virgin of Guadalupe. In an amazing overhead shot, from what appears to be the start of the march on the Zócalo, the camera films the photographers and cameramen rushing around with their tripods to find the best position. In another, it captures a remarkable view of Zapatista soldiers on horseback or on foot mingling with their city supporters. Two scenes separate these parade shots. The first is a series of panning shots on Emiliano Zapata, President Eulalio Gutiérrez, and

Pancho Villa at the celebrated banquet in Chapultepec Castle. The other shows Villa's visit to the tomb of Madero and singles out from the crowd an elegant *soldadera* (camp follower; women who went to war with their husbands) and Madero's widow interacting briefly with Villa.

Like the photographers who recorded this parade, the filmmakers draw on what was by then a well-established trope to visualize the encounter between rural and urban Mexico. The sight of troops in peasant clothes marching in ceremonial formation and masses taking over the streets of Mexico City is a spectacular projection of collective agency. Through composition and framing, these images reveal the shifting positions of city inhabitants viewing the parades and the cameramen recording them. The spectator-participant dynamics are reflected in the symmetrical design of the parade shots and the swarming effect of the crowd scenes. The combined feelings of awe and curiosity that greeted the arrival of the armies of Villa and Zapata manifest themselves in the impulse, by the cameramen and the city inhabitants, to be merged into one body with the soldiers. In the shot of the Zapatistas and their admirers described above, the effect is that of a fluid mass of white hats that evokes a later photograph by Tina Modotti titled *The Workers' Parade* (1926). By highlighting movement, the iconic Zapatista hats become, as Noble writes on the sombreros in the Modotti image, "a symbol of the continuing surge of popular power" (2000, 93). Faced with this show of military discipline, the cameramen offer their allegiance to the peasant troops. In this way, these scenes document an astonishing civic response that casts away the imagery of recklessness and savagery of the Villista and Zapatista armies disseminated earlier by the press (De los Reyes, [1983] 1996, 159). In December 1914, following the political defeat of the Carranza faction in Aguascalientes that forced its leaders to retreat to Veracruz and thrust the rest of the country back into war, the capital became an open city. Although uncertain about the outcome of this battle for the heart and minds of the Mexican people, the cameramen and the crowds at these parades were firsthand witnesses to and players in a momentous event. Once again, the cameramen's skill in recording attitudes and responses allow the imagery to break from the constraints of partisanship to side with the multitudes who participated in what Gilly describes as "one of the finest and most moving episodes of the entire revolution, an early, impetuous yet orderly expression of mass strength which has left its mark on the country" (1983, 148).

The scenes of *Epics of the Revolution* discussed here reveal the paradox that lies at the heart of compilation documentaries. On the one hand, the film images are decontextualized and turned into a visual support for an official discourse. Shaped and regulated by voice-over, editing, and music, the images become a tool for a state-promoted view of the revolution as a force sustained by the sacrifice and heroism of Mexicans and a synthesis of diverse ideological currents. On the other hand, the scenes shot by Abitía and the Alva brothers are a cinematic testimony to the attitudes and responses of participants and spectators, including their own, to the Mexican Revolution. The wealth of meanings of the images fracture the homogenizing control of the official discourse. What is more, their aesthetic and narrative properties enable an appreciation of how Abitía and his colleagues understood the historicizing potential of cinema when they recorded the different aspects and experiences of the revolution, despite the partisan dimension that dominated the production and reception of films after 1913. In the case of Abitía, the filmed scenes and the postcards reveal a versatile and multivalent use of the media. Perspective is not limited exclusively to representing the events but integrates the observer organically.

PUBLIC AND PRIVATE *Memories of a Mexican*

The documentary image of the revolution received official approval on June 27, 1967, when *Memories of a Mexican* (1950) was "declared a national monument by an act of Congress" (De Orellana, 1990, 212). Subsequent rereleases on video in 1976 and 1996 have confirmed the film's canonical status. With the gradual rediscovery of film materials from the period, Mexican film historians and archivists have identified the provenance of most of the film's footage and rectified the erroneous assumption that Toscano is the sole author. They have reconsidered his pioneering role as a collector since, in addition to producing and exhibiting, he purchased and compiled footage shot by his associates Ocañas and Echáñiz Brust, as well as by the Alva brothers, Rosas, and Abitía.[5] As Miquel writes in his detailed Toscano biography, "The engineer's merit was to patiently gather all those materials and organize them sequentially for a project he had fine-tuned already in 1912 and brought to fruition as a silent film in 1935, and which his daughter Carmen in some way took up again as a sound film in *Memories of a Mexican*" (1997, 95). Despite the confidence expressed in a letter to his wife, Enedina Escobedo de Toscano, when he undertook another version of his *History of the Revolution*, the compilation films he produced in 1927 and 1928 yielded modest revenues (see Miquel, 1997, 87). As Miquel points out, these films "barely managed to run for three days. Cinematic language had changed some time ago and to see these fixed shots of processions and cannon fire proved unbearably boring for ordinary spectators who were used to the dynamics of Hollywood cinema, and also for those connoisseurs who had, for example, enjoyed Eisenstein's *Battleship Potemkin*" (1997, 88). The updated 1935 version received limited circulation because Toscano lacked the monetary resources for marketing and assembling a sound version as distributor Ignacio Rangel had advised (Miquel, 1997, 90). The rereleases of *Memories of a Mexican* have also led to a greater appreciation of Toscano de Moreno's achievement. She managed to reverse her father's two failed attempts, and the positive reception of her film enabled her to establish the Toscano Historical Cinematographic Archive. Renamed the Carmen Toscano Foundation in 1992 and headed since by her daughter, the historian Alejandra Moreno Toscano, this family-run archive has become a prestigious repository of early Mexican documentaries. It has been fundamental in raising awareness of the need to safeguard the integrity of archival materials from misuse for partisan and mercantile purposes and to acknowledge their cultural and monetary value.[6]

Writing on the rerelease in 1996 of *Memories of a Mexican*, the reviewer José Joaquín Blanco noted that "to have that video at home is like keeping a family album," because it offers a testimony of daily life in Mexico, its pageantry, misery, and violence, from the Porfiriate to the Revolution (1996). This broad chronological scope distinguishes this compilation from *Epics of the Revolution*, and highlights its singularity as the only extant evidence of the altering effects of visual technologies on Mexico's social and political identities. The extended segments containing footage from the Toscano-Ocañas collaborations *Fiestas del centenario de la Independencia* (Festivities of the Centenary of Independence) (1910), *Toma de Ciudad Juárez y el viaje del héroe de la Revolución Mr. Francisco I. Madero* (The Fall of Ciudad Juárez and the Trip of the Hero of the Revolution D. Francisco I. Madero) (1911) and *Decena trágica en México* (aka *La revolución felicista* or *La caída del gobierno de Madero*) (Ten Tragic Days in Mexico aka The Felicista Revolution or The Defeat of the Madero Government) (1913) warrant a detailed discussion. These segments reveal how documentary images were used to organize events, places, and personalities into a compelling story whose power derives, as I argue, from a compulsion to turn the newsworthy instant into a memorable visual archive of Mexico's history.

The Toscano de Moreno compilation validates this role of film as an archival artifact in restoring and preserving personal and collective histories. The footage is structured around a male voice-over narration read by the prominent children's radio personality and announcer Manuel Bernal that begins in 1897 and ends in 1950. The events are organized sequentially and conclude with a montage sequence condensing the postrevolutionary period around images of seven presidents, from Plutarco Elías Calles (1924-1928) to Miguel Alemán (1946-1952).[7] The voice-over accompanying these images recalls the family history of the fictional narrator and the lives of prominent public figures. Even though the narration is personalized, the speaker remains unseen and his own connection with public figures not shown. As Margarita de Orellana writes, this device "is a simulation of 'collective memory' that manifests itself in this cross between the voice of the 'Mexican' and the documentary images" (1990, 213).

While this collapsing of personal and collective history is not unusual in commemorative films, what sets this film apart is a meta-archival component whereby biography, cinema, and national history converge. This convergence is reflected in the narrator's opening remark about being born in 1897, the year marking the arrival of cinema in Mexico (and the start of Toscano's professional activity), and the pronouncement, "How many things have happened since!" This convergence also sets up a framework for viewing the materials included in the film and manifests itself, as García Riera writes, in "a historical perspective that assumes itself at once as singular and plural" (1994b, 355).

The most explicit articulation of the film's meta-archival drive can be found in the closing segment. With the narrator explaining his return to Mexico in 1950, the memorializing role of documentary images is ascertained by means of a superimposition of shots of Mexico's urban modernity with the emblematic images of the revolutionary armies entering the capital in 1914. The double exposure functions as a trope for the fusion of individual recollection and public history, resolution of family and social conflicts, national reconciliation and progress. "Present and past, modernity and memory," Noble writes, "are bound together in these multiple exposures in delicate equilibrium" (2005, 66). Rather than simply validate the modernization agenda of the Alemán presidency and the nationalist discourse of the postrevolutionary state, the phantomlike appearance of the armies and the final shot of the Monument to the Revolution located on Mexico City's Plaza de la República visualize the formative role of the archive in the preservation of identities. What is more, the voice-over reinforces "the temporal imperative (before it is 'too late')" that drives the conservation of filmic images (Doanne, 2002, 222). It imprints the archival images with historicity, not just as artifacts, but as a presence threatened by loss when the narrator says, "I have the impression of seeing the images of the past flow through the city's arteries and I feel that something of me will endure as long as the recollection of what I have lived may palpitate in the memory of every Mexican." Noble offers a complementary opinion: "Memory as presented here exists then as a configuration of film and revolution which, in turn, is also a (curiously) family affair" (2005, 59).

Porfirian Modernity: Images of the Centenary

The brief exposition of life at the turn of the twentieth century in the opening segment of *Memories of a Mexican* exemplifies the role of cinema in the formation of individual and collective identities.[8] The combined effect of image and sound reveals a country pressing ahead on an accelerated path toward modernization. Family anecdotes enrich the descriptive voice-over and complement scenes highlighting the diverse sites and activities that made cinema attractive to cameramen and audiences. Referring to these early nonfiction images as "views," the narrator says that they could "transport the spectator to faraway places ... without even having to move from his seat." Shots of city and provincial landscapes, popular entertainment and travel, local and official festivities reveal features of daily life that are at once modern and picturesque. Scenes of the training of army reservists, a boating mishap at an outdoor festival, and the flight of Tomás Braniff in 1910 complement shots of traditional indigenous dances recorded in different locations, a pilgrimage to the Virgin of Guadalupe sanctuary, and allegorical carts pulled by oxen at a parade in Mexico City in 1904 to offer a view of a society and culture where, according to the narrator, tranquillity and prosperity prevail.

This alignment of the cinematic image with the slogan "Order, Peace and Progress" of the Porfirio Díaz presidency is disrupted by the narrator's account of the political disagreements between his (fictional) father and uncle. If, for Nicholson, "this device is historically correct, since many families were thus divided at the time" (1953, 15), it also draws attention to the scarcity of period materials showing social conflict and political repression. The reading of a letter from Uncle Luis describing his deportation to Quintana Roo is set to picturesque jungle and plantation shots from a later film titled *Territorio de Quintana Roo* (Territory of Quintana Roo) (Toscano with Ocañas, 1917). The incongruity produced by using exotic imagery to illustrate an account of the wretched conditions in the infamous penitentiary only makes sense if seen in relation to the systemic evasion of "disagreeable events" in the cinema of the Porfirian decade (De los Reyes [1987] 1997, 27). The deployment of scenes from a travelogue-type film designed to attract investors and settlers to the region constructs a cinematic record of the systemic suppression of political dissent out of generic images and reinstates what is missing from the archive.

Scenes from *Entrevista Díaz-Taft* (Díaz-Taft Interview) (Alva brothers, 1909) in Ciudad Juárez and El Paso illustrate the preference of cameramen for recording the pomp and circumstance of the public appearances of President Díaz. In the shots depicting the meeting with President William Howard Taft, for instance, their cameras capture the comings and goings of officials on the steps of the Customs Building in Ciudad Juárez. The slightly low angle position accentuates the staged effect, with the honor guard in their plumed hats framing the climactic moment when the presidents are filmed together. What these shots also ratify is the self-assured performance of a ruling class that embraced cinema with relish, just as it had previously adopted photography, to legitimize its power and further its claims to being modern. As De los Reyes stresses, quoting from an illustrated newspaper, to be "imprinted on film ... will be the golden dream of the Mexican aristocracy" ([1983] 1996, 94). Nowhere is this investment of the bourgeoisie in filmic representation more evident than in the numerous scenes of *Festivities of the Centenary of Independence* (Toscano with Ocañas, 1910) incorporated into *Memories of a Mexican*. Shots of inaugurations, speeches, banquets, and excursions visualize the affectation of the bourgeoisie with the camera. Alongside the attending foreign guests, diplomats, military officers, academics, and financiers, members of this class present themselves to the gaze of the camera and the curious crowd wearing their finest clothes—the men in ceremonial dress and top hats and the women in the latest French fashions. The narrator's statement, "It was a memorable day for women who like my mother liked those sumptuous dresses and enormous hats with feathers," adds intimacy to the shots of couples mingling at what appears to be a garden party. This display of wealth and privilege projects a social identity that, like the new sumptuous buildings erected in the capital, asserts itself as difference. The glamour of the bourgeoisie is but a pretense, as Carlos Monsiváis comments on their photographs in the Casasola Archive: "Perfect clothes, Parisian education, these are the badges of their otherness: we are *less* Mexican than the rest, and could pass for Europeans" (1984, 40; original emphasis).

The scope of the monthlong celebrations in Mexico City in September 1910 is also illustrated in this ten-minute segment. The obsession with appearance over substance characteristic of the period is rendered cinematically through compositions and framing to reveal how ornate monuments and avenues were turned into a stage for the performance of a narrative of modernity. As Olivier Debroise writes, "It also 'appeared' that this was erected for the delight of the photographers," who, like the cameramen, "were the greatest beneficiaries of the festivities" (2001, 171). Despite the reported attendance of more than fifty thousand spectators at the Independence Day parade of September 15, the cameras of Toscano and Ocañas stand above the crowds. Placed on the upper floor of buildings on the remodeled Paseo de la Reforma, the cameras record what the narrator describes as the "historical pageant." High-angle shots accentuate the choreography representing the three historical periods that were promoted by the state as the foundational moments of Mexico's identity as a modern and sovereign nation. Costumed performers act out the encounter of Moctezuma and Cortés, the "Paseo del Pendón" procession to commemorate the conquest, and the entrance of the Army of the Three Guarantees led by Agustín de Iturbide into Mexico City on September 21, 1821. As the historians Robert M. Buffington and William E. French point out, it is this parade "that most clearly reveals the use of history both to invent tradition to teach nationalistic values and to portray the Porfiriate as the culmination of tradition—the end point of progress and the herald of modernity" (2000, 426). Moreover, the visual arrangement of the parade scenes evokes the genre paintings and illustrations of the mid-nineteenth century. About this mode of representing Mexico, Erica Segre writes, "The *cuadros de costumbres* [pictures of customs] delighted in the theatricality of the local in a disrupted post-colonial order, with framing devices which favored emblematic traditional scenes viewed from balconies, windows, street benches, carriages and theatre scenes" (2007, 13). As in the scenes filmed by Toscano, the frame-within-the-frame structure establishes the viewer reflexively both as producer and as spectator of the spectacle of communal identity.

The placement of footage from *El grito de independencia o el grito de Dolores o sea la independencia de México* (The Call for Independence or The Grito of Dolores, That Is, the Independence of Mexico) (Felipe de Jesús Haro, 1907) at the end of this segment generates intriguing aesthetic associations between early filmmaking practices and the civic rituals of the final years of the Porfiriate. Scenes of this early fiction film are introduced by the narrator's comments on the crowds assembled to watch the official commemoration of the *Grito* (the call) of Independence. Over night shots of the illuminated buildings on the Zócalo, he says, "The bright lights made them think of the film they had seen being made in the town of Dolores de Hidalgo." In both films, location shooting and crowd participation are indicative of a cinematic investment in the spectacular display of nation-

FIGURE 1.6. Memories of a Mexican, *frame enlargement*

alist and didactic imagery. Hence the accent is on the theatrical qualities of the patriotic and religious emblems, as the gun carriage displaying the uniform of independence hero José María Morelos in the *The Festivities of the Centenary of Independence* and the Virgin of Guadalupe banner in the scenes reconstructing the call for independence in *The Grito of Dolores*. In both cases, the symbolic meanings of decorated floats, costumes, and accessories are revealed as constructs that allow the actual crowd and the troupe of actors respectively to reenact the past and reimagine themselves as a national community. Factuality (or lack thereof) may not have been of concern to the Díaz minister who had proclaimed, "Oblivion, and I would say that even historical falsity are essential factors in the formation of a nation" (Buffington and French, 2000, 427), but it bothered a journalist who at the feature's initial release identified numerous "inaccuracies in art design" (De los Reyes, [1987] 1997, 250).

Notwithstanding the nostalgic views expressed now and then by the narrator of *Memories of a Mexican*, the segments on the Porfiriate are more than just an evocation of the belle époque. They reveal the ideological role of images during a regime obsessed with visual display that manifests itself in the persistence of traditional themes and the deployment of patriotic and religious emblems for nationalist purposes. The anecdotal and romanticized images of customs and scenery in this early part of the film hark back to the mid-nineteenth century when "the slogan was to generate a discursive and visual image of *lo propio*," as the art historian Angélica Velázquez Guadarrama (1999, 159) writes, by means of *costumbrista* painting (the Mexican equivalent of genre painting). The cinema expanded literally and figuratively the meanings of these images by packaging and circulating them massively as "views" taken from reality. For the emerging film industry it was more cost-effective to record reality because it "knew beforehand that more people would attend to see themselves on the screen" (De los Reyes, [1987] 1997, 25). Moreover, film became an effective medium for reproducing the historical discourse of the regime. "Actualities" showcasing official events replicated in cinematic terms the narrative constructed in *Mexico throughout the Centuries* (1884–1889), the groundbreaking collaborative five-volume history designed by Vicente Riva Palacio. The symbolism of patriotic images is magnified, this time, by the medium's capability to capture the most spectacular and theatrical dimensions of the nationalist narrative. In *Festivities of the Centenary of Independence* and *The Grito of Dolores,* the Porfirian iconography of identity and power is offered for mass consumption as an experience of movement and space that is as ephemeral as it is memorable. In effect, as Miquel indicates, the success of the Centenary festivities prompted Toscano to release portions of his film as they were being processed, and the popularity of the completed film enabled him to maintain it in exhibition until 1912 (1997, 51–52).

A New Way of Seeing: The Madero Years

Toscano de Moreno stated in an interview with Berta Reyes Nevares in 1973, "Cinema serves to tell stories, but also to tell history; in other words to gather what really happens, and record on celluloid the features of the protagonists, the fashions, the attributes of the streets, the gestures of apprehension or happiness" (43). This outlook on the historicity of moving images is not exclusive to *Memories of a Mexican*. As remarked earlier, other Mexican filmmakers whose footage is included in *Epics of the Revolution* share this outlook. Yet the broad chronological framework in Toscano de Moreno's film points to ways in which this outlook was modified at the onset of the revolution. At this time, as Noble remarks, "the revolution not only generated new kinds of images—locomotives packed with combatants, multitudes gathering to greet the arrival of a revolutionary *caudillo*—it also provided unprecedented points of view, breaking with the circumscribed modes of seeing associated with the Porfiriato" (2005, 51). The segments dealing with the triumph and defeat of the Madero revolution reveal new modalities of representing social and political identities by means of a substantially different perspective on how events were experienced by common people and cameramen, as actors and spectators. As I argue, these modalities constitute a series of rearrangements rather than a break from the approach instituted during the Porfiriate.

These rearrangements are exemplified by contrasts between scenes of President Díaz's official tour in *The Inauguration of International Traffic in the Tehuantepec Isthmus* (Toscano, 1907) and Madero's train ride to Mexico City recorded in *The Fall of Ciudad Juárez and the Trip of the Hero of the Revolution D. Francisco I. Madero* (Toscano with Ocañas, 1911). The vignette-like views of Díaz and his officials traveling to Yucatán are replaced by a compelling representation of popular mobilization. With the camera placed aboard the train carrying Madero and his supporters, the train is at once the subject and the agent of representation. Adding excitement to what was basically a filmed reportage of Madero's trip reconfigures the objectified icon of Porfirian modernity (Miquel, 1997, 57). The dramatic range of the train imagery is expanded in the scenes identified by the narrator of *Memories of a Mexican* as occurring in Allende, Saltillo, and León. The camera registers the enthusiasm of the crowds; of women in nursing outfits lining the tracks, people perched on top of railcars, men on horseback or on foot swarming a station. It preserves the instant in which the train passes and, more significantly, links in dynamic ways the forward movement of the train to the shifting political and social landscape.

In the scenes of Madero's arrival in Mexico City on June 7, 1911, the camera assumes a variety of positions. Sometimes placed high above, sometimes just slightly over the heads of the people or at eye level, it provides magnificent views of the masses filling the streets, surrounding Madero's car and perched on public monuments. No matter the camera's vantage point, the focus is on spontaneity and immediacy. The blurring effects of movement and compression as men on horseback ride past the camera, as people wave hats and flags, jostle for a better spot, or walk facing the camera, compound this focus. This accumulation of ephemeral moments endows the scenes with historicity because it expands the perceptual and affective field of the cinematic image. This investment in history is persuasively articulated in the observation made about this imagery in the video *The Maderista Revolution: A Media Triumph* (2003.) As the narrator explains, "The people's euphoria on the screen produced a new perceptual field. Society saw itself differently. The filmed revolution became part of

FIGURE 1.7. Memories of a Mexican, *frame enlargement*

the modernity to which it aspired. These images seen and remembered, and seen again, reproduced the meaning of the Madero triumph: the victory of political freedom, the perception of apotheosis."

This "perception of apotheosis" is worth reconsidering because it applies as well to the imagery of Zapatista troops parading in Mexico City in December 1914. It touches concurrently on already tested modalities of narrative and spectatorship and the visualization of modernity as a shifting and dynamic experience. With the revolution, filmmakers took an "idiosyncratic" approach to continuity to "its ultimate consequences" (De los Reyes, [1987] 1997, 43). In the last years of the Porfiriate, and mostly to make up for the technical or practical constraints of shooting, filmmakers edited scenes in terms of narrative rather than chronology. They also embraced the motif of the apotheosis—or the tableau-style finale that George Méliès successfully integrated into film from popular theatre—for dramatic effect and hence used it more than once and not always as the closing shot (De los Reyes, [1987] 1997, 44–45). For audiences accustomed to seeing events out of order and multiple scenes of apotheosis, the documentaries of the revolution offered new ways of interacting with the screen. In the Mexico City welcome scenes of *The Fall of Ciudad Juárez and the Trip of the Hero of the Revolution D. Francisco I. Madero,* the central

FIGURE 1.8. Memories of a Mexican, *film still from storybook. Courtesy of the Archivo Toscano, Mexico*

actor of the apotheosis scenes is the people, not the ruling class. The crowd is represented as a spatially situated and diverse social force with common desires and aspirations, enabling spectators to project themselves into the crowd, not just as viewers, but as actors of history.

The confidence of cameramen to represent what was happening in Mexico extends to documenting the brutality and chaos of the revolution, notably the only episode of combat in Mexico City, which occurred in February 1913. *Memories of a Mexican* includes a twelve-minute segment on the uprising that ended with the assassination of President Madero and Vice-President José María Pino Suárez. As noted above, it contains mainly footage from *Ten Tragic Days in Mexico* (1913). In contrast to the imagery of class privilege and popular empowerment discussed so far, the scenes in this segment reveal a city traumatized by a fierce power struggle and shattered by warfare. Mood and affect are mediated by a diverse range of shots, many mobile but others static and with masking effects recalling the earlier "views." Panning and tracking shots obtained by a camera mounted on a car showing the deserted downtown streets with their boarded-up shops convey feelings of foreboding that are eloquently summarized in the narrator's comment on the Zócalo looking like "an enormous cemetery." Long-shot compositions turn the urban locations into the central player of a tragic drama that took place on city streets, not just in army barracks. Scenes of intense street battles visualize the bravado of the soldiers firing their guns and the curiosity of civilian onlookers. The inevitable and brutal consequences of war are depicted in two series of shots. One shows the buildings and city landmarks damaged by mortar shots and fire. The other documents the loss of life by means of horrific shots of corpses loaded on the back of a cart and displayed on the street.

The dramatic inflections of the voice-over personalizing or historicizing the account enhance the imagery's affectivity. Over shots of men waving their hats to the camera, for instance, the narrator says, "The people asked themselves what will be the fate of the leaders of Mexico." To use this mundane urban image to make a claim on the impact of Madero's murder is not gratuitous considering the narrator's double function, as an eyewitness and as an interpreter of Mexico's history. In this particular segment, the "we" substitutes the first-person pronoun as Uncle Luis shares the eyewitness role, and the voice-over presages the altering effects of these tragic ten days. The narration invests with anxiety the shots of soldiers and camp followers in the courtyard of the National Palace and the row of cannons aimed at the Zócalo. As Miquel points out, Toscano and Ocañas conceived the film from which these scenes are taken as a *"requiem* to the Maderista period" (1997, 65; original emphasis). Hence the sense of mourning that pervades even the most sensationalist imagery, like the shots of the smoldering pyre of human remains and grieving crowds on the site of the Madero and Pino Suárez murders. Here the narration confirms the archival intent of *Memories of a Mexican*. It rearticulates the meanings of scenes that have come to epitomize the tragedy of those ten days by implicating the contemporary viewer in a mode of seeing that is foremost meditative. It breaks away from the expectations placed on documentary and abandons distance and discretion to probe into the distress and pain contained in the images of daily life militarized, democratic ideals betrayed, and human life annihilated by chaos and violence.

The value of the Toscano de Moreno compilation resides in its ability to illuminate as well as reflect on how the documentary of the revolution chronicled its momentum and brutality. Its broad chronological framework reveals how cameramen repositioned themselves in the midst of crowds and projected onto the screens the large urban and rural sectors that they excluded (willfully or not) in their zeal to register "the dream of the Porfiriate of a flourishing and wealthy Mexico" (De los Reyes, [1983] 1996, 89). While the fictional narrator is the primary narrative agent in *Memories of a Mexican*, the commentary highlights the distance that time

FIGURE 1.9. Memories of a Mexican, *film still from storybook. Courtesy of the Archivo Toscano, Mexico*

imposes on how these archival images can be read. It is this historicizing perspective that ultimately validates the film's agenda: to reexperience Mexico's history as a visual event by revealing how moving images allowed a society and culture to imagine itself. Moreover, the scenes discussed here are valuable evidence of how Mexican cameramen expanded the perceptual and affective field of the cinematic image, used immediacy and identification effects to replicate the visual and sensory sensations of modernity, and visualized it as a shifting and dynamic experience. Hence these diverse filmed materials exemplify a documentary practice that evolved into a distinctive form of expression during the Madero presidency because, as De los Reyes states, "the public and the themes were unified. The cameramen portrayed ordinary people, and these people attended the cinematograph to see themselves or to admire their favorite leaders (1977, 46).

In all probability, viewer responses to this film, and a decade later to *Epics of the Revolution,* was quite different from those described in 1914 by Guzmán. Audiences who went to see these compilation documentaries consisted of people who either experienced the conflict firsthand—as combatants, bureaucrats, policy makers, as perpetrators or victims of violence, and as bystanders—or gleaned knowledge of it from the testimonies of participants and witnesses because they were born near the end of the armed struggle or soon after. Even if they did not conduct themselves in the boisterous manner reported by Guzmán, the revolution—in Noble's words—"represented a potent memory text. Both categories of spectators would arguably have been better acquainted with the conflict in representational forms other than the spectacle of the moving image of early actuality films" (2005, 50). Be that as it may, screenings of *Memories of a Mexican* and *Epics of the Revolution* enabled spectators to partake again, or to partake for the first time, in the public memorializing of this event. Showings in subsequent years (mostly on television but retrospectives, festivals, and other specialized venues too) afforded audiences the opportunity to grasp their value as historiography. As I have remarked in this chapter, the images recorded by Mexican filmmakers and photographers are a visual statement on modernity and a testimony to the role of film in constructing a collective identity whose representative agents were the rural and urban masses, not just their leaders. In spite of their fragmentary nature, the images in these compilations project a changing relationship between producers and consumers and reveal how visual technologies altered the ways Mexican society saw itself.

Chapter 2

Historicity and the Archive
RECONSTRUCTION AND APPROPRIATION

Photographers and cameramen became the earliest historiographers of what Americans called the Mexican war. Alongside diplomats, politicians, and journalists, the art historian and curator James Oles writes, "they would participate in the visual reduction of an amazingly complex historical scenario—marked and obscured by shifting alliances, by trainloads of misinformation created by all sides, and by a wide range of competing personalities—into a comprehensible construction for the American public" (1993, 59). Although the accounts of the radical activists and journalists John Reed and John Kenneth Turner remain the most well known, their bearing on mainstream public opinion was minimal. By and large, the American public continued to view Mexico through the prism of prejudice. The historian John A. Britton explains, "The U.S. media were filled with derogatory depictions," and the "racist explanation of Mexican character reduced the revolution to a mere series of violent explosions engendered by instinctive urges that had no counterpart in . . . Anglo-Saxon legal and constitutional traditions" (1995, 25, 29). These views affected in predictable ways how visual materials were produced and consumed, including those related directly to the Villa-Mutual deal.

On January 5, 1914, following the occupation of Ciudad Chihuahua by the troops of Pancho Villa, the *New York Times* reported the signing of a contract between Harry E. Aitken of the Mutual Film Company and the Mexican revolutionary. The *Times* described it as a business partnership whereby Villa would facilitate the production of films "in any way that is consistent with his plans to depose and drive [General Victoriano] Huerta out of Mexico and the business of Mr. Aitken" (2). Camera crews were given exclusive rights to record the military campaign, and Villa would receive 20 percent of the exhibition profits of the films. On the official document, provisions were made that guaranteed safe conduct, duty-free import of film equipment and train transportation on controlled territories, and food and living quarters for men and horses.[1] The cameramen were to record newsworthy events, battles, and troop movements, subject to directives issued by officers and Villa on security, strategy, convenience, and safety. "There was absolutely no mention of reenactment of battle scenes or of Villa providing good lighting," Frederick Katz writes (1998, 325). Mutual was to release the films promptly and negotiate profitable exhibition deals. After the unsatisfactory results of filming the Ojinaga battle in January 1914, Mutual and Villa agreed to undertake a more ambitious project. It was a seven-reel film titled *The Life of General Villa* that combined actual combat with dramatic scenes.[2] On May 10, 1914, the *Sun* published a note that stated, "All the horrors of war are revealed, with none of the accompanying pomp and circumstance.... Also [appear] stretchers loaded with the dead being taken away from the battle scene, while other corpses were burned. The burning of a woman who had followed her husband to war was especially horrifying" (quoted in De los Reyes, 2001a, 37–38; see also De los Reyes, [1985] 1992, 170). As the concluding statement makes clear, the anonymous writer was less impressed with the reenactment scenes and dismissed them as having no entertainment value.

If this contract turned Villa into a media celebrity and boosted his standing worldwide, it also generated narratives and representations that minimized its significance. Claims of battles delayed and public executions staged for the camera to accommodate technical limitations cast doubts on the authenticity of the war footage and the political impact of filming on the battlefields. Sensationalist accounts by cameramen in Mutual publicity materials, with opinions expressed by film reviewers, fed prevailing stereotypes and discredited Villa's role as the initiator of the deal. Shifts in U.S. foreign policy and engrained attitudes hampered the revolutionary leader's ability to promote his social agenda and cement his political and military leadership within the Constitutionalist forces. In Mexico, in a propaganda effort to undermine Villa's achievements, enraged rivals in the Carranza camp disqualified Villa as being "more a creation of the mass media than... a substantial revolutionary force" (Anderson, 2000, 44). By making light of his own awareness of the power of visual media to reconfigure identity, he was turned into a commodity deprived of social agency and burdened by historical reductionism and mythology. As a cinematic hero, Villa came to embody at once the most heroic and most brutal traits of the Mexican Revolution.

Two recent films engage with these issues by drawing on the extant visual archive and current historiography to tell the story of the now-missing film *The Life of General Villa*. Produced by Home Box Office (HBO) and first telecast on September 7, 2003, *And Starring Pancho Villa as Himself* (Bruce Beresford) re-creates anecdotes of the Mutual deal and replicates early cinematic practices. In keeping with its metahistorical aims, the film draws attention to historical modes of spectatorship linking vision and identity to rehabilitate Villa's persona (played by Antonio Banderas) and redress filmic stereotypes. *The Lost Reels of Pancho Villa* (2003) is an experimental work by the Mexican film- and video maker Gregorio Rocha documenting his quest for the missing film. It investigates foreign (mainly U.S.) depictions of Villa and the revolution found in archives and libraries in Europe and North America, including those that reconfigured him into the archetypal Mexican bandit following the Columbus raid in March 1916. It recounts the making of *The Vengeance of Pancho Villa*, a film made in the 1920s from a variety of materials by Félix and Edmundo Padilla.

While both films explore the meanings and value of the archival evidence on the Villa-Mutual deal and the ensuing film, they treat the materials differently. Historicity in the Beresford film is shaped by an investment in apparatus-mediated representations of identity, even if the meanings of the Villa-Mutual deal are relocated into current debates surrounding media politics and war reporting. Notwithstanding its action-packed sequences, melodramatic effect, and archetypal imagery that risk derailing the film's revisionist design, what emerges is a multilayered representation of Villa as a mass-mediated construct that is contingent on narrative slippages between what is historically verifiable and fictional. In the Rocha film, reflexivity is put at the service of alternative modes of historicity. Characters and events of the past are represented as cultural and social projections, their agencies unstable and contingent on the material frailty of the archive and the paradox of historicity. Moreover, reassemblages of extant film materials point to the film's strategies of reclamation aimed at reimagining Villa's subjectivity and cinematic identity as a Mexican hero.

"PANCHITO VILLA SELLS A WAR": VISION AND IDENTITY IN *And Starring Pancho Villa as Himself*

A short synopsis of the Beresford film is in order.[3] With D. W. Griffith's (Colm Feore) approval, Harry Aitken (Jim Broadbent) sends his nephew Frank Thayer (Eion Bailey) to Mexico. The Mutual Film Company will accept Villa's (Antonio Banderas) offer to film his campaign against Huerta. After signing the deal, Thayer and his crew shoot their first battle in Ojinaga just across from Presidio, Texas. The poor response by the New York press does not deter Aitken from pursuing the deal, now as a fiction feature to be called "The Life of General Villa."[4] In the wake of the murder of the British rancher William Benton (Anthony Head), both Villa and Aitken stand to gain by countering William Randolph Hearst's pro-intervention propaganda campaign. Only after tough negotiations, a larger crew is dispatched to Mexico. Shooting begins with William Christy Chabanne (Michael MacKean) directing, Raoul Walsh (Kyle Chandler) playing the young Villa, and Teddy Sampson (Alexa Dávalos) playing the sister. Marred by disagreements, it ends successfully just as Villa's army moves against Torreón. Following Villa's decision after a disastrous daytime attack on the Federal garrison to launch the final offensive at night, Thayer can only record the bloody aftermath. At the New York premiere on May 9, 1914, Thayer meets with John Reed (Matt Day) again. Both voice their disappointment with Villa and their misgivings about the propagandistic use of war imagery. Thayer returns to Mexico after Villa's assassination in 1923 to show "The Life of General Villa" at the request of his former Mexican film trainee, Abraham Sánchez (Cosme Sánchez).

By means of a variety of visual effects, the film highlights vision as a primary mode for negotiating identity and difference. Digitally generated or not, masking reveals an agency shifting between what Thayer and the viewers see, what the Mutual cameramen Charles Rositer (Carl Dillard) and Hennie Aussenberg (John Wharton) record, and what Beresford re-creates for the film-within-the-film. No matter how often the camera registers Thayer's expressions of awe and dread, his responses to the thrills and horrors of war are conveyed most effectively when he assumes the position of film viewer and watches the black-and-white images of "The Life of General Villa" on the screen. How Villa enters Thayer's field of vision in the early sequences is symptomatic of an apparatus-mediated representation of identity. Whether his figure is reflected in field glasses during a battle in Ojinaga across from Presidio, Texas, or silhouetted against the doorframe of the room where Thayer is waiting, the effect is similar. Fearlessly masculine on horseback or plainly menacing in the darkness, he embodies desire and abjection. Only when both characters meet face to face does the phantasmagoric projection give way to subjectivity. In this scene, to which I will return, agency is repositioned by means of a series of renegotiations worth considering because, as Thayer's closing remark—"I have never seen a man like that"—implies, they are anchored in the vast visual archive that links identity and spectatorship.

The Mexican Revolution, as Debroise writes, "was photographed from every point of view, both geographically and ideologically" (2001, 181). As noted, visual media reconfigured the public sphere and generated a new

FIGURE 2.1. And Starring Pancho Villa as Himself, *frame enlargement*

iconography from existing formal structures. For the subjects (leaders and common folk), posing and good clothes became validating gestures, not just signifiers of political and social legitimacy. When Emiliano Zapata posed for Hugo Brehme in an elaborate version of the customary *charro* attire and when Villa replaced his wide-brimmed hat and gun belts for a tailored jacket and pith helmet, they transformed themselves into subjects of their own histories. They defied stereotypes, breaking with the Indian peasant and outlaw types of Mexican folklore and the "greaser" bandit figure of American pulp culture to project their leadership and military qualities. The photographs of Villa wearing an army uniform taken prior to the battle of Torreón in May 1914, like the attack strategy he implemented, reflect "in spectacular ways a recently acquired cinematic consciousness" (De los Reyes, [1985] 1992, 13). This ownership of the image extends to numerous group pictures whose subjects, albeit anonymous, enact a powerful belief that no matter how trivial, the moment is worth recording. As the American war correspondent Timothy G. Turner recalls in his memoirs, "The lure of a camera was great in Mexico in those days. It was all so new and so exciting and so romantic. Everybody enjoyed it hugely and wanted everyone else to share the fun. Were not photographs souvenirs, and should not one let friends as well as visitors have souvenirs? That was more important than fighting any time" (1935, 80).

Whether everybody shared in this feeling of excitement and adventure, or how long it persisted given that the war lasted another decade, may in the end be less significant than the awareness that photography afforded

FIGURE 2.2. *"Francisco Villa on Horseback," D. W. Hoffman, ca. 1900, photograph. Courtesy of the Special Collections Department, University of Texas at El Paso Library*

HISTORICITY AND THE ARCHIVE || 45

FIGURE 2.3. *"American Sightseers Near Madero's Camp,"* D. W. Hoffman, June 26, 1911, postcard. Wayne Brendt Collection, Courtesy of the Specials Collection Department, University of Texas at El Paso Library

common people a place in history as actors and witnesses. Nowhere is this rendered more eloquently than in their presence as onlookers in the Mexican-produced still images and the film materials included in the compilations *Epics of the Mexican Revolution* and *Memories of a Mexican*. Conversely, in American images, spectatorship constructs a mirror image of the curious and souvenir-hunting gaze of the camera described by Turner. This gaze was commodified in numerous postcards that show citizens of border cities observing the insurrectional forces camped or in combat on the Mexican side of the Rio Grande. As Claire F. Fox explains, not even the danger of being hit could "stop hundreds of people from flocking to battle scenes anyway, and behaving as though they were watching a play or a movie rather than a war" (1999, 81).

Villa: Identity as Spectacle

Given the metahistorical intent of *And Starring Pancho Villa as Himself*, it should not come as a surprise that Villa's first appearance is an explicit citation of this curious tourist phenomenon. These scenes reconstruct a postcard with the caption, "On the Roof Garden of Hotel Paso del Norte. The only Hotel in the World Offering Its Guests a Safe, Comfortable Place

FIGURE 2.4. *"Americans View the Battle of Ciudad Juárez from the Hotel Paso del Norte in El Paso," postcard. Jane Burges Perrenot Research Center. Courtesy of the El Paso County Historical Society*

to View a Mexican Revolution." Even if bartenders, soldiers, women, and young children are added to what is in the postcard a largely male crowd, and a title printed on the frame names the setting as the "Rio Grande, The Texas-Mexico border," the ensuing scenes historicize the anecdote. While iris shots single out Villa as the main attraction, other iris shots expose the politics suppressed in this visual equation of warfare and spectacle by panning on embattled town streets and burning American oil wells. To Thayer's remark, "It feels almost like watching a show from up here, doesn't it?" a man who promptly identifies himself as "John Reed, Metropolitan Magazine," responds: "It is more than play acting, sir; what you are watching is a dictatorship in the throes of dying." Benton's disdainful categorization of Villa as "the bloody Robin Hood of Mexico" even before Thayer sees him diverges from Villa's own elation ("The movies have come to Pancho!") when he sights the red cloth that Mutual representative Eli Morton (Saul Rubinek) waves to announce the film crew's arrival.

Villa's representation in this sequence is burdened by historicity, with visual and written sources that give priority to sight and display getting in the way of a critical treatment of this imagery of revolution as a spectacle. Equally reliant on ocular effects (the attention-grabbing reflection of the horse-riding Villa on Thayer's field glasses) and stereotype repositioning (Benton's denigration of a familiar moniker), the treatment of this encounter of curious yet incompatible gazes confirms historical positions. Whereas for Mexicans the revolution was politically and historically meaningful, "from the U.S. point of view, [it] was a drama, and its soldiers were actors" (Fox, 1999, 83). Americans equated prevailing responses to the camera to backwardness and projected deeply internalized prejudices onto the visual apparatus. An instance of this reaction is found in a review of the Mutual "Mexican war pictures" printed in *Moving Picture World* on February 17, 1914. W. Stephen Bush wrote, "I saw General Villa, General [Toribio] Ortega, Manzanillas and other generals mentioned by the gentleman who explained the pictures and I have not a just conception of what a Mexican general looks like. They were all pleased to be kinematographed [sic]. Villa and Ortega posed as meekly as any novice before a camera and obediently took off their hats when told to do so by the photographer" (1914, 657).

Although he had proven to be a successful yet unconventional military leader, the depiction of Villa as naive, self-indulgent, or vulgar reduced his identity and agency to an affectation with the apparatus. Naturalized under the accumulated weight of mythmaking and hagiography, this image has endured in history. Terry Ramsaye, commenting on the Mutual deal in 1926, asserted that "Villa rode to battle and conquest because he loved the vision of himself on horseback" (1964, 670). Edgcumb Pinchon saw Villa on his horse as a photogenic embodiment of visuality itself. In the 1933 biography titled *Viva Villa!* he described Madero's camp on the Rio Grande in 1911 as "a glorified Barnum and Bailey circus" where journalists and common people mingled to get "a furtive glimpse of a pre-moral order." There, he wrote, "'bad men,' donning their most ferocious smiles, obligingly pose for their pictures; 'generals' affix flourishing signatures to colored picture-postcards of themselves in heroic attitudes; and even Pancho Villa, up for a military caucus, reins in his plunging stallion long enough to leave on a strip of film a sun-record of brutal force, vitality and horsemanship" (152–153).

These representations of Villa originate in the vast photographic archive produced during his victorious 1914 campaign. Made up primarily of publicity materials prepared by the Mutual Film Company for trade periodicals, it also included production stills that, issued to press agencies, guaranteed their worldwide circulation as journalistic images (De los Reyes, [1985] 1992, 12–13). This marketing strategy explains why some of the most frequently reproduced images of Villa present him in action, sometimes literally in a freeze-frame, rather than in the conventional style of portraiture. The most celebrated of these stills shows Villa on horseback

FIGURE 2.5. *"General Villa after the Battle of Ojinaga,"* 1914, photograph. John D. Wheelan Collection of Mexican Revolution Photographs. Courtesy of the Cushing Memorial Library and Archives, Texas A&M Libraries

after the battle of Ojinaga and appeared first in the *New York Times* on January 23, 1914.[5] It has been reprinted innumerable times on handbills, posters, and book covers and in magazine articles and illustrated histories of the Mexican Revolution. It was used as a source for monuments in Durango and Chihuahua due, most likely, to an erroneous attribution to the Mexican photographer Agustín Víctor Casasola and inclusion in the first edition of *The Graphic History of the Revolution 1900–1940*, edited and published by Gustavo Casasola, Agustín's son and director of the prestigious Casasola Archive.[6]

Disruptions of the objectifying power of vision serve to renegotiate differences and rehistoricize Villa's identity in *And Pancho Villa Starring as Himself*. Having been led blindfolded and under the cover of darkness across the Rio Grande to meet Villa, Thayer first sees a table laden with desserts. After being subjected to the disapproving gaze of soldiers, among them a stern-looking *soldadera*, a belligerent Villa antagonizes him. With Sam Drebben (Alan Arkin) translating and disputing Morton's admonition not to look Villa in the eyes ("That's a pile of crap, they don't stop telling stories about this guy"), Thayer's agency is put to the test. His self-assurance collapses, and his identity is destabilized. When Villa sees the Harvard crest on his necktie, a perceptual shift occurs. He switches from English (he calls Harvard "the school where they make presidents") to Spanish (a joke about having enough sons to fill all the colleges in America). Next, in the contract-signing scene, and by donning eyeglasses, his identity is aligned with rationality to offset the image of Villa as an illiterate simpleton driven by instinct. He comes across as commercially astute and politically informed. He forces an adjustment from 10 to 20 percent in profits and declares his confidence in moving images to counter the Hearst press-led misinformation campaign. After his remark about sharing the same name with Thayer (Francisco and Frank), the self/other structure of identification breaks down. Despite the character's sporadic outbursts of aggressive and roguish behavior, Villa's agency is resignified by self-identification to minimize difference. It is ultimately narrative agency that enables the production of new knowledge. While the impetuosity and belligerence associated with Villa as a brutal chieftain are integral to Banderas's performance, these traits are contained by the weight given to the character's social and political motivations.[7]

Even if this sequence seems to steer clear of the standard elements of Villa's filmic portrayals by resorting to archival evidence, it combines two different sources. On the one hand, it refers to the personal recollections of Ivar Thord-Grey, a Swedish-born officer who joined briefly the Villistas and later the Constitutionalist army commanded by Obregón. The artillery and intelligence expert writes about being struck by the sight of the flower bouquet that "stood in front of Villa, stuck in an expensive blue Chinese jar from the Ming period, a beautiful museum piece," and the leader's reaction: "When he saw me his face turned to a scowl, almost anger, associated, it seemed to me, with arrogance or contempt. His whole attitude was a challenge, startling although not altogether objectionable" (1983, 54). As in the memoir, the scene relies on Thayer's bewildered response to seeing the lavish table and then being overtly antagonized by Villa.

On the other hand, this scene contains allusions to Raoul Walsh's semifictional autobiography, *Each Man in His Time: The Life Story of a Director* (1974), regarded by film historians as unreliable or at least "highly colored" (Brownlow, 1979, 577 n. 17). The Hollywood veteran recounts how Villa's lieutenant Ortega (mistakenly named Manuel instead of Toribio) told him "apologetically" that he had to cover his eyes and made him wonder, "Why did I have to be blindfolded when every child in [Ciudad] Juárez and most of their parents certainly knew of Villa's whereabouts? Whatever reason, it added more drama to the situation" (Walsh, 1974, 87). The account that follows is "fantastically cinematographic" (De los Reyes, 1985, 24).[8] As in the scene of *And Starring Pancho Villa as Himself*, the representation of Villa and his men is highly mediated. However, identification is based on visual fallacy, with Walsh claiming he "recognized him at once from his pictures" in a then-nonexistent biography he read on the train ride from southern California (Walsh, 1974, 88). His views waver between condescension, bewilderment, and alienation. Ignored by Villa and positioned as bystander rather than participating agent, Walsh sees the revolutionary leader at first as "the classic example of a Mexican bandit," adjusting his perception ("Here was a man's man") only when he watches Villa's lively interaction with Ortega (88).

Villa and the Mutual Contract

To the extent that Walsh's story functions as a bridge between contemporaneous testimonies and fictionalized recollections of Americans in Mexico, it underlines the burden placed on the film's historicity by the incomplete nature of the extant archival evidence on the Villa-Mutual deal. With most of the films lost, to revisit the deal film historians have had to content themselves with still photographs, handbills, reviews, and articles. As De los Reyes makes clear in *Con Villa en México*, the narratives fashioned around the contract offer multiple and overlapping perspectives that matched the views promoted by the popular press in the United States ([1985] 1992). Besides profit, these promotional materials were intended to create audience anticipation through details on the making of the films and accounts of the hardships and dangers encountered by the cameramen. Although genuine anecdotes and gossip are impossible to tell apart in these testimonies, their historical dimension resides, as the Mexican film historian Margarita de Orellana states, in their reflexivity: "Symbolically what they went to observe and report disappears, and their camera turns on its imaginary 180-degree axis to film them in the act of looking. In those moments, Pancho Villa and his men form a kind of scenography that projects the personal characteristics of the observers" (1999, 86).

Moreover, by favoring their own agency, the narratives of the cameramen reveal to what extent apparatus reductionism diminished the part played by Mexicans as subjects and protagonists of the films. Not even Villa was spared. At best, they treated him with condescending respect. In an interview that appeared in the May 9, 1914, issue of the Mutual Film periodical *Reel Life,* cameraman Herbert M. Dean offered the following description of Villa: "Sometimes in action he would ride by and stop to watch us at work. Taciturn by nature, he would say nothing but his sunny smile indicated that we amused him hugely. If we wished to photograph him, he would rein in his horse, and in the fraction of a second would be on his way again" (11). For Walsh, Villa's behavior was "unpredictable. When he was angry, he would gallop past the camera, raising dust and making it impossible to follow him" (1974, 97). At worst, accounts about filming in Mexico passed derogatory judgments on military leaders as "being more vain than movie actors" and "willing to reenact a battle after it was over, with corpses still on the ground" (Wagner, in De los Reyes, [1985] 1992, 240). It did not matter that additional battle scenes were most likely staged for "The Life of General Villa" (De los Reyes, [1985] 1992, 20). Claims of faked footage became part of the lore surrounding the Mutual deal, and they resurfaced again in the 1970s in Walsh's fanciful filming anecdotes (Walsh, 1974, 95–97).

While *And Starring Pancho Villa as Himself* exhibits the same penchant for autobiographical agency and daring exploits found in the cameramen's accounts, it steers clear of the claims of war being re-created for the cameras. It restores Villa's position as initiator of the deal that brings Thayer to Mexico and the movies to the revolution. He partakes in the film's emphasis on visual agency with most moments of conflict revolving around his desire to control representation. Whether the effect is dramatic or comedic, he is shown as being responsive to the visual apparatus both as a naturalized and as an imaginary projection of identity and history. Scenes dealing with the arrival of the actors, shooting fictional sequences for "The Life of General Villa," and later his clash with Thayer over the screenplay make apparent the historical Villa's "clever, if ironic, responses" to American stereotypes (Anderson, 2000, 14). They show a skeptical, impish, and outraged Villa. Although he mockingly acquiesces to the blond Irene Hunt (Barbara May) playing his mother and only approves of Walsh after testing his abilities to ride a horse and fire a gun, he repudiates the idea of being portrayed as president of Mexico. Shooting up the screenplay may be a melodramatic gesture, yet it fits the film's attempt to highlight Villa's awareness of the already proven power of media to reconfigure identity. By calling "lies" what Thayer deems artistic license, Villa comes across as an unwilling partner in a venture that falsifies his past and denigrates his motives to suit the profit-driven motives of film producers and the thrill-seeking expectations of audiences.

Antonio Banderas Performing Villa

If vision has been central to the historical construction of Villa's identity, its objectifying function is further disrupted in *And Pancho Villa Starring as Himself* by charismatic performance and narrative catharsis. Banderas conveys the weight of history and legend on Villa. Through a dynamic and highly sexualized performance of gender and ethnic difference, he endows the character with a transnational identity that is marked equally by the actor's professional trajectory and global Latino icon status.[9] Body language and speech blend action and melodrama, despite the irritating shifts from Mexican to peninsular Spanish vernacular and the actor's propensity to mutter. "Some of his facial distortions," Juan Bruce-Novoa writes, "could be read as parodic tributes to [Wallace] Beery's unique repertoire of grimaces and hand-to-face gestures"(2005, 8). The reference to the actor who played in *Viva Villa!* suggests to what extent Banderas's performance hinges on that of previous Hollywood actors who have portrayed the Mexican leader. It reaffirms, in the words of Charles Ramírez Berg, the "eroticism, exoticism, [and] tenderness, tinged with violence and danger," that have defined since Valentino Hollywood's representations of Latino masculinity (2002, 76). Excessive and unruly, at times bordering on silliness, the acting reflects Banderas's own attraction to the character. "From a dramatic point of view," he said in an interview posted on the film's official Web site, "Pancho Villa is a dream. He's flexible. You can stretch him as much as you want. You can do practically anything that comes to your mind. . . . Because everything is acceptable" (2004, n.p.). This potential is appealing to the Spanish actor. It allows him to go beyond his and the character's persona to restore his own transcultural identity and Villa's historical agency as a cinematic hero.

The coming together of narrative agency and fetishized spectacle is visualized in two important moments that rely on high melodrama for effect to replicate historical modes of spectatorship. In the quarrel over the screenplay, Villa's outburst at being compared to General Ulysses Grant is a visceral projection of how Mexicans have viewed U.S. contempt for their own people. He calls Grant a "drunk dogface; he killed *mexicanos* like he killed his whiskey bottles," and reacts angrily to Thayer's admission that he did not know. The aggressive and sexualized performance turns Villa into the key player and Thayer into the mediating figure of desire. This position is upheld by camera placement and lighting, despite the change of register that occurs later when Thayer confronts Villa about the Benton killing and makes a case for what can be gained politically by self-

FIGURE 2.6. And Starring Pancho Villa as Himself, *frame enlargement*

promotion. Seen in long shot, his figure bathed by light coming from the open roof of the train car, Banderas's lively gestures and hypermasculine pose contrast with Bailey's soft voice and subservient bearing. The scene alluded to by the film's title revolves as well around display and spectatorship. Having bowed to Thayer's request to play himself as president, Villa arrives on the set in a white suit and whiteface makeup with kohl-rimmed eyes and powdered moustache and hair. Visual effects call attention to artifice, and the histrionic performance reflexively alludes to silent film acting. The reverse shot of the internal audience restores the emotional resonance of image production and consumption of the Mexican Revolution. Even if Villa's performance sways precariously toward parody, the men, women, and children of his army approvingly applaud their leader's performance. The thrilled responses of the American film crew are summarized again by the fawning Thayer, who says, with Reed at his side, "Is there anything the man can't do?"

Although this scene is utterly fictional, its credibility depends both on historical evidence and on Banderas's skillful interpretation of Villa's own role in packaging himself as a cinematic hero. As Anderson writes, by the time the revolutionary agreed to Mutual's request to don military garb, "the construction he now presented to the public had become more fully a conscious production that included a package (self-reliant, rugged, uniformed warrior), a content (friendship at any cost), and a pitch (honesty, virtue, courage, love of democracy and fatuous praise of the United States and Wilson)" (2000, 61). By embracing an acting style grounded on performance, Banderas validates the revolutionary leader's historical and legendary persona at once as an intercultural icon and an agent in the construction of his own mythology.

Translators and Spectators

Notwithstanding the transcultural dimensions of Banderas's portrayal of Villa, the translation of cultural difference falls primarily to the gunner Sam Drebben, nicknamed "the fighting Jew," and the journalist John Reed. Whether in their habitual role as narrative catalysts or as historical figures, the Americans are central to the film's revisionist designs and, with the latter as a secondary character, perspective on media politics. Through Drebben, and Alan Arkin's characterization, the film illustrates the participation of U.S. soldiers of fortune in the Mexican Revolution and takes a pragmatic view of war devoid of the patriotic overtones of Hollywood action movies. In a sense, he is Thayer's mature alter ego. Skilled in the rules of combat and cultural exchange, he is energized by the revolution because it is an adventure and an opportunity to come into his own as an individual. In the end, having lost an eye and an arm in Torreón, Drebben is a battle-weary veteran. He is a custodian of memory and a Cassandra-like figure who foretells the fate of Mexico. Yet the bond between the characters is knocked off balance because he is at once decoder and actor of the violence that Thayer witnesses. After the Ojinaga battle, for instance, neither the reasons provided by Drebben nor the actions of Villa dispel Thayer's revulsion at the sight of hanging corpses and the unbridled hostility he encounters as he strolls through the ravaged town. Accompanied by Reed, he watches Rodolfo Fierro (Damián Alcázar) killing two Federal officers with a single gunshot ("It saves ammunition," says the journalist) and then Drebben extracting a gold tooth from one of the corpses with pliers. In the next scene, during a joyful night party and escorted by Reed, Thayer gains knowledge on what drives the various actors of the revolution. The journalist characterizes the U.S. and Mexican followers of Villa according to their compassion, idealism, and brutality. "Healing Jews and fighting Jews," is how Reed refers to Maurice Rauschbaum, "a surgeon from Indiana," and Drebben, "the machine gunner from the Bronx." Reed uses the same symmetry for General Felipe Angeles (Diego Sandoval), the cultured military and idealist, and Rodolfo Fierro, who, as he says, "gets ugly unless he kills at least one prisoner before breakfast."

Reed (like Drebben) acts as a go-between, his interventions providing a reflexive counterpoint to the visual reductionism that has turned the popular mobilization of the revolution into a spectacle. Echoes of archetypal images and sounds abound in this sequence: the earthy hues imitate the sepia-tinted or discolored look of old photographs and the "Adelita" song on the sound track. Yet the tracking camera restores historicity to the vignette-like shots. The social and political dynamics of revolutionary community are revealed by choreographed movement and framing that favor interactions among the diverse actors. Matching moments disrupt the objectifying gaze, give agency back to the characters, and expose the visual transactions and narrative deferrals hidden behind the spectator-based imagery of the Mexican Revolution. Two scenes with Villa merit attention. The point of view shots of Villa dancing and singing the familiar refrains of "Adelita" around a campfire bind Thayer and the film viewer to evoke the investment of apparatus-mediated vision in the constructions of Villa as a cinematic figure. Yet this bond is broken in the scene of Thayer's failed attempt to have Charlie take a picture of a grief-stricken widow expressing her gratitude for having been given money. Thayer's repositioning as observer is made more explicit for Charlie, who is presented as an agent of representation in the opening scene of this sequence as he sets up his camera and magnetic flash to photograph a group of four soldiers.

Reed is a witness, as well as a socially and politically responsive interlocutor. With Thayer at his side, he is addressed as "Juanito" when Villa solicits his feedback on what Americans will think of the movies. He prompts Villa's own account of why Edward Doheny and William Randolph Hearst have reasons to be nervous about the events in Mexico. Although there is no mention of the Mutual deal in Reed's accounts published in the *Metropolitan* and collected in *Insurgent Mexico,* his presence in the film is crucial.[10] The film relies on his historical standing, first as an eyewitness whose romantic and sympathetic vision is put to the test by the brutal realities of war and later as a radical committed to Communism. In this capacity, he provides crucial historical information. A notable example is the Presidio sequence where Reed's remarks contextualize the action, explaining events and anecdotes not shown in the film (Bruce-Novoa, 2005, 9). Positioned as an informed bystander, the fictional Reed is both a foil to Thayer's star-struck and naive idealism and a savvy critic of the media's complicity with U.S. interests in Mexico. In the only scene where Reed is shown as a working journalist, he says, "Clearly more people would discover Pancho Villa from a few feet of this crude historic film than from the reams that have been written about his struggle to rid Mexico from its greedy robber-barons, the only ones to profit from their marriage with rapacious American interests." Thus reconfigured, Reed is the mediating agent of the film's present-day outlook, which is articulated best in the screening sequence of "The Life of General Villa" (see below).

A significant metahistorical component of *And Starring Pancho Villa as Himself* is the diverse reactions of crew members and the revolutionaries who observe the shooting and the New York and Mexican audiences who view the newsreel and "The Life of General Villa." Through this emphasis on spectators, the film exposes a complex process of acquiescence and resistance that implicates contemporary viewers as well in the work of the image and its competing truth-claims. At the press showing, for instance, the New York journalists greet the Ojinaga footage with perplexity and amusement. They dismiss Aitken's pitch about "never seen [battle] footage" with "never seen . . . you still can't see it," and make fun of Villa's jovial acknowledgment of being filmed. This scene registers the negative responses to the 1914 newsreel. As De los Reyes writes, "There were no good, exciting battles; Villa did not wear an elegant military uniform but old, dirty city clothes and a three-day beard which made him look like a common bandit, not a General; and the clouds of dust raised by the action obscured the images" (2001b, 37). Conversely, in the closing segment, a Mexican audience greets with enthusiasm the scene of Villa as president. A letter from Abraham Sánchez to Thayer prompts the screening. But it is the official refusal to grant a hero's burial to Villa after his assassination in 1923 and Sánchez's question posed offscreen—"How will the sons of Mexico remember Pancho Villa?"—that aligns the representation with popular memory. Reaction shots capture the affect-charged effect of the fictional images and legitimate the legendary leader's place in the social imaginary.

At the New York premiere of "The Life of General Villa," the well-heeled public greets the war images with puzzlement and outrage. Used to complement acted scenes about Villa's early life, these images are a shocking and spectacular intrusion into what is otherwise a trite story of revenge. Their effect on Thayer and Reed is significant as well. Through their subsequent discussion, the film constructs what is ultimately its message. At issue is the veracity of the image and the anxiety resulting from its manipulation for political purposes. To have Reed invoke Senator Hiram Warren Johnson's notorious pronouncement from 1918, that "the first casualty of war is truth," the film's historicizing agenda is projected into the present. The Mexican Revolution as a mediated event and Villa's role in fashioning himself into a cinematic hero are displaced onto contemporary debates over the various meanings of "reality" and repositioned within a renewed anxiety about the media and the representation of war.

This should not come as a surprise. Both the director, Bruce Beresford, and the scriptwriter, Larry Gelbart, have tackled the topic of war before, and reviewers have ensured that analogies with reality TV, celebrity spin, and "embedded" journalism are not overlooked (Gilbert, 2003, 1). What the British film historian Kevin Brownlow describes as "one of the most curious and remarkable deals in film history" (1979, 91) is put at the service of current debates on media fabrication. Moreover, *And Starring Pancho Villa as Himself* falls short of what I believe are genuine intentions to rehabilitate the most complex figure of the Mexican Revolution — and the most notoriously demonized by Hollywood cinema. In spite of its reflexive emphasis on vision and identity, its historicizing position remains uncritically aligned with the numerous narratives circulated first by American journalists and cameramen and later by film historians about Villa and the Mutual deal. What remains is nothing more than a made-in-Hollywood spectacle that uses the revolution as a pretext for moralizing statements on war and representation.

COUNTERMEMORY AND APPROPRIATION IN
The Lost Reels of Pancho Villa

As De Orellana points out, "The history of the revolution through the fictional and newsreel films of North America is simply the history of a self-directed gaze and its transformations, the history of a circular look" (1993, 14). If cinema turned events and their protagonists into a reflective mirror in which Americans could view themselves as other, then it is legitimate to ask, what is the meaning of these representations for Mexicans? This question is explicitly addressed in *The Lost Reels of Pancho Villa* (Gregorio Rocha, Mexico, 2003), a formally imaginative, multivocal, and personal work that deals with the archival object. Its value comes from its political and affective investment in historicity and strategies of reclamation. Rocha's on-camera presence and first-person offscreen address establishes him as protagonist and narrator of a search to locate "The Life of General Villa." He describes events, characters, and images and articulates the questions guiding his quest. "I like to ask questions of old pictures. Who are you standing there in front of the camera? Who took your picture? Where were you? What was going through your mind? . . . So General Villa, what happened to the movie you shot in 1914?" says the filmmaker early in the film over a montage of period images, including the footage known as "Unknown Seffens" depicting Federal army refugees in Presidio, Texas, after the battle of Ojinaga.

FIGURE 2.7. The Lost Reels of Pancho Villa, *frame enlargement*

To explore the stories hidden behind extant period images of the revolution, Rocha enlists the silent film scholars and archivists Kevin Brownlow (London, England), Paolo Cherchi-Usai (Rochester, New York), and Fernando del Moral González (Mexico City); the historians Rubén Osorio (Ojinaga, Mexico) and Stephen Bellmore (London); the grandson of cameraman Charles Rosher, Langdon Morrell (San Diego, California); and the exhibitor Edmundo Padilla (El Paso, Texas, in a previously taped interview). To find the lost reels of the Villa film, Rocha sets out on a journey that is part wandering and interrogation and involves trans- and intercontinental travel by airplane, train, car, and foot. In the process, the desire to rescue the past is repeatedly put to the test. Visits to film archives and libraries in New York, London, Amsterdam, and El Paso bring mostly disappointment but yield some unexpected results. By far the most exciting discovery is made in El Paso. Among the deteriorating film reels kept by the family of the itinerant movie exhibitors Félix and Edmundo Padilla, Rocha finds the hitherto unknown *The Vengeance of Pancho Villa*, which is made up of segments from a variety of silent films, including one from *The Life of General Villa*. Produced in the 1930s, the Padilla film appropriates Villa as a popular Mexican hero by reconfiguring his legendary filmic identity from the numerous fictions that turned him in 1916, after the attack on Columbus, New Mexico, into a ruthless and bloodthirsty bandit (Rocha, 2002, 26–27).

Not having found what he is looking for, Rocha transforms failure creatively. He integrates into the film still photographs and documentary and fictional footage, as well as a variety of printed items.[11] Rather than simply confirm long-established opinions on the systemic objectification and racism in U.S. depictions of Mexico, he places these materials at the service of alternative modes of historicity. His statement, "I want to believe that Utopia is to be found in the shape of an archetypal image, one that refuses to disappear despite the wear and tear of the years," echoes the film historian Jay Leyda's insights on reconstructing the past out of old newsreels expressed in his pioneering study of compilation films, *Films Beget Films* (1964). Whether used as evidence or reorganized into filmic montage segments, the archival materials provoke reflections on their historicizing value and purpose. Their diverse iconographic and narrative features and shifting spectator positions enable meanings to be scrutinized, deconstructed, and reformulated. "History in film," as the filmmaker aptly remarks over the earlier-mentioned shots of refugees, "does not necessarily coincide with history of reality. Rather, film records the history of the imaginary." This caveat is sustained not just by the revisionist opinions of the interviewees but also by the reflexive treatment of the film's various components. By means of technological, aesthetic, and rhetorical mediations, characters and events of the past are represented as cultural and social projections. The caption replicating period postcards on the film poster reads, "Gregorio Rocha and Pancho Villa caught by the camera while filming his documentary." Villa also appears literally as a ghost reflected on a Parisian subway car window and a metal container filled with corroded film reels. He also enters the film as a disembodied voice summarizing the plot of *The Life of General Villa* over water-stained pictures, perhaps the only extant visual record of the lost film. If iris shots of a spinning record on an old gramophone expose the artifice, then first-person address, diction, and vernacular idioms infer a subject in control of his own, albeit fictionalized, life story.[12] Revealed in this way, the revolutionary leader haunts the film's discourse: its dialogue with an elusive subject in danger of melting away, like images bearing the telltale signs of nitrate decay, and an absent agent of his own representation waiting to be rediscovered.

Those who recounted filming the revolution are also invited to partake in this dialogue between what is lost and what waits to be reconstituted. As Rocha says, images "tell the stories the film makers want us to

FIGURE 2.8. The Life of General Villa, *film still*, *Mutual Film Company*, 1914. *Courtesy of the Specials Collection Department, University of Texas at El Paso Library*

see," even if some may be true. Whether depicted or vocalized, historicity and agency are shown as unstable constructs, contingent on historiography and mediated by affect. As noted, cameramen's testimonies were mainly vehicles for promoting newsreels dealing with events in Mexico. To enhance their own standing, cameramen circulated misleading stories, sometimes based on rumors or anecdotes told by colleagues working for Mutual or other film companies (De los Reyes, [1985] 1992, 21). To what extent genuine anecdotes and gossip are indistinguishable is demonstrated in the Brownlow interview segment that involves perusing photographs and viewing footage in an editing room. Matching film and still images are used as proof of reliability of the stories told by the famed Mutual cameraman Charlie Rosher. Other accounts are shown to be inconsistent, if not outright fabricated by self-attribution or visual trickery. Rocha deconstructs the notorious account of his arrest in Ojinaga by orders of the Federal army general Salvador Mercado as a misappropriation of a comparable incident recounted by the freelancer Charles Pryor (Brownlow, 1968, 256). New evidence modifies perceptions, not solely assessments, as the film historian's reactions reveal. He marvels at Rocha's discoveries, the detention scenes and Rosher's letter describing Pryor's arrest, yet is utterly repulsed by the graphic violence of the imagery of executions and doctors tending badly wounded soldiers in the Seffens collections.

By means of digital animation the figure of Rosher at his tripod-mounted camera is moved from one picture into another to illustrate Brownlow's anecdote of having come across a faked photograph of the U.S. cameraman with Villa. If visual trickery replicates here the notorious tendency to counterfeit images during the revolution, in other instances the visual effects of silent cinema are used reflexively. In the combat shots complementing Osorio's account of the Ojinaga battle as having started at seven o'clock in the evening, the deep-blue tinted images restore the temporality of Villa's attack and contest the stories about the Mutual film contract. In *The Lost Reels of Pancho Villa,* the disclosure-refutation rhetoric of competing claims of authenticity and historical agency generated by the imagery of the Mexican Revolution is particularly significant. If some of these claims are invalidated, the film does not resolve the uncertainty surrounding faked footage. Instead, the images themselves become the focal point for negotiating the essentialism of ubiquitous assertions that all war films shot before World War I were faked.[13]

The newsreel footage makes clear the blending of spectacle and actuality in silent films. In the Ojinaga scenes, for example, the yellow-tinted shot of U.S. soldiers with field glasses standing on a roof, their backs turned to the camera, evokes the spectator-themed imagery of the Mexican Revolution. Coloring is also a reminder that visual effects in this period were cosmetic enhancements. Like battle reenactments that, in De Orellana's words, "seemed more convincing dressed up in the studio than photographed direct," technical mediations were aimed at intensifying the reality effect of newsreels (1993, 7). What is more, a present-day outlook on the constructed nature of representation sustains the handling of archival footage. Visual effects and editing denaturalize the indexical properties of the footage to reveal image making then and now as a process, rather than a willful deception, and promote readings that are more consistent with current silent film historiography.

Period Imagery: Fact and Fiction

For this reason, period images in *The Lost Reels of Pancho Villa* deserve detailed attention. As indicated earlier in this chapter, they are evidence of diverse points of view on Mexico and revolution. Produced during the phase called transitional by silent film historians (i.e., 1907–1917), these images demonstrate the joint impact of apparatus and narrative-driven identifications in shaping a social spectator. In the U.S.-produced documentary footage, as De los Reyes states, "what prevails is a scrutinizing gaze on the human side of events, people and leaders. The epic was marginalized by their authors maybe because their gaze as foreigners compelled them to record habits, customs, and behaviors of people who were strangers to them" ([1985] 1992, 11). The Seffens materials of the Federal troops in Presidio illustrate the suffering and brutality of war and construct a point of view that betrays curiosity and compassion. The long shot composition accentuates the desert landscape. Group shots express in dramatic ways distress and isolation, such as the scenes of soldiers wearing rough wool blankets to protect themselves from the winter cold. All the refugees acknowledge the camera, even the women and young children standing behind a crude fence described as *corrales* (animal enclosures) in Osorio's present-day account of the disastrous Federal army retreat in January 1914. Framing reveals the refugees' vulnerability and, like the border imagery of the period, "indicates an anxiety about containing the Mexican population within the United States" (Fox, 1999, 74). Panning breaks momentarily the controlling and objectifying gaze of the stationary camera. The refugees' agency is realigned with a narrative about life in the makeshift camp in the scenes of a man receiving a bundle of firewood from a woman camp follower and groups of men looking at U.S. Army officials inspecting seized ammunition. With scenes of soldiers burning the dead, the affect of the imagery shifts to mourning. A spectacular panoramic shot of a caravan of people and animals escorted by U.S. troops across the sand-swept desert from Presidio to Marfa illustrates what has passed into history as the march of sorrows.

In contrast to this affect-laden representation of a defeated army, the footage of the Federal maneuvres on the outskirts of Mexico City in 1914 is primarily a military spectacle. Located at the British Film Institute (London), it may well be the film shot by the Austrian-born cameraman Fritz Arno Warner on a commission by the U.S. subsidiary of Pathé. As Rocha says, it was recorded "so [that] the American president Woodrow Wilson could see for himself that [Victoriano] Huerta was still the strong man in Mexico." Framing and composition point to controlled conditions and confirm the cameraman's account published on April 14, 1914, in *Moving Picture World*. The apparatus-mediated aesthetics of militaristic display and authoritarian agency are exemplified by a long shot of a photographer in a dusty field, his back to the camera. Horsemen pulling cart-mounted artillery guns and a cavalry officer respectively in the rear and front of

FIGURE 2.9. The Lost Reels of Pancho Villa, *frame enlargement*

the image surround him. The image of a well-equipped, disciplined, and efficient army is reinforced by shots of a cannon being fired, a trench with soldiers shooting, as Rocha says, at "invisible enemies," and a bridge being built over a canal. In the battle drill scene, a narrative dimension is added with below-the-waist shots of soldiers jumping over a "dead" soldier lying on the stony ground of a hill. The objectified performance is made more explicit by reenactment where, as De Orellana writes, the camera "was like an extension of [Huerta's] army: a weapon manipulated by the cameraman" who had been made "A General for a Day" (1999, 50).

This depiction of war as spectacle is sustained in fictional dramatizations by narrative and generic devices familiar to film audiences in the silent period. As the fictional films included in *The Lost Reels of Pancho Villa* demonstrate, spectacle is placed at the service of representations of gender, class, and racial difference. Moreover, the film insinuates the merits of viewing these materials as a broad canvas on which the history of foreign (largely U.S.) representations of Mexico can be retraced. By means of an extended montage combining various films, Rocha carries out Leyda's imagined but unrealized project on the Mexican Revolution using footage shot by foreigners. The filmmaker may well have taken a cue from the historian's plan to have the "entire factual heart of the film... framed with non-factual material to show less tangible things, attitudes, prejudices, inspirations" (Leyda, 1971, 113).[14] Yet he takes this idea further. The mosaic-like assembly of archetypal images is central to the film's politics of reclamation. Over shots of the Seine in Paris, Rocha says, "Today, in the city of the manifestoes I proclaim my right to challenge the demeaning image the foreign film industry has projected of me. I proclaim my right to see myself through the stereotypes (the savage, the half-breed, 'greaser') they made of me. I proclaim my right to the images of the past; to make them mine and bring them back to life."

The montage consists of Kalem Film Manufacturing Company productions, *The Mexican Joan of Arc* (1911) and *The Colonel's Escape* (1912), found in London and Amsterdam, respectively; the Wagner footage; and a Dutch film, *The Mexican Telegram* (1914). The story line eliminates good-versus-evil dichotomies and dispenses with melodramatic catharsis. Instead of brutality and retribution, it focuses on thrilling and dignified actions.[15] This narrative rearrangement works against the grain of the rescue motif, and its attendant fantasies of restoring the threat posed by gender and racial alterity, in silent westerns and female-centered adventure serials. As a result, characters and their agencies are reconfigured. The revenge-seeking widow in *The Mexican Joan of Arc* becomes an ingenious young woman at ease with trains and horses, a fearless but compassionate revolutionary leader.[16] Rather than the arrogant foreigner who saves Mexicans from oppression in *The Colonel's Escape,* the bravery and patriotism of the gun smuggler (and real-life Welsh-born mercenary) Caryl Rhys Price equals that of the other rebels.[17] The military unit from the army maneuvers film that surveys the mountainous landscape with field glasses is turned from enemy into passive spectator. With his cruel tormentors out of sight, the Dutch settler Willem's distress is revealed as nothing more than a mental image conjured by an anxious elderly father.[18]

One may argue that using films that depict the revolution in sympathetic ways because they draw on factual incidents and characters facilitates Rocha's reclamation of archetypal images of Mexico. However, he does more than just substitute negative with positive images. The western-style train robbery, battle reenactments, and trick film–style fantasy scenes in the montage point to the hybrid features of period silent film practices that mixed authentic locations of newsreels with stage setups of studio filming (Hansen, 1991, 46). Intertextuality and crossing genres, in Miriam Hansen's words, "acknowledge a diversity of viewer interests" and "a more open relationship with the arena of public discourse... that allowed that discourse to be contested and interpreted in alternative ways" (1991, 48, 94). Hence the montage segment revisualizes, albeit briefly, silent film spectatorship out of temporalities and identities dispersed around the world in film archives. The restructured narrative enables multiple identifications, reinstating the pleasures lost when early films are hidden from view. The resulting effect is a subject that is at once positioned and transitory, local and global.

Recycling as Resistance

Having said that, Rocha pays homage to Félix and Edmundo Padilla as pioneers of recycling as a strategy of cultural resistance. As noted earlier, they made *The Vengeance of Pancho Villa* in the 1930s from fragments of existing films about Villa and the Mexican Revolution. By integrating this film, along with outtakes found in the family's garage, the filmmaker rescues the work of this Mexican American father-and-son team of itinerant exhibitors as an early example of Mexican and Chicano cinema practices in the United States. Moreover, he uses the story of these other lost reels as a metaphor for the frailty and paradox of historicity. Recurrent shots of an unidentified figure in a blue smock and protective headgear, white gloves stained with brownish powder, oxidized reels, and brittle film stock turned into a whitish mass function as a visual trope for a salvage project literally at risk from hazardous and fragile materials. This "compilation of compilations," as Rocha calls it, is what countermemory is to historicism: an idea rather than an object, a construct made up of differing temporalities. The Padilla film is a political gesture of self-affirmation, as the divergent imagery of Villa used in the poster and the discarded outtakes exemplify. Wearing a white shirt and northern hat pushed slightly to the back of his head to reveal a jovial face, the legendary hero is revisualized. As an explicit quote of an archival photograph, it reinstates his historical persona and counteracts the filmic image equating Villa with a vicious predator by means of a ghostly superposition of his face with a mountain lion.

The Vengeance of Pancho Villa contains a segment from *The Life of General Villa* on Mormon settlers being attacked by bandits and requesting Villa's assistance.[19] A scene recorded by the Alva brothers showing Villa in Mexico City at Madero's tomb in December 1914 and a dramatized reconstruction of Villa's murder in 1923 shot by the Padillas with the help of friends in 1930 are also included. There is also footage from *Liberty, Daughter of the United States* (Jacques Jaccard and Henry McRae, 1916), a Universal serial of which only three of the twenty episodes seem to have

FIGURE 2.10.   La venganza de Pancho Villa, *poster. Courtesy of the Specials Collection Department, University of Texas at El Paso Library*

survived. Changes in attitudes toward Villa, President Woodrow Wilson's recognition of the Carranza government in 1915, and the public outrage over the Columbus, New Mexico, raid are graphically displayed in the exhibitor-aimed advertisement reproduced in De Orellana's book, *La mirada circular*. The serial was a timely melodrama intended to appeal to patriotic sentiments at a time when "all eyes [were] on Uncle Sam's boys along the Mexican border" (1999, 149). The National Guard soldier with a bugle against a backdrop of army tents, with the caption "Is Your Boy on the Border?" is a visual reminder of General John J. Pershing's punitive expedition into Mexico. Geographically undefined, the border is turned into a space where an "archetypal confrontation between Anglo and Mexican" occurs and "in which racial and physical contrasts are hyperbolized" (Fox, 1999, 72). The story line combines crude analogy and allegory, idealized femininity and ominous alterity. Liberty (played by Mary Walcamp) is the Anglo heiress of an enormous Mexican property that must be freed. Pancho López is the ferocious-looking, brown-faced bandit in dire need of money to finance his revolution who kidnaps her for ransom. And Mayor Rutledge is the all-American hero sent by Washington to rescue her and destroy the bandits who have attacked the U.S. town of Discovery.

As Rocha discovers in an editing logbook and among the outtakes, the Padillas eliminated Liberty as the main character, cut blatantly racist scenes and titles, used real names for characters and events, and created bilingual Spanish- and English-language titles. In keeping with the Mexican-centered perspective of *The Vengeance of Pancho Villa,* as Rocha says, "Pancho López became Pancho Villa, the Mexican hero. Discovery was changed back to Columbus." The image of victimized Americans was discarded in favor of fearless Mexicans, such as the title celebrating Villa's elite corps, the famed Dorados, which complements the fictionalized battle shots from films dealing with the Columbus raid. The representation of gratuitous violence is not associated with the New Mexico attack but the U.S. invasion of Veracruz in 1914 by means of the title "Lo mismo aquí, que en Veracruz, nuestros hermanos han sido sacrificados! Here as in Veracruz, our brothers have been sacrificed!" and the scenes from various films that follow. Villa's gaze is humanized. Instead of sadism and lasciviousness, it expresses determination in the Mormon segment of *The Life of General Villa,* despite the eerie effect produced by the contrast between Raoul Walsh's blue eyes and his brown-face makeup. It projects serenity in the 1920 footage documenting the talks in Sabinas, Coahuila, that lead to Villa's surrender. Respect and compassion are elicited by the title "Paz a sus restos. Rest in peace" and the shot of Villa's dead body slumped over a car window. Notwithstanding the addition of the period photographs and postcards that the shot replicates, the affect of these last images of the Padilla film enables an alternative historicity. What the viewer is left with is a multifaceted and mediated image of Villa, ephemeral, dynamic, and changing as Rocha's split-frame triptych of movable film frames suggests. Villa's subjectivity and identity as a cinematic hero are revisualized, reimagined, and reclaimed.

"More than a mere case study for film preservationists," Rita Gonzalez writes, "*Lost Reels* is a meditation on film's role in the field of history. The search for 'lost reels' unsettles so much dust in the archive that other film histories come to light" (2006, 2). It alters the salvaged-from-oblivion inferences driving the rescue and preservation of lost images. Out of divergent and dispersed temporalities, *The Lost Reels of Pancho Villa* constructs new identifications overlaid with the affect of memory, estrangement, and cultural activism. The documentary is at once a work of historiography and of memory. Although it does not resolve the pervasive assumptions about faked footage, it offers a unique opportunity to reexamine the competing representations and narratives generated by Villa's association with cinema. What is more, the reflexive treatment of period imagery and archetypal figurations signals their signifying power as imaginary projections, yet open to be reclaimed. By drawing attention to countermemory and appropriation, this film is far more effective in addressing the filmic constructions of Villa's historical persona than is *And Starring Pancho Villa as Himself*. The film's revisionist aims are undermined by the priority given to sight and display. Whether explicitly quoted as historical or inscribed by narrative, spectatorship is central in Beresford's film. Characters and film-within-the-film audiences function as agents of the American fascination with Villa and the Mexican Revolution. Villa's representation depends at once on Bandera's ability to portray him as an agent in the making of his own mythology and on replicating historical modes of spectatorship that turned him into a movie celebrity and the revolution into a commodity.

Chapter 3

Pancho Villa on Two Sides of the Border

In *The Eagle and the Serpent* (1928), Martín Luis Guzmán writes, "My interest in Villa and his activities made me ask myself, while I was in Ciudad Juárez, which exploits would best paint the Division of the North: those supposed to be strictly historical or those rated as legendary; those related exactly as they had been seen, or those in which a touch of poetic fancy brought out their essence more clearly. These second always seemed to me truer, more worthy of being considered history" (1965, 163). This view of the historical credibility of legend is key to Villa's mythology and to his standing as the most popular and best-known figure in Mexico's modern history. The mystery of his early years and the transformation from outlaw Doroteo Arango into revolutionary leader were indispensable factors. Class, race, and gender made Villa at once picturesque and threatening and imprinted his celebrity and reputation. In the Villa "legend-creation process," as John Rutherford contends, "there is not that alternation between legend and counter-legend found in the cases of Madero and Zapata, but a continuous coexistence of the two, and to a certain extent an overlapping of them" (1971, 152).

In this sense, Mexican and American historiography coincides. Out of the Villa legend emerges a historical agent that is variably a murderous bandit, a lower-class rogue and political adversary, a social outcast, and an untrained but gifted military leader. For those who loathed, admired, or identified with him, for those bent on defeating him, enthralled by his charisma, or who followed him into war for land and justice, "Villa was the stuff of fantasy" (O'Malley, 1986, 89). Only spectacle and romance could contain the paradoxes that overdetermined the legend, and, as I argue in this chapter, only popular mass culture could ingrain the legend in the collective imaginary. In the first part of the 1930s, and as Villa's historical legacy and status as hero of the Mexican revolution were being disputed in the political arena, the burgeoning radio and music recording industries disseminated *corridos,* the folk ballads that told episodes of his life, recollected victories and defeats, and mourned his passing. The rapidly growing tabloid press, which specialized in lurid stories of violence, sex, and romance, circulated testimonies and fictionalized accounts (O'Malley, 1986, 100). The cinema contributed as well to keeping the legend alive, notably by means of two films, very different in aesthetic and political terms, which were produced one decade after his assassination on July 20, 1923, in the town of Parral in the state of Chihuahua.

In the United States, David O. Selznick of the Metro-Goldwyn-Mayer (MGM) studios bought rights to the fictionalized biography, *Viva Villa! A Recovery of the Real Pancho Villa. Peon . . . Bandit . . . Soldier . . . Patriot*, by Edgcumb Pinchon and Odo B. Stade (1933).[1] In Mexico, the director Fernando de Fuentes, with the poet and playwright Xavier Villaurrutia, adapted the first third of Rafael Felipe Muñoz's novel *¡Vámonos con Pancho Villa!* (1931). *Viva Villa!* (1934) and *¡Vámonos con Pancho Villa!* (1935) created visual archetypes and story lines that remain classic to this day. In both, the aesthetic and discursive resources of filmmaking mediate the multiple meanings and competing narratives that turned Villa into a larger-than-life figure. Iconography and narrative echo processes of image and legend construction in which historical and fiction-driven modes are implicated in revisualizing situations and actors. Moreover, both films reveal the combined power of and the inconsistencies within the "black," "white," and "epic" legends identified by the historian and Villa biographer Frederick Katz. Brutality, victimization, and heroism coexist to give historical legitimacy to the narrative. Heavy on epic spectacle and melodrama, representation in these films favors the responses elicited by Villa in the United States and Mexico, which Katz describes as consisting of a "mixture of love and hate, respect and contempt" (1998, 2). These affective and perceptual disparities historicize representation: in *Viva Villa!* they reinforce the revolutionary leader's appeal as a cinematic hero, and in *Let's Go with Pancho Villa!* they are used to scrutinize the legend by critically reconfiguring its themes of bravery and loyalty.

In the early years of sound cinema, Hollywood and the nascent Mexican film industry were differently drawn to Villa's legend. Hollywood sought to capitalize on the renewed political and cultural interest in Mexico and increase its market share in that country. After a decade of offensive films (and production companies) being banned and official protests, as the cultural historian Helen Delpar indicates, "Mexican characters began to return to motion picture screens" (1992, 169). Now the industry could count on the bilateral agreement signed in 1922 by the Motion Picture

Producers and Distributors of America (MPPDA) and the Mexican government and the Production Code established in 1930 by the MPPDA to safeguard itself from censorship and protect its expansion into overseas markets (including Latin America).[2] In De los Reyes's words, the result of bilateral agreements and the MPPDA rules "did not mean a meeting of cultures but an accommodation" designed to ensure market access rather than transform in any substantial way Hollywood's portrayal of Mexico (1996, 35). The ways in which this accommodation operates in *Viva Villa!* are discussed in this chapter.

To counteract negative stereotypes of Hollywood films, including those aimed at Spanish-language markets, and to secure audiences, Mexican cinema drew on its diverse roots in popular theatre, music, and literature. It also made the most of the tableau of identity, a construct of folkloric rural themes and character types, promoted as "typically" Mexican by the postrevolutionary state since the 1920s. As in the silent films dealing with the recent past, the *charro* replaced the revolutionary figure, embodied and sustained primarily by the Villa and Zapata legends. Moreover, these films filtered out the social, moral, and political complexities of the revolution, reducing it to a series of spectacular incidents and stereotypical characters. While features of this reconfiguration can be found in *Let's Go with Pancho Villa!* it avoids what Andrés de la Luna calls the "totalizing historical impulse" characterizing then (and since) the cinematic representations of the revolution in Mexico (1995, 175). To explore the film's approach, I address the following questions: How does the film signal the mediated features of Villa's historical and cinematographic persona? What is the impact of the visual motifs of *charrería* on the film's representation of heroism and death?

THE LEGEND ACCORDING TO HOLLYWOOD: *Viva Villa!*

As noted in the previous chapter, the U.S. film industry discovered Villa in 1913–1914. He became the main actor of the drama being played out south of the border who used media as a political tool to refashion himself as a revolutionary leader. Two years later, as De los Reyes writes, "the image of Villa as the Robin Hood and Napoleon of Mexico who fought heroically against the usurper Huerta, and of a peon who could become president of the republic, was converted into a barbaric, savage, and murderous bandit who killed defenseless Americans during his *raid* [in English] on Columbus" (1996, 24). In an ironic twist of fate, his role as the initiator of the historic deal with the Mutual Film Company was obliterated from public memory and his filmic identity reverted to suit the prevalent stereotype of the Mexican "greaser" created by turn-of-the-century pulp literature and early cinema.

Filmgoers rediscovered the Mexican leader in 1934 when Wallace Beery portrayed him in *Viva Villa!* Although the film ranks with *Viva Zapata!* (Elia Kazan, 1952) as one of the few attempts to render the Mexican Revolution with a certain measure of respect, it also attests to Hollywood's inability to overcome historical attitudes and perceptions. In spite of the steps taken by MGM to appease Mexican concerns, the film contains the best and worst features of the Hollywood spectacle. It relies on the stylistic and narrative protocols, and audience expectations, of the historical and biographical film genres. The unnamed film reviewer of *Time* magazine described the film as "a superbly mounted spectacle which combines most of the advantages of Eisenstein's [sic] *Thunder Over Mexico* and David Ward Griffith's antiquated *Birth of a Nation*" (1934, 45). It blends epic spectacle, melodrama, and comedy to accommodate the competing meanings and changes in public attitudes toward Villa and validates the overdetermined meaning of the legend by means of an opening title that reads, "This saga of the Mexican hero, Pancho Villa, does not come out of the archives of history. It is fiction woven out of truth and inspired by a love of the half-legendary Pancho and the glamorous country he served."

If early segments set up a context for Villa's life story, by the closing scene of his assassination just about all the social, political, and psychological elements that give factual validity to the plot have vanished. A young boy (Phillip Cooper) is a witness to his father's (Frank Puglia) futile complaint about a government's order that community land be turned over to hacienda owners. After seeing his father whipped to death, he kills the foreman. The boy's destiny is sealed when he flees into the mountains to become Villa, the bandit intent on avenging injustice and restoring land and dignity to the peasants. He is accompanied on this quest by his volatile deputy, Sierra (Leo Carrillo), and an American journalist working for the *New York World*, Johnny Sykes (Stuart Erwin). Summoned by Francisco Madero (Henry B. Walthall), who sees him as a victimized peon, he leads an army of peasants into the revolution. When Madero boards the train that will take him to Mexico City and the presidency, Villa complies with the order to dismiss his men. He settles on a farm with his bride-to-be, Rosita (Katherine de Mille), and the letter writer Emilio Chavito (George E. Stone). During a trip to a bank, Sierra kills the clerk, and Villa is arrested. Abandoned by Madero and humiliated by General Pascal (Joseph Schildkraut), he nearly escapes the firing squad when an order is delivered that sends him into exile.

After Sykes arrives in El Paso with news of Madero's murder by Pascal, Villa crosses the border. The revolutionary army is now an agent of vengeance. When the troops raid a hacienda, Villa runs again into its owner, Don Felipe (Donald Cook) and his sister, Teresa (Fay Wray). With the brother calling the Villistas a "pack of beasts" and the sister fighting off Villa's amorous advances, a confrontation is inevitable. She fires at Villa but is fatally wounded in the ensuing scuffle with the brother. In the wake of the Torreón battle, Villa orders his deputy to toss a honey-covered Pascal onto an anthill. Villa enters victorious into Mexico City. After signing Madero's Land Restoration bill, Villa gives up the presidency. On a trip to Parral to get a birthday present for Rosita, Felipe and his friends gun him down. As he lies wounded, he asks Sykes to write his story. To the question about what his final words would be, the journalist responds, "Good-bye my Mexico, said Pancho Villa, forgive me for my crimes. Remember if I have sinned against you it is because I loved you too much." Holding the medal given to him for liberating Mexico from a cruel dictator, Villa says as he expires, "Forgive me . . . Johnny: what have I done wrong?"

"Delicious ending!" wrote Alejandro Aragón about this scene in an article titled "¡Muera Villa!" (Death to Villa!) that appeared on April 16, 1934, six months before the film's Mexican release, in the daily *Ilustrado*. As the journalist puts it, in spite of what is said about Hollywood's anxieties to deal with Mexican subjects "because of our exasperating sensibility," the film gets it wrong. Now that the damage has been done, he writes, "we have no other choice than to resign ourselves and sigh" (quoted in García Riera, 1987b, 216). This opinion reflects the mixture of annoyance and resignation that characterized Mexico-Hollywood relations in the early 1930s and manifested itself during the film's production. The notoriety of *Viva Villa!* rests mainly in actor Lee Tracy's outrageous behavior on November 19, 1933, during the Anniversary of the Revolution festivities. Journalists alerted Don Eddie that the inebriated actor was shouting obscenities at the parade participants from a Hotel Regis balcony. "I got there just in time," the production unit member writes, "to see him urinating on the cadets of Chapultepec, the West Point boys of Mexico" (quoted in Haver, 1980, 151). This incident turned into a public relations nightmare.[3] A crash of a plane outside El Paso carrying exposed footage made matters worse. These problems were resolved after apologies from Louis B. Mayer to Mexican President Abelardo L. Rodríguez; staff reassignments with Conway taking over from Howard Hawks, the actors Stuart Erwin, Fay Wray, Leo Carrillo, and Donald Cook stepping in for Tracy, Mona Maris, Irving Pichel, and Donald Reed, respectively; script changes; and reshooting in Hollywood and Mexico.[4]

Even if these measures were meant to appease public opinion in Mexico, criticism of the film revolved mainly around historicity and characterization. An unsigned article in *Ilustrado* on November 23, 1933, stated, "[The film] is not denigrating for our country because nothing is done that may cause us embarrassment. Only the historical truth is undermined.... *Viva Villa!* does not insult our people, it makes a romantic and sentimental novel out of an event that was tragic and bloody" (quoted in García Riera, 1987b, 216). When the film was released on September 4, 1934, at the Regis Cinema and exhibited for a customary two-week run, Cube Bonifant called "nothing but the product of publicity frenzy" the campaign alleging that the film was offensive and sporadic comments by elected officials that a ban be considered (quoted in García Riera, 1987b, 217). The influential critic who signed her weekly column in *Ilustrado* with the pen name Luz Alba acknowledged the film's good intentions. "Out of the strange mixture of fact and fiction," she wrote, "the figures of Villa and Madero stand out. They are neither psychological nor even material portraits of two Mexicans; they are two characters of American cinema, with their own life, strong personality, and grand sense of purpose" (quoted in García Riera, 1987b, 217). This distinction between the historical and the cinematographic agent is revealing. It underlines to what extent the reviewer is familiar (and assumes that Mexican film audiences also are) with Hollywood characterization. These judicious comments made by Mexican film critics provoke the question: how does the film reconstruct an event and its actors according to Hollywood norms and yet manage to be moderately inoffensive?

From Epic to Comedy

Visual themes taken from period images and Mexican folklore and western films are used in *Viva Villa!* to make the Villa legend comprehensible to a global film audience.[5] A train sequence in the early part of the film exemplifies how this diverse imagery reinforces a shared historical narrative about the revolution as epic spectacle. It starts with a series of picturesque vignette-like crowd scenes that show men in *charro* outfits loading horses on a train, watching a cockfight, and performing rope tricks, children milking a goat, *soldaderas* cooking, and a mother rocking her baby on a swing made of bullet belts. The series ends with a by-now-classic frontal

FIGURE 3.1. *"Federal Troops under the Command of Carlos Rincón Gallardo,"* photograph. © CONACULTA-INAH-SINAFO-*Fototeca Nacional, Mexico*

FIGURE 3.2. Viva Villa! *frame enlargement*

long shot of a locomotive adorned with a "Viva Villa" garland. Each scene singles out the social, cultural, and gender formations that came together in the revolution, with framing and camera movement aimed at translating the mass mobilization in cinematic terms.

With shots of Villa sitting in a bathtub on the roof of a railroad car and Sykes being pulled onto the departing train, the epic is supplanted by comedy. In the next scene, the journalist's blabbing sets in motion a spirited exchange about a newspaper headline, accompanied by a photograph of Villa, announcing: "Villa captures Santa Rosalia. Important Federal Stronghold falls before Peon Leader . . . vivid eyewitness account." In the game of denial and acquiescence that ensues, and in part due to Beery's acting, the revolutionary leader turns into a man-child, bewildered and eager to please his American friend. Wrapped in a blanket that hardly covers his bare chest and wearing a *charro* hat tilted backwards, he is no longer a commanding figure of authority, even though he towers above Sykes.[6] The journalist comes across as a conniving drunk who refers to himself as "the guy who faked the biggest battle yarn of the century: Johnny Sykes, the newspaper Judas," and acts offended to pressure Villa into agreeing to attack the town.

Sykes stands in for the *San Francisco Examiner* and *New York American* correspondent John W. Roberts, who served also as a publicist in Villa's media campaign against Carranza in 1914 (Anderson, 2000, 51). It is not clear whether the screenwriter, Ben Hecht, created his character, as McCarthy claims, just to comply with Production Code rules and ensure exhibition approval in Mexico (1997, 191). At any rate, the journalist is a mediating agent who, as noted, is entrusted by the dying Villa to write his last words, and as such corroborates the role of the media in legend making. He acts as a narrator who explains Mexico and relays the story of Villa's trek from El Paso to an *Evening Post* colleague, the jovial Calloway (Ralph Bushman). While his boyish antics provide comic release, the clownish nature of his friendship with Villa sweeps aside the history of the mutual distrust and antagonism that characterized American-Mexican relations in that period. As well, the zany repartee in the train sequence turns leadership and decision making into a farce, undermining Villa's agency and transforming the officers, civilian aides, and musicians around him into bit players in a vaudeville show.

While it is arguable that the shift of mood from epic spectacle to slapstick sustains Hollywood's demeaning figurations of Mexicans, it suits the affective and perceptual disparities of the Villa legend that historicize representation in *Viva Villa!* This fluctuation facilitates viewer engagement by enabling forms of recognition that belong at once to the social imaginary and the fictional world of cinema, even if the historical spectacle of disenfranchised masses thrust into history is eclipsed by comedy. What is more, this fluctuation is crucial to the film's agenda. To deserve being immortalized by Hollywood, Villa must become a heroic figure. He needs to be represented as a social and political outsider and a champion of the people; in other words, he must be an underdog fighting for social justice and paying the ultimate price for his determination.

The palace segment in the last part of the film endorses a fiction depicted in the now-lost feature produced by Mutual in 1914 and recorded in the U.S. press after Villa's assassination—that an "educated Villa might have been president of the republic" (quoted by Katz, 1998, 768).[7] Comedy dominates in these scenes, with ludicrous situations revealing Villa's naïveté and ignorance of the affairs of state and exposing the officials' arrogance and maliciousness. In one fell swoop, the entire state apparatus is lampooned. By ridiculing the government and its agents, *Viva Villa!* reinstates the *opéra bouffe* image of Latin American revolutions that circulated in the United States in the 1905–1914 period (Britton, 1995, 13). Moreover, the banquet scenes update this representation by relocating Villa and Mexico's ruling class within the fairy tale world of musicals. Two scenes evoke the European refinement and intruder-in-the-palace themes found in *Love Parade* (1929) and *The Merry Widow* (1934), by the German American director Ernst Lubitsch. In one, the gold-embroidered vests make the various officials who bestow an award on Villa, for having rescued Mexico, look like characters in a Viennese operetta. In the other, the chic lady sitting next to Sierra (in a fancy jacket with epaulettes) is horrified when he reveals the identity of Villa's dinner companion as "the French manicurist of the Regis Hotel." Authenticity is achieved by incorporating the iconography of power and privilege found in the photographs and newsreels of the Porfiriate. If this layering appears, at first glance, to be a factual error, it is primarily a distancing device with a dual function. It enables the film to parody class identity and signal, by virtue of being visually anachronistic, that it is the Porfirian elite that is represented, not the postrevolutionary and nationalist class.

The climactic moment of the banquet scene comes when Villa accepts the medal. After announcing his intention to leave Mexico City, he threatens to return with his Dorados and "hang everyone by his whiskers" if the commitment made in Madero's Land Restoration bill to distribute land to the peons is not kept. By confronting this well-appointed crowd, he acts on his awareness of being isolated; by resigning from the presidency, he acknowledges that the establishment will never accept him. This episode is in line with the narrative strategies of the Hollywood biographical genre and the populist features of the Villa legend. It reinforces the representation of Villa's agency and actions as being shaped by his marginal position within and struggle against the traditional power structures established in the early scenes of the film. Except with Madero, whom he calls "little feller" (and who sees him as a wayward and capricious child), he is shown reacting with defiance to the complacency, loathing, and even overt abuse of the *hacendados*, politicians, and career officers. These gestures cement Villa's status as a popular hero and inform the film's re-creation of his entry into Mexico City in December 1914.

The montage insert that precedes the presidential palace segment captures the epic scope of the Mexican Revolution. It begins with the title, "Starting with four men who joined him at the Rio Grande, Pancho Villa entered Mexico City three months later as a conqueror at the head of an army of sixty thousand." Scenes filmed in Hollywood personalizing Villa's interaction with the people looking at the spectacle on the street below are combined with crowd and parade shots recorded in Mexico City.[8] Explicitly quoting period footage and inserting shots of Beery and Carrillo over images of familiar landmarks sustain the historicity and authenticity of these scenes.[9] Were it not for some awkward scale differences, the effect would be spectacular; the image of a victorious leader responding to the adoring crowds, notwithstanding the bashful grin on Beery's face, validates Villa's position as a historical agent.

Citation and Visual Production

The length of the initial screenplay led MGM to consider producing a two-part epic (Haver, 1980, 148–149). To make it into a single feature, contentious incidents were omitted, such as the conflict with Carranza, the Columbus raid, and the defeat of the remnants of Villa's army by Obregón, and montage inserts were used to maintain the focus on Villa's celebrated rise to power.[10] With titles mimicking the florid rhetoric of Pinchon's book, these formally distinctive inserts favor picturesque images that were, as Ruth Vassey notes, "staple ingredients of Hollywood production" in this period. In films set in foreign locales, these images "offered audiences the chance to become 'American' tourists in a fictionalized and romanticized world" (1997, 227). Yet in *Viva Villa!* the picturesque is remarkably stylized, even reflexive in its overt investment in image and legend production.

Of these montage inserts, the most memorable is titled "Villa's call to arms" and is credited to director and transition specialist Slavko Vorokapich (*Time*, 1934, 45; Haver, 1980, 151). Multiple visual and literary sources are used to condense into four and a half minutes Villa's march from El Paso to Torreón and the armed offensive against the Federal forces.[11] History becomes an operatic performance of popular determination, heroism, and brutality whose protagonists are the landscape and the people. The link between Mexico, the revolution, and Villa's destiny is reinforced aurally (the orchestral arrangement of the song "La cucaracha" by Herbert Stothart) and visually (dissolves, wipes, chiaroscuro lighting, canted frames, and printed titles, some of which increase in scale). Shots of guns raised against cloud-filled skies, soldiers riding, and peasants marching along stony roads flanked by ancient churches and adobe walls are staged against the backdrop of iconic desert and village landscapes, evoking the period imagery shot by Toscano that is included in *Memories of a Mexican*. Groups of women and children in the foreground, their backs to the camera, act as the mediating agents of the mass spectacle.

The title "With the gentle Madero silent, Pancho Villa fought his own way. The vanquished were slaughtered. The wounded were slain" opens the second part of this montage insert. The relentless sound of rolling drums over shots of desolate buildings set against ominous night skies draws attention to the wanton cruelty of civil war. As in the gruesome postcards of mass graves and firing squads first marketed by the U.S. postcard maker Walter H. Horne, the victims, agents, and witnesses of violence are interchangeable. By far the most disturbing scene is the mass execution of Federal army officers. With Sierra figuring prominently, this scene alludes to well-known anecdotes about Rodolfo Fierro, the Villa lieutenant renowned for his brutality, who is said to have lined up prisoners in rows so that he could kill several at a time with a single bullet.[12] As rank after rank of officers is felled, pathos gives way to a grotesque sensationalism, whereby the combined effect of formalist elements (graphic symmetry, silhouette, and lighting effects), the garish makeup of the officers, and the histrionic performance of Sierra result in what can be best described as a *danse macabre*.

This scene confirms Sierra's position as a primary perpetrator of violence. Yet throughout the film he comes across as a narcissistic, dim-witted clown with a violent streak. His villainy is mocked every time Villa orders him, either to be silent or to hold fire. His compulsive grooming with a handheld mirror insinuates a latent homosexuality that makes him even less palatable than Fierro, his historical alter ego, because it explicitly aligns

FIGURE 3.3. *"Zapatista Column,"* Memories of a Mexican, *film still from storybook. Courtesy of the Archivo Toscano, Mexico*

FIGURE 3.4. Viva Villa! *frame enlargement*

FIGURE 3.5. Viva Villa! *frame enlargement*

humiliation and brutality to sexual deviance. While these features do little to improve the "greaser" stereotype, they are not devoid of ambiguity. Vestiges of Carrillo's earlier career as a vaudeville dialect comedian are found in the makeup, speech, and body language. The pastiche-saturated acting draws attention to the bandit-as-buffoon as an ethnic construct and is a gesture of self-parody of the actor's public persona as a proud descendant of Spanish settlers and advocate of California's Hispanic traditions dating back to Mexican rule in the eighteenth century.[13]

Wallace Beery Performs Villa and the Charro

Wallace Beery's characterization and performance exhibit similar ambiguities. The comic actor who specialized in sentimental roles plays the Mexican revolutionary as a scruffy-looking rogue with a disarming grin. His impish behavior neutralizes the compulsive womanizing and the brutish treatment of subordinates and enemies. No wonder Howard Hawks was displeased. Todd McCarthy quotes the director as saying, "I tried to make a strange man, humorous but vicious, out of Villa, as he was in real life, but Conway's version had Wallace Beery playing Santa Claus"

(1997, 196). Whether or not one agrees with this view, the acting register disrupts the hyper-*macho* image popularized by the Villa legend. With joviality counterbalancing violence, Villa's screen identity is reconfigured as a comic bandit, a Mexican character type launched on the American stage in the 1920s and introduced to film in the 1930s to counteract "the vengeful, cowardly 'greaser' of tradition" (Delpar, 1992, 166).

A key element of this reconfiguration is the *charro* hat, the fetish object of Mexican identity. In the 1930s, as Noble points out, the ornate widebrimmed hat worn by Emiliano Zapata in the Brehme portrait "predominates in the visual vocabulary" of Mexico (2000, 101). The promotion of folklore by the Mexican state reinstated the *charro* figure as a nationalist and gendered signifier of authenticity, making possible the revalorization of the hat as a novelty item by tourists and foreign visitors. Yet *Viva Villa!* reinforces earlier meanings. During their first meeting, Madero shows the map of Mexico to Villa, who merrily declares, "It looks funny, it looks like a sombrero upside down." Surely, the generic wide-brimmed hat is far more visually appealing than the image summoned by Pinchon when he writes, "The map of Mexico recalls a leg of mutton standing on its knuckle-bone" (1933, 270). It alludes to the multiple representations of the sombrero as a symbol of Mexico and the revolution, reducing the country's identity to a garment popularized as a genuine Mexican artifact. The same process of reduction is revealed in Beery's costume. Even though photographs taken after 1911 show Villa in a range of military-type hats, his screen image reverts to the banditlike figure of the Ciudad Juárez pictures. Except in the Mexico City and death sequences, where he is dressed in an officer's uniform and the Texas-style cowboy hat preferred by northern revolutionary leaders, the actor appears in an embroidered *charro* hat. Yet the grimy hat and the casual manner in which he wears it evoke the generic sombrero used by "greaser" bandits in silent films and worn by "Mexicans" in caricatures and pictorials depicting U.S.-Mexican relations during the revolution.

The *charro* hat also figures prominently in promotional materials. A drawing by the caricaturist and art designer Matías Santoyo, printed in the daily *Excelsior* at the time of the film's release in Mexico, shows Beery wearing an enormous hat. The actor's ample chest and the oversized hand resting on a gun holster make his thighs look stunted. There is no hint of what the Mexican adviser who designed the title credits calls the "magnificent and vigorous" interpretation by Beery in his short article. In fact, his body is devoid of virility and rendered grotesque by the distortions of caricature. A comparable effect of regendering can be found in a trade

FIGURE 3.6. Viva Villa! *frame enlargement*

advertisement produced by MGM especially for industry publications, depicting Beery in an oversized hat with a woman seductively reclined on the wide brim (see Haver, 1980, 151). The hat's reddish dark brown color, curved shape, and indented peak evoke the desert and volcanoes of Mexico's Central Valley. The black gown and bright red shoes of the female figure add a touch of Hollywood glamour to an already gendered visual theme and draw attention away from Beery's rugged face. The zigzag pattern of multicolored lines on the actor's chest is playful and, like the raucous laughter on his face, in tune with the film's approach. The gendered and picturesque imagery is thoroughly modern, not just in its design. It reveals a strategy of accommodation whereby the normative associations of the *charro* hat with Mexico and Villa are readjusted without substantially disrupting their normative meanings.

In view of this strategy, it is imperative to move beyond a narrow understanding of historicity in *Viva Villa!* Fluctuations between comedy and spectacle, humor and pathos, set up the terms by which the revolutionary leader's historical and screen identity can be rehabilitated. Humorous situations reconfigure Villa as a picturesque and jovial figure, and epic spectacle restores him as a key figure in the visual culture of the Mexican

Revolution. To transform the vengeful peon into a champion of the dispossessed and a popular hero, the narrative must invest him with Hollywood values of individual resolve and social justice, and the imagery must evoke the overdetermined meanings that constructed the character and the event into a spectacle. Even as the representation of Villa's agency and actions accommodates competing, if not opposing, attitudes and responses, the film collapses under the weight of its own contradictions. The closing title—"Out of the years of battle arose a new Mexico, dedicated to justice and equality. The wild heart had not fought in vain"—is accompanied by shots of a Mexican army regiment on parade.[14] This imagery alludes, of course, to the incident that jeopardized the film's production, exposing to what extent *Viva Villa!* is driven by Hollywood's attempt to make amends but, in the end, without radically interfering with historical attitudes and perceptions about Mexico and the revolution.

HEROISM AND DEATH IN *Let's Go with Pancho Villa!*

As 1936 drew to a close, audiences in Mexico City were able to see two films directed by Fernando de Fuentes. Those who attended screenings of *Allá en el rancho grande* (Over There on the Big Ranch) were able to immerse themselves in hacienda life, to love, suffer, and sing along with handsome *rancheros* and beautiful *chinas* (young women wearing traditional costumes that originated in Puebla). Those who went instead (or also) to see *¡Vámonos con Pancho Villa!* at the Palacio Cinema in the week starting December 31 were exposed to the sights and sounds of battlefields, to tales of male bravery and futile death. Were it not for the diverging trajectories of these films, this coincidence may not be worth recording. *Over There on the Big Ranch* premiered on October 6 at the Alameda and, despite a slow start, became an unexpected commercial success at home, in Latin America and Spain. The public largely ignored *Let's Go with Pancho Villa!* and the most expensive film produced up to that point in Mexico failed at the box office. These contrasting outcomes led producers to capitalize on the popular appeal of melodrama, folklore, and music. They turned the *comedia ranchera* into the most "Mexican" of film genres; a vehicle to idealize rural identities and traditions at a time when their continued existence was considered in conservative circles to be threatened by the agrarian reform policies of the Lázaro Cárdenas regime (1934–1940). In these circumstances, the prospects of a somber and thought-provoking film on the country's recent past were grim. It would be three decades before *Let's Go with Pancho Villa!* was fully appreciated in Mexico and celebrated for its ability to represent, as García Riera writes, the revolution as "chaotic, contradictory, and implacable" (1994a, 200).

This film is the last of a trilogy that includes *El prisionero trece* (1933) and *El compadre Mendoza* (1933). By drawing on literary and visual models, this trilogy focuses on the themes of betrayal, violence, and death. It resignifies incidents and agents, as Julia Tuñón notes, "from the perspective of the thirties, sufficiently distant to be critical, but close enough to still be hurtful" (1996, 57). Its moral position counters the rhetoric of national reconciliation, collective memory, and political consensus that wrote the Revolution with a capital letter. To quote John Mraz, the films "exude a disenchantment with the revolution's shortcomings, instead of celebrating its achievements" (1997a, 94). Noble complements this view: "By focusing on interpersonal relationships that turn on the bonds of allegiance and trust and which ultimately end in tragedy, all three films provide a bold critique of the revolution's fratricidal factionalism" (2005, 56). While sharing these features, *Let's Go with Pancho Villa!* signals the mediated features of Villa's historical and cinematographic persona by making a group of *rancheros* the collective agents of the film's discourse. It capitalizes on public familiarity with *charrería* culture and performance to question the reified representations of heroism and sacrifice embraced by state nationalism to further its modernizing agenda.

In contrast to the other films dealing with Villa that I have considered, he personifies the revolution but is not its leading protagonist (García Riera, 1994a, 200). The plot revolves around a group of friends who decide to join the revolution after the youngest, Miguel Ángel del Toro (Ramón Vallarino), barely escapes from being executed by a Federal army officer. They gather at the home of Tiburcio Maya (Antonio R. Frausto) and set off to meet the Villa army at a rail crossing. Máximo Perea (Raúl de Anda) is killed when he presents the machine gun he captured to Villa. Martín Espinosa (Rafael F. Muñoz) demonstrates his bravery by blowing up a fortified enemy position. After the death of another one of their friends, Melitón Botello (Manuel Tamés), Rodrigo Perea (Carlos López, Chaflán), and Tiburcio are sent to negotiate with a Federal army officer. Sentenced to hang, they are led to the firing line. The corpulent Melitón, who is called *panzón* (Big Belly) by his friends, avoids death when the rope breaks, and Rodrigo is killed by a stray bullet during the rescue attempt. Villa rewards the remaining Leones by promoting them to his elite corps, the Dorados. In the cantina of a recently occupied town, Tiburcio, Becerrillo, and Melitón are pressured to participate in a circle of death, a Mexican variation of Russian roulette. Hit in the stomach, Melitón takes his life. On the trip to Zacatecas, Tiburcio takes care of Becerrillo, who has been infected with smallpox. When Villa finds out, Tiburcio is notified by Fierro (Alfonso Sánchez Tello) to dispose of his friend's body. After shooting him and burning the corpse, Villa orders him to stay behind. Disappointed by his leader, the last of the Leones walks into the night, away from the train and the revolution.[15]

Let's Go with Pancho Villa! was an ambitious project. It is based on the first third of a homonymous novel by Rafael Felipe Muñoz. The Chihuahua-born journalist and novelist had briefly joined the Villa army (in 1913 and 1915) before supporting Obregón and covered the story of Villa's assassination for *El Universal Gráfico* in 1923. The film brought together a prestigious director and crew, screenwriters, and musicians. Among them was the playwright Celestino Gorostiza (artistic supervisor), the poet Xavier Villaurrutia (co-scriptwriter), the author Rafael Felipe Muñoz (in the role of Martín), and the composer Silvestre Revueltas (musical score, and in a cameo role as the cantina piano player). On-location filming took place in October 1935, in the states of Chihuahua, Coahuila, and Guanajuato, and continued in November in Mexico City at the newly built Cinematográfica Latinoamericana (CLASA) studios. It benefited from a big budget (Mex $1,000,000 or U.S. $200,000) and state-of-the art technology (Mitchell cameras, sound synchronization, and film processing equipment) and official support (monetary and military). Production was suspended between December and January 1936 when De Fuentes became sick, delaying the completion.

Visual Production and the Villa Legend

When the film was finally released in December, it failed to attract audiences. The historian Ilene O'Malley speculates that the film "did not give the public the Villa that had proven so popular in the literary versions of Muñoz' story" (1986, 110). Indeed, the film's antiheroic treatment validates this opinion. Character construction and the performance by Domingo Soler avoid the sentimentality and lurid violence that made novels dealing with Villa so appealing to readers and profitable for writers.[16] While the film draws on the affective power and contradictions of the legend, it adopts a critical stance in regard to popular narratives bent on preserving the rebel *guerrillero* image and government efforts in the 1930s to recuperate Villa as an embodiment of the *macho* ideals of the revolution. This is achieved by shifting viewer identification onto the Leones of San Pablo. They are the collective agents of the film's discourse and personify the at-

FIGURE 3.7.   Let's Go with Pancho Villa! *film still. Courtesy of Filmoteca UNAM, Mexico*

titudes and values of those who joined *la bola*.[17] In the course of the film, their resolve and loyalty are put to the test. They must not only prove their bravery in battle but also struggle to preserve their humanity, even if in the end all but one lose their lives. What they see conveys their investment in the revolution, drawing attention to the part played by Villa's followers in legend making.

This dual role is represented early on in the film when they ride up together to the train junction. Long-shot compositions are used almost exclusively for the entire sequence, until the group introduces itself as "the Leones" and Villa adds "of San Pablo" (their place of origin) to their moniker. The shift to personalized close-ups and address occurs as each man identifies himself by name, and the leader gives the nickname Becerrillo (Little Calf) to Miguel Ángel because he is too young for his surname, del Toro (Bull). A collective point of view also brings Villa into the narrative. The scene that shows him distributing corn refers explicitly to an image that figures prominently in the recollections of Northern Division veterans to support their view of Villa as a champion of the poor (Katz, 1998, 295). Yet multiple camera positions integrate the beneficiaries of this populist representation. The scene begins with sounds of people over close-up shots of upturned hats held aloft and is followed by an upward pan that reveals Villa framed in the door of a boxcar. After asking the crowd to quiet down, he explains why he is fighting. Reaction shots individualize the men and women in the crowd, disrupting the mediating (and by and large fetishistic) function of the gaze.

Villa's transformation is equally conveyed by the Leones' point of view. In the last scene, at night in La Calera, Fierro and the doctor (Miguel M. Delgado) advise Villa that there is a smallpox outbreak on the trains bound for Zacatecas and that Becerrillo is among those stricken. After Tiburcio executes the order to dispose of Becerrillo, he sits on the edge of the boxcar and lights a cigarette. Just as in the first appearance, the sounds of conversation announce Villa's presence. Tiburcio reacts, and sees the leader escorted by officers, wearing a pith helmet, and wrapped in a serape. When Tiburcio points toward the burning remains, Villa's concern about what has been done to Becerrillo changes to hostility. He recoils at the sight and abruptly orders the last remaining member of the Leones to stay behind. This scene matches in its affective power that of Villa's first appearance. Here, the joint effect of subjectivity and detachment sets off "an ideological critique in images that destabilizes the myth of Pancho Villa" (De la Luna, 1984, 231). Instead of being caring and confident, he appears as a cruel and fearful leader.

As Mraz points out, these scenes are proof of the capacity of cinema to visualize Villa's famed charismatic qualities and director Fernando de Fuentes's ability "to communicate the sensation of charisma through the actor Domingo Soler" (1997b, 109). The actor explained the challenges to Mario Galán, a journalist whose report on the film appeared in the *Ilustrado* on February 13, 1936. "In regard to the part I play," he said, "it is artistically the most risky because anybody who interprets on the screen or the stage such a renowned figure as Pancho Villa has to please those who imagine him in one way or another.... And not many men are imagined so diversely as Pancho Villa!" (quoted in Garcia Riera, 1984, 36). The actor creates a complex figure without resorting to folklore or melodrama. Gone are the *charro* hat and the facial mannerisms of Beery's figuration in *Viva Villa!* Soler wears the Texas-style felt hat (or a pith helmet), soft-collared shirts, khaki pants, and knee-length leather leggings that signal his character's regional identity as a northerner.

Shifts in emotional register enable the actor to visualize the psychological and moral traits that endeared Villa to his followers and those that his detractors exploited to demonize him. An example is the scene that follows the promotion of the Leones. After they step out of the cantina, an officer conveys a message from General Urbina to Villa. To the question of whether a band of captured musicians should be executed, Villa responds, "No, man, how barbaric. Poor musicians, why would we shoot them?" Yet the fate of the prisoners is determined by military efficiency, not empathy. Informed that all units already have a band, he reverses the order: "Well, then shoot them. Why are you bugging me with this?" The objective point of view and Soler's sober performance in this scene may have unsettled film viewers in the 1930s. "They were enamored," as O'Malley notes, "of Villa the daring Robin Hood, the satyr and the monster, the unpredictable deviant, the grimy *guerrillero* and outlaw with an uncanny power over men" (1986, 111). Although Soler's characterization is built around the contradictory combination of attributes admired by the public, the acting detaches the character from the mythical subject. In this way, the actor delivers what is still considered the most nuanced and authentic portrait of the revolutionary leader.

From the Archive to the Heroic Charro

García Riera proposes another explanation for the commercial failure of *Let's Go with Pancho Villa!* Audiences misunderstood the film because they were conditioned by the populist predisposition of Mexican cinema to "mummify" the revolution by reducing it to a folkloric display of patriotic sentiment (1994a, 202). This assessment demands that the issue of how De Fuentes visualizes the revolution be explored. He draws on period footage and photographs that recorded the military campaigns of 1913 and 1914, as well as on imagery of *charrería,* the equestrian practices of lower-middle-class rural workers that became a symbol of Mexican nationalism in the 1920s, and treats them reflexively and critically. The cinematographer, Jack Draper, re-creates the iconography and, at times literally, the modes of spectatorship found in the Toscano and Abitía footage. The scene showing the triumphant entry of Villista troops into an unnamed city, for example, consists of overhead shots of people watching from windows and balconies and eye-level shots of regiments marching on the streets.

At other times, Draper made the most of camera technology, mainly mechanical devices designed to improve mobility and composition. In the train junction scene in which the Leones meet up with Villa's army, lateral movement brings to life the Casasola and Brehme photographs of troops riding the trains. Yet the subjective point of view of the panning shots confirms the Leones as agents of the gaze and conditions the meta-

FIGURE 3.8. *"Train Carrying the Headquarters of Gral. de Obregón between Colima and Jalisco,"* 1914, Jesús H. Abitia, postcard. Courtesy of the Fondo Juan Barragán, Centro de Estudios Universitarios—Archivo Histórico de la UNAM (CESU-AHUNAM), Mexico

archival impulse of period re-creation to the needs of the narrative. Hence the train becomes more than just a setting to represent the daily life and social interactions of the men, women, and children of the Villista army. It is primarily a backdrop for the characters' tragic fate: when the Leones are captured, they march along the tracks on the way to be hanged; Miguel Angel dies of smallpox in a railroad car; Tiburcio walks along the ties after he abandons the Villista army. As Mraz points out, "The train begins by promising much and ends up being the site of disillusion; it too is the revolution" (1997b, 116).

The imagery of *charrería* is introduced in the credit sequence by means of drawings that blend visual motifs of the *ranchero* (the wide-brimmed hat, horse saddle, guitar, desert landscape, and cacti) and revolutionary cultures (the cartridge belt and revolver). These familiar motifs reappear throughout the film, first and foremost as fetish objects that symbolize the core values of the *charro* code of honor: bravery and gallantry. De Fuentes deploys them strategically to question their reified meanings and to represent the cruelty and trauma of the revolution. Before detailing the function of these motifs, an explanation is in order. As warfare devastated the Mexican countryside and peasant communities revolted against the social order of the haciendas, the landowning class migrated to the cities.

Without land and divested of political power and social identity, this class turned to customs and values honed since colonial times in rural work and warfare. It used them to invent a tradition—*charrería*—and forge links with the postrevolutionary state. In the process, to quote Cristina Palomar Verea, this class "lost its political position, its potential as a group affected by the Revolution and land redistribution, in other words, its antirevolutionary standing; and gained a symbolic place in the new social order and recognition as a cultural group, a compromise sealed with the elevation of the *charro* figure as a nationalist emblem" (2004, 26). For the emerging state, this link meant that social peace and national unity could be guaranteed by neutralizing class resentment and regionalism. *Charrería* resurfaced in cities as a competitive sport and an idiosyncratic expression of Mexicanness that, in the words of Juan José Doñán, "possessed a certain epic quality that seemed perfectly suited to represent not what our country was then but what it wanted to be" (2000, 93).

The battle sequence that culminates with Máximo's death illustrates the use made of the performance and iconography of *charrería*. The Leones rush out of the trenches to knock out a machine gun that is wreaking havoc on the Villista ranks. As they distract the Federal army soldiers,

FIGURE 3.9. Let's Go with Pancho Villa! *frame enlargement*

Máximo comes up from behind and executes a stunning *mangana a caballo* (roping a horse from horseback) to lasso the weapon. The real-life *charro* and actor Raúl de Anda performs one of the high points of the *charreada*.[18] The fictional battlefield is transformed into a *lienzo*, the keyhole-shaped arena and its adjacent spaces (the stands and holding pens) where *charrería* competitions are held. Blocking, that is, the visual organization of the scene, re-creates the various components of the routine, and continuous shooting with two cameras reinforces the effect of spectacle. Multiple perspectives invite the film viewers to participate and cheer along with the Villista soldiers. As in a live show, a drumroll announces Máximo's entrance on a galloping horse and twirling the *reata* (lariat). As he reaches the target, the focus shifts initially to the lasso looped around the weapon and dragging it across the field, then to the excited audience assembled in a circle, and finally to the *charro* hat flying off the rider's head and the trail of dust left behind by the horse in the concluding dash (see figure 3.9).[19]

As noted in chapter 2, displays of horsemanship were integral to the visual construction of Villa's persona. Foreigners and Mexicans who wrote and reported on his campaigns were just as enthralled with the rancheros-turned-soldiers. John Reed, for instance, described a mule roundup as follows: "And now the Tropa instantly went back to their native profession—they became *vaqueros*. It was a pretty sight, the rope-coils swinging in the air, the sudden snakelike shoot of the loops, the little horses bracing themselves against the shock of the running mule" (1969, 44). The final moments of the scene I have been discussing shatter this romanticized view. As the rider approaches the trenches, the camera reveals the corpses scattered on the field, foreshadowing his fate. While doing the silent *charro* salute (the right hand turned outward) in front of Villa, the wounded Máximo collapses facedown and dies. As the leader lifts the head and walks away from the body slumped over the weapon, he is no longer the fearless *charro* but another casualty of war.

Charros and *charreadas* appeared in melodramas and action films in the 1920s, as a result of a partnership (if not formal, at least in spirit) between the budding film industry and the conservative sectors that took it upon themselves to revitalize the character and the spectacle as a competitive sport. Producers opted for displaying authentic traditions in natural landscapes. Filming "beneath Mexico's skies" reflected their obsession with raising the prestige of Mexican cinema at home and abroad (De los Reyes, 1993, 211). *El Caporal* (Miguel Torres Contreras, 1921) and *Rosario's Wedding* (Gustavo Saiz de Sicilia, 1929), for instance, used the hacienda as a setting to idealize rural life; romance, adventure, and male comradeship to

FIGURE 3.10. Let's Go with Pancho Villa! *film still. Courtesy of Filmoteca UNAM, Mexico*

block out any references to social conflict.[20] Thus the recent past vanished from the screen, for the same reason that "city people wanted to forget [the revolution] because it was the cause of the nightmare they endured since 1913" (De los Reyes, 1993, 209). Another factor was the belief, as Noble writes, "that the revolution played a significant role in the deterioration of Mexico's image abroad (particularly in the U.S.), an image that the state was keen to 'sanitise'" (2005, 52).

If in the previous decade the public was drawn to the awesome sight of Villista and Zapatista troops in Mexico City, its curiosity shifted in 1921 to another attraction: the *charreada* at the Condesa racecourse sponsored by the newly founded National Association of Charros for the Centenary of the Achievement of Independence festivities. Held during the Obregón presidency, this event was significant because it started the drawn-out process of incorporating the *charro* into the nationalist discourse (Palomar Verea, 2003, 99). It culminated during President Pascual Ortíz Rubio's tenure (1930–1932), when for the first time a contingent of *charros* closed the athletic parade, the main event of the November 20 celebrations of

Revolution Day in 1930 in Mexico City and *charro* attire was proclaimed a symbol of *mexicanidad*. To revalorize the display of equestrian skills as a sport and patriotic spectacle and turn *charro* dress into a fetish of identity required that the iconography of *charrería* be refunctionalized and references to the past resignified. Notable is the revolver, a remnant of the participation of *charros* in the rural militia corps of the Porfiriate. A steadfast companion of the *charro*, just as his horse was, it is a utilitarian artifact and a symbol that, as Palomar Verea writes, "guarantees the gallantry of the *charro*, in some way 'completing' him" (2003, 79).

Charro *Iconography and the Representation of Death*

Let's Go with Pancho Villa! counters these meanings in two sequences that focus on Melitón, a character whose lumbering, portly figure and constant wisecracking set him apart from the other Leones. Manuel Tamés plays with great gusto the comic ranchero popularized by Leopoldo Beristaín on the vaudeville stage and the silver screen. To be recognized as a genuine fighter, not just a jovial simpleton, he must master the revolver. His apprenticeship is illustrated in the film's only humorous scene. After a battle, Rodrigo offers Villa a gun in a chiseled leather holster, similar to the one seen in a credit sequence drawing. He turns down the gift, demonstrating instead how to fire a revolver without removing it from the holster. The awestruck Melitón fails to emulate his leader's prowess. Not even the promise to be made a general and his friends' cheering make it easier to hit the prickly pear cactus. Each time he misses, he moves closer to his target. Exasperated, he knocks off the fruit with the butt of the revolver. He fares better after becoming a Dorado. On the way to the pay office, he aims at a box being sold on the street and hits the tightly packed fruit dead center.

Gunplay ultimately determines Melitón's fate. In the next sequence, he turns a gun on himself to prove that he is not a coward. As the Leones celebrate their promotion in a cantina, El Flaco (Max Langler) notices that there are thirteen men sitting around the table. To determine once and for all who is fated to die, the Dorados agree to play the circle of death game. Even though Tiburcio objects, he tosses the loaded revolver into the air so that it can randomly select one of the men. What happens next confirms Melitón's anxiety about being a good target. Hit in the stomach, he appeals for silence. "I'll show you my fear," he says. Reaching for his gun, he invites everybody to "watch how a Leon of San Pablo dies." The mise-en-scène visualizes death as a spectacle of camaraderie, staged in a darkened saloon at midnight and witnessed by those who themselves are waiting to die. Also watching are the bartender and two soldiers. Their function as spectators (and stand-ins for the film audience) ends when they duck behind the counter. The panning camera reveals the emotions of the men arranged tightly in a circle, as if holding each other close would make the inexorable outcome more bearable. The close-up of Tiburcio's shocked reaction and the offscreen gunshot reiterate that death, no matter how anticipated, is horrifying. These two sequences question the masculine ideals represented by the revolver. Not only is Melitón mortified because he cannot match Villa's skill; he is robbed of agency. After being singled out by the gun, he acts in accordance with the game's logic. He acquiesces to the superstitious (and still disgruntled) El Flaco, who pronounces, "There must be a death."

Let's Go with Pancho Villa! adheres to the critical outlook of Muñóz's novel, in which the revolution is seen as a struggle without ideological motivation and depicted, in Mistron's words, as "a *círculo de la muerte*—a violent game which is played in order to prove masculine valor, and which results in senseless carnage" (1983, 7). Circularity as a visual motif and narrative device is germane to the film's representation of death. The semicircular arrangement in the battle and cantina scenes construct a stagelike setting where reckless and misguided actions are displayed and the ideals of male bravery enacted in the horse roping show and symbolized by the revolver are questioned. Death unites the authentic and the wannabe *charro*. For Máximo, the glory is short-lived; for Melitón, courage is an empty gesture.

Each time one of the Leones dies, the narrative is brought to a halt by extended shots of their bodies. The proscenium-like effect achieved by composition and lighting invites film viewers to witness death, to quote Ayala Blanco, as "gratuitous, banal and stupidly heroic" (1985, 30–31). What is more, the shots make tangible the image each man created in his mind and put into words in the early part of the film. Sitting around a fire, the friends respond to Tiburcio's reflections on the transitory nature of life and the certainty of death. Máximo wishes to die fighting; Martín wants his body to be left wherever he falls; Rodrigo wishes to be surrounded by his friends; Melitón wants not to be frightened; Becerrillo hopes that his glorious death will be honored by music and pageantry. Narrative rules, the guarantee to make these premonitions happen, do not diminish the horror of corpses discarded on the battlefield (Máximo and Martín) and the cantina floor (Melitón), cradled in Tiburcio's arms (Rodrigo), and set ablaze (Becerrillo.) The beam of light on Martín's body and the bugle tune played by a young man standing on the roof of the railcar as Becerrillo's body is consumed by fire insinuate pathos. It is worth noting here that the shot of the dead Martín sprawled on a maguey plant, a cigar clenched in his teeth, evokes the imagery found in *The Horrors of the Revolution,* a series of drawings and a lithographic version known as *Mexico in the Revolution,* made by Orozco during his New York stay in the mid-1920s (see chaps. 4, 5). Yet the overwhelming affect is abjection. By accentuating the grotesque, this imagery deglamorizes death, enabling the spectator to interrogate the characters' inadequate attempts to conform to idealized views of male heroism.

Let's Go with Pancho Villa! was produced at a time when *charrería* shows were as common as bullfighting in Mexico City and other large urban areas. By then, the invented tradition (viewed at first with suspicion, if not outright hostility) had become a feature of national authenticity, and "popular consciousness began to substitute mythical reality—everything it represented—for actual reality" (Doñán, 2000, 93). This familiarity and status (alongside the concurrent release of *Over There on the Big Ranch*) prompts the question about the use of this imagery in a film about Villa. De Fuentes treats *charrería* strategically. Performance and fetish objects become catalysts to expose, in a detached yet profoundly compelling manner, the cruelty and trauma of the revolution. The poor showing of *Let's Go with Pancho Villa!* and the popular success of the *comedia ranchera* proved to what extent audiences predisposed to put aside the past had embraced *charro* culture as an imaginary projection of what they wanted to be.

Nevertheless, the film's emphasis on disillusion and death was a major factor in its rediscovery. Since then it has been celebrated for representing the revolution "without folklorism and *cucarachas*" (Ayala Blanco, quoted in García Riera, 1984, 82).[21] Its sober approach and minimalist aesthetic have inspired filmmakers interested in representing the communal quotidian of war instead of glorifying mythical figures. Conversely *Viva Villa!* remains an example of Hollywood's inability to overcome historical attitudes and perceptions about Mexico and the revolution, notwithstanding the intention of its producers to accommodate Mexican sensibilities. Shifts from spectacle to comedy, like the combined traits of violence and joviality in Beery's characterization and performance, reinforce the overdetermined meanings of the Villa legend. As I have argued, the visual and narrative protocols of historical drama and biography are put at the service of the film's agenda: to rehabilitate the revolutionary leader without substantially altering the normative constructions of his historical and screen persona.

Avant-Garde Gestures and Nationalist Images of Mexico in Eisenstein's Unfinished Project

Chapter 4

On December 6 or 7, 1930, the Soviet filmmaker Sergei M. Eisenstein crossed the border from California into Mexico by train accompanied by Grigori Alexandrov and Eduard Tissé, his assistant and cinematographer. He had secured funding from the socialist writer Upton Sinclair and his wife, Mary, to make a film in Mexico. What the film was going to be neither Eisenstein nor his financial backers knew. What none of them suspected was that fourteen months later, on February 23, 1932, Eisenstein and his crew would recross the border, to Texas this time, because the film was suspended, to remain forever unfinished.[1]

Nevertheless, the extant footage of *Que Viva Mexico!* and the history of its failure remain to this day an object of fascination for film historians worldwide. Over the past two decades, as the extensive literature and ongoing restoration efforts attest, attention has shifted away from the director's trials and tribulations. Soviet, European, and North American scholarship is now driven by the need to relocate the project within the director's creative trajectory and explore its aesthetic and ideological agenda (Noble, 2006; Robé, 2006).

Concurrently, Mexican scholars have produced a multilayered narrative aimed at reconfiguring Eisenstein's place in the history of Mexican cinema. As Eduardo de la Vega Alfaro has remarked, "Even at a distance of 68 years, the arrival of Eisenstein in Mexico continues to be one of the most affecting episodes of the history of film and, undoubtedly, one of the events that marked, for better or worse, the course of [Mexican] national cinema" (1998, 8). Most of the recent historiography was generated by the various events organized in the years leading to the hundredth anniversary of the birth and the fiftieth anniversary of the death of the Soviet director, commemorated in 1998.[2] Notable and invaluable both in substance and propositions is the work of the film historians and scholars De la Vega Alfaro and De los Reyes, who separately documented unexplored and neglected facets of Eisenstein's project. The first has provided new insights into the project's aesthetics and its relation to Mexican visual culture (De la Vega Alfaro, 1997). The second has written a suggestive account of the sources that shaped the film's conception based on the books and illustrated magazines preserved by Naum Kleinman, curator at the Eisenstein Museum in Moscow (De los Reyes, 2001a, 2002, 2006).

The extant footage, together with production stills, frame enlargements, and Eisenstein's drawings, demonstrates to what extent this unfinished project is symptomatic of the complex and diverse ways in which images of Mexico and the Mexican Revolution were constructed and negotiated in the postrevolution period by Mexicans and foreigners alike. To this effect, I begin with a brief description of *Disaster in Oaxaca,* a documentary that Eisenstein made shortly after his arrival in Mexico. What could be regarded as a minor work is in fact an example of the range of the director's activities, as well as of his goal to turn his impressions as a traveler into a creative investigation of the country's contrasting realities and histories. Next, I examine the sources and meanings of the imagery intended for what Eisenstein described as the "Maguey" episode, and which is the only one of those filmed that approximates the time frame of the revolution. Set in the historical Santiago de Tetlapayac estate, where the "rough outline" and first screenplay were written, "Maguey" is a reenactment of the autocratic politics, social inequity, and brutalization of the peasantry that led to the nationwide insurgency in 1910 against the Porfirio Díaz regime.

Since Eisenstein was never granted the opportunity to edit his materials, my remarks are based on the restored version of *Que Viva Mexico!* produced by Grigori Alexandrov and released in 1979. The extant footage is presented in the following order. Peons assembled in a courtyard set out to work in the maguey fields. An elderly couple arrives to entrust María (Isabel Villaseñor) to Sebastián (Martín Hernández). The couple heads back to the hacienda. On the way to present his fiancée to the owner, the rancheros block Sebastián's way and escort María to where the *hacendado* and other men, all wearing the typical *charro* attire, are gathered. The owner's daughter Sara and her cousin Julio (Julio Saldívar) arrive, and the peasant girl is briefly forgotten. When she walks away, a guest intercepts her and pulls her into a room. A servant then alerts Sebastián, who rushes to the door. He is whipped by the man (Nicolás Nuñez) standing outside. When María emerges, she runs to her fiancé. As he confronts her rapist, Sara and her father arrive. María is locked up, and Sebastián is injured when he is pushed down the stairs. At a party, the workers and owner drink pulque. To rescue María, Sebastián and his friends steal rifles and ammunition. The assault fails, and they flee into the maguey fields. A posse sets out. During the firefight several peons are shot and Sara is killed. Two peons are apprehended. Sebastián is trapped in a gulley and dragged back to the hacienda. In the courtyard, the captured peons are forced to pay their respects to the dead Sara. Her cousin Julio surveys the digging of holes in which the peons are then buried up to their shoulders. A boy hiding behind a maguey plant looks away when the rancheros' horses decapitate his friends. María is freed from her prison, runs out into the fields, and kneels in front of Sebastián's body. The peons mourn their companions' death.

The imagery of "Maguey" elicits a range of questions about Eisenstein's investment in the postrevolutionary debates about Mexico's culture, society, and politics. Hence I consider the influence of Anita Brenner's book, *Idols behind Altars*, and *indigenismo* on the project and the way in which Eisenstein reformulated visually the place of the Indian in the nationalist narrative. Also explored are the affinities with the artistic practices and visual culture of the period. First, I comment on the participation of Isabel Villaseñor to reinscribe her subjectivity as artist and actor and clarify the confusion about her identity originating from Marie Seton's erroneous claim that she was an art student (Seton 1978, 215). The director's drawings of Villaseñor suggest an assimilation of vernacular forms and his rapport with the expressions of Mexico's emerging vanguard. Second, I discuss how the publication of production stills and frame enlargements in Mexican newspapers in 1931 facilitated the project's incorporation into debates on Mexicanness. This process occludes the critical dimension present in the "Maguey" episode. As I argue, the imagery reconfigures the physical and human geography of the hacienda. It counters romanticized views of the landscape by rehistoricizing its picturesque features through citations from a series of drawings by José Clemente Orozco. It represents the *charro* as an agent of violence to expose the tensions resulting from the integration of this iconic figure associated with the landowning class into the postrevolutionary discourse on national reconciliation. What these reflections reveal is the extent to which Eisenstein's project was reshaped by his contact with the political, social, and cultural conditions that existed in Mexico in the early 1930s. The remarks on the materials related to this episode bring to light the multiple convergences at work in the project and serve to untangle the complex processes of cultural exchange and debates on Mexican identity that inform *Que Viva Mexico!*

SETTING THE STAGE: *Disaster in Oaxaca*

Eisenstein's arrival in Mexico coincided with an acute crisis in the country's incipient film industry, spurred in part by the technological and economic demands accompanying the transition to sound (De la Vega Alfaro, 1998, 8). Notices about his visit in the local press were extremely positive. To have a foreign filmmaker of Eisenstein's stature come to Mexico to work with Mexicans on a film about Mexico was a welcome development. The statements made prior to his departure from Los Angeles impressed nationalists of all political persuasions. In Mexico, the filmmaker stated in a newspaper interview published on December 11 in *El Nacional Revolucionario* that he intended to dispense with images of "*charros* with guns on their belts" and the distorted views of the revolution circulated by "the sensationalist American yellow press" (quoted in De la Vega Alfaro, 1997, 17). In another report, published on December 9 in *El Universal,* the director said that he intended to "study the Mexican *ambiente* [surroundings]" and enlist the collaboration of Mexican artists and photographers (quoted in De la Vega Alfaro, 1997, 18). A few days later, on December 12, the same newspaper printed a caricature on its front page relative to Eisenstein's statement that he would use local people instead of professional actors.

Additional coverage came on January 14 in the form of news that "various cinematographic experts" (Eisenstein and his crew) had traveled to Oaxaca on a commercial flight to record on film the destructive effects of an earthquake that had struck the region the previous day. Four days later, *Excélsior* published on its front page what it claimed was the first eyewitness report of the collapse of the San Pablo de Guelatova church in the village of Zimatlán, along with a photograph attributed to Tissé.[3] Also noted was Eisenstein's horrified response to the "spectacle that cemeteries present where, through openings in the walls and crypts, countless human remains can be sighted" (De la Vega Alfaro, 2000, 348). The public relations potential of the article did not escape Hunter Kimborough, managing director of the project. "Headlines tremendous Eisenstein story all newspapers here today, is scoop," is what he communicated in a telegram addressed to his brother-in-law, Sinclair (Geduld and Gottesman, 1970, 44).[4] Barely five weeks in the country, the Soviet director and his crew had made what would paradoxically be their only complete Mexican film within an eight-day period: the twelve-minute documentary titled *Disaster in Oaxaca*. In a record forty-eight hours two thousand feet of film had been shot, and in two days the material was developed, assembled, and

—¿Pa onde mero le jala asté, don Chema, con ese traje de asbestación tan garigoleado?
—Pos meramente voy a devisar al siñor Eisenstein, el de las piliculerías rusas, pa que me dé mi chambita en la vista esa que quere sacar de puritito ambiente mexicano...

FIGURE 4.1. *Caricature*, El Universal *(Mexico City), December 12, 1930*

screened to a select group of government officials. On January 21, the final version was ready for exhibition approval by the Censorship Commission. Two days later, the film was premiered at the Iris Theatre during a fundraising event for the earthquake victims that consisted mainly of a variety show featuring the legendary revue star María Conesa (De la Vega Alfaro, 2000, 354).

Six decades would pass before the film was screened again in Mexico City, at the Restored Memory festival organized by the Filmoteca of the Autonomous National University of Mexico in 1996. Programming of the print preserved and restored by the Museum of Modern Art in New York provided an opportunity to assess its import. It also elicited a reflection on its relationship to footage shot two months later on the Isthmus of Tehuantepec, the tropical region of the state of Oaxaca. As De la Vega Alfaro notes, the aesthetic features of *Disaster in Oaxaca* "reveal the transition from a cinematic concept associated with the newsreel or the 'live' film reportage to another where a much more complex 'pictorial' concern dominates, inevitably filtered by composition, framing, and editing" (2000, 356). This tendency toward abstraction evokes the work of contemporary Mexican or foreign photographers, namely, Manuel Álvarez Bravo, Agustín Jiménez, Edward Weston, and Tina Modotti. Apocalyptic associations sustained by recurring shots of angel figures are confirmed by the title of the last section, "Angel of Death" (356). To show the effects of the earthquake, static shots of buildings and people are intercut with aerial views of the Popocatéptl and Iztaccíhuatl volcanoes and surrounding landscapes.[5] Like the religious statuary placed against the background of bell towers and cupolas, the Indian villagers standing motionless by the ruins of damaged buildings seem to be "waiting for the return of the cataclysm" (356).

With its emphasis on human and material devastation, grief and mourning, the imagery of *Disaster in Oaxaca* stands in overt contrast to the footage intended for the "Sandunga" episode of *Que Viva Mexico!* The idyllic and eroticized portrayal of village life in Tehuantepec is aligned with the romantic primitivism and ethnographic impulse that drove both Euro-American and Mexican representations of traditional societies during this period. As De la Vega Alfaro writes, "What appear to be antagonistic ways of visualizing Oaxaca complement each other perfectly insofar as they present a broad and suggestive filmic panorama of the region in the early 1930s, a time when the debate on tradition and modernity acquired a new and defining momentum in our country" (2000, 364). Rather than simply the first impressions of a foreign filmmaker seeking out the traces of Mexico's colonial and indigenous heritages, these two sets of footage visualize the precariousness of these legacies. The sense of transience in the shots of destitute people wandering among the ruins of fortresslike churches in the earthquake film transcends the impulse to document how, as noted in the journalistic accounts of the time, "in Oaxaca, sleeping, eating and living is done in the open air" (quoted in De los Reyes, 1994, 26). Similarly in the footage destined for *Que Viva Mexico!* a sense of melancholy saturates the paradisiacal imagery of the landscape and the ancestral matriarchal traditions in Tehuantepec to depict a history and culture on the verge of disappearance.

Seen in this way, Eisenstein's work in Oaxaca suggests an initial stage of a process wherein reality and discourse are simultaneously implicated. Whether it records a recent disaster or the tenous survival of Zapotec customs, Eisenstein's edited earthquake footage preserves antithetical but complementary visions of a region that in those years symbolized the ongoing conflict surrounding the dual poles of national identity between hispanists (champions of religious and cultural traditions) and indigenists (secular modernists and advocates of an indigenous Mexico). Moreover, *Disaster in Oaxaca* and the footage destined for the "Sandunga" episode hold a significant place in Mexican film historiography. Among only a handful of surviving films of this period shot in Oaxaca, they represent a substantial contribution to regional film history and, in the words of De la Vega Alfaro, are the "inevitable reference and main challenge" for the filmic image of Oaxaca (2000, 364).

CONVERSATIONS ACROSS BORDERS:
SOURCES AND CONTACTS

Although Eisenstein arrived in Mexico without a developed concept for his film, he brought with him more than simply intuition about what he expected to find there. In the preceding years, his curiosity was spurred by the stories told by the poet Vladimir Mayakovsky after his trip to Mexico in 1925 and by the 1927 visit of Mexican painter Diego Rivera to Moscow. He would also have been familiar with John Reed's *Insurgent Mexico* since his film *October* (1928) was based on the American journalist's testimony of the Soviet Revolution, *Ten Days That Shook the World*. "His interest turned into an obsession," De los Reyes said, after seeing an article written by Dr. Alfons Goldschmidt containing three photographs of the Day of the Dead festivities taken by his wife, Lina, and published in Berlin in the *Arbeiter Illustrierte Zeitung* on November 16, 1927, and which he filed with the notation *Berliner Illustrierte 1927-1928* (2001a, 154). After his visit to Berlin in 1929—the first leg of the extended period of travel that took him to Mexico via Hollywood—Eisenstein became an avid collector of illustrated journals and books dealing with Mexico.

Once in the country, he supplemented his knowledge by touring various regions, mostly south of Mexico City, in the company of both Mexican and foreign-born artists and writers. All became friends and collaborators, and all belonged to the various groups that constituted the Mexican avant-garde. Prominent figures included the muralists and painters Jean Charlot, Roberto Montenegro, Diego Rivera, and David Alfaro Siqueiros and the designer and folk art specialist Adolfo Best Maugard. Although Maugard also participated informally as a crew member, he also acted in the capacity of officially appointed adviser-censor (De los Reyes, 2002, 164). Among the emerging figures were the muralists, painters, and engravers

Fernando Leal, Pablo O'Higgins, Gabriel Fernández Ledesma, and Isabel Villaseñor, along with the photographers Manuel and Lola Àlvarez Bravo. These friends and advisers came to consider Eisenstein "the 'pioneer' of the 'Mexican image' in the cinema" (Pérez Montfort, 1994b, 361).

The enduring appeal of the imagery shot by Eisenstein for *Que Viva Mexico!* is the result of a series of conversations across cultures. Some are consistent with the cosmopolitanism that contributed to making Mexico an important place for the modernist vanguard in the 1920s. As detailed in chapter 7, the country and its capital were key destinations for intellectuals, artists, and writers who wanted to experience firsthand the confluence of modernism and politics that was reinventing the country's cultural landscape. Other conversations, apparently provoked by direct contacts, seem to permeate the entire project. Examples can be found in the tropes used by the director to formulate its concept and, as discussed below, in the extant footage of the "Maguey" episode. In both cases, the conversation is at once an appropriation of and engagement with the ideas articulated by the twenty-four-year-old Mexican-born anthropologist and writer Anita Brenner in *Idols behind Altars* (1929). Illustrated with photographs by Edward Weston and Tina Modotti, this book circulated a modernist and postrevolutionary vision of Mexico in the United States and, to a lesser degree, in Mexico. It offered a synthetic, dynamic interpretation of the country's history and culture, articulating in visual terms the relationship between contemporary and precontact-period social realities and forms of popular expression. "Without the need for translation or a story sequence," Brenner wrote, "Mexico resolves itself harmoniously and powerfully as a great symphony or a great mural painting, consistent with itself, not as a nation in progress, but as a picture, with certain dominant themes, certain endlessly repeated forms and values in constantly different relationships, and always in the present, like the Aztec history-scrolls that were also calendars and books of creed" (1929, 15).

Eisenstein purchased *Idols behind Altars* in Los Angeles at the Hollywood Bookstore, owned (or managed) by Odo Stade, who presented himself as a veteran of Villa's army and who later collaborated as a researcher in Edgumb Pinchon's 1933 book, the source for the script of *Viva Villa!* Copious notations on the signed copy preserved at the Moscow archive are evidence of how the director used Brenner's book. De los Reyes remarks, "It offered an explanation, a handle to grab onto a complex being and arrange the images he began taking on the march; and, besides, Anita Brenner was attempting to explain the complexity of that country which had captivated both, despite its social contrasts, dirt and garbage" (2001a,

FIGURE 4.2. Que Viva Mexico! *"Maguey" episode, frame enlargement*

167). By singling out the above quoted passage in Eisenstein's annotated copy, the Mexican film historian confirms the import and influence of the book for the film's conceptualization (2001a, 168). Indeed, it validates the project's primary metaphor, the one instigated by the director's question, "Do you know what a 'Serape' is?"⁶

Filmed materials intended for the "Maguey" episode, specifically, the images of the maguey plant, allude directly to Brenner's narrative on the survival of indigenous culture. As James Oles writes, for Brenner "the maguey represented the drama of Mexican life—hardy and strong, even aggressive, yet ultimately powerless" (1993, 149). Visiting and local painters and photographers were fascinated by the hardy succulent that thrives in the semidesert, infertile soil of Mexico's highlands, depicting it as a national symbol. Extant scenes of the "Maguey" episode (see fig. 4.2) detail the labor required to extract the *aguamiel,* the sweet sap used for fermenting pulque (*octli* in Náhuatl), a thick, foamy, and cloudy alcoholic drink consumed since ancient times. They show Sebastián and the other peons separating the ripe *pencas* (thick, fleshy, grayish-green spears edged with hooked thorns and a single straight thorn on the tip), making an incision in the heart of the plant to facilitate the flow of the *aguamiel,* and sucking up the viscose liquid with the dried-out casing of the emptied *guaje* (large squash). The stylized framing with its dramatic contrasts and sculptural qualities turns the whole process into allegory. The ethnographic dimensions dissolve in the face of the symbolic power of the images to represent a ritual in which, as Brenner writes, "something of the old religion holds" because "with each successive gesture of this ceremony, the *tlachiquero* [laborer] murmurs invocation and prayer" (1929, 172). If what attracts Eisenstein in Brenner's account is the continuity and survival of indigenous cultures, he rehistoricizes the meanings of the maguey. As Chris Robé writes, the scenes destined for this episode reveal "the alienating production system for harvesting pulque that keeps peons dispossessed of their land and in a constant state of abject poverty" (2006, 15). Thus the visual motif for representing the ancient and mystical bond with the land serves to dramatically reenact the harshness of daily life and labor in the pulque-producing haciendas of Mexico's Central Valley.

THE IMAGE OF THE INDIAN AND COMPETING NARRATIVES OF MEXICAN IDENTITY

Foreign artists with an ethnographic interest may have been surprised to find peasants instead of the Indians in feather headdress depicted in the novels by Karl May and Jack London. Yet their paintings, photographs, and illustrations idealized the peasant of Indian and mestizo heritage as an archetype of a vanishing world and constructed a racialized image that erased class difference. "Despite the mobilization of the rural peasantry during the Revolution," Oles remarks, "images of these people by visiting American artists in subsequent years overwhelmingly omitted any indications of violence, seeking out instead the exotic and untroubled nation that many remembered from before the war" (1993, 75). As this art historian points out, caricature-like images of Mexico and Mexicans are rare in the work of foreign artists who traveled across Mexico: theirs are "stereotypes of selection rather than distortion" (55).

A drawing by the German American artist Winold Reiss, *Zapatista Soldiers* (1920), for example, offers a stark contrast to the period imagery of the civil war produced by photographers and postcard makers. "Cartridge belts or not, Reiss's soldiers symbolize a revolution that was no longer to be feared but rather memorialised through art" (Oles, 1993, 71). In spite of the wide-brimmed hat worn by one soldier and the gun belt of the other, the image conveys nostalgia by calling attention to what is absent:

FIGURE 4.3. Que Viva Mexico! *"Maguey" episode, frame enlargement*

the white shirts traditionally associated with the Mexican peasantry. The visual prominence of the striped shirt and pastel-colored bandannas divests its subjects of historicity, linking them to an idealized farm laborer rather than to the millions of peasant-soldiers of Indian or mixed-race origin who joined Emiliano Zapata. Even those artists who brought some degree of political consciousness to their work were barely able to overcome this predisposition. The photograph *Men of Santa Ana, Michoacán* (1933), by Paul Strand, for instance, shows peasants by an adobe wall that looks as weathered as their faces. They look straight at the camera, sternly if not with hostility. To the extent that this image, like most of those published in Strand's 1940 *Mexican Portfolio,* was obtained by using a trick camera that made the subjects unaware of being photographed, it throws into question the authenticity of the exchange between subject and photographer. What we are left with is a clear acknowledgment of the ambiguities and contradictions of trying to represent the dignity and moral strength of Mexican peasants who, in Strand's own account, were averse to being photographed.

Eisenstein's imagery of peasant culture reflects in some measure the practices of other visiting artists and, when viewed in these terms, is "less 'flawed' than symptomatic of the cultural milieu of the age in which he lived" (Noble, 2006, 180). Yet there are differences due to a cinematic strategy commonly known as montage-within-the-shot wherein editing elements are included in the otherwise formalist treatment of individual shots in order to construct meaning. An instance of this method is found in the "Maguey" episode. The shot preceding the *aguamiel* extraction sequence shows the peons in wide-brimmed hats, serapes, and huaraches walking past a rancher who reclines against a massive stone gate. The mise-en-scène points to their place within the hacienda system. Their backs to the camera and their slow movement toward the distant maguey fields signify their condition as exploited laborers (see fig. 4.3). The tension between the darkened archway in the foreground and the luminous peak of a volcano dominating the landscape in the background reinforces this meaning, investing the peasant body with a symbolic value closer to the indigenist positions of Mexican cultural nationalism.

The Mexican anthropologist and cultural historian Ricardo Pérez Monfort explains that the Indian was recognized in the postrevolutionary period as the "foundational member of the *Mexican people*" and "a stereotype capable of embodying the defining features of Mexicanness" (1994a, 352, 353; original emphasis). Here "Indian" refers actually to the mestizo and "the people" designates peasants and indigenous sectors, in other words, the marginalized majority who had participated in the revolution.

To address the racialized representations in Eisenstein's project, it is necessary to consider briefly what *indigenismo* meant. Although the revolution had been waged to reconcile class differences, in the 1920s the operative terms of the state's agenda of national reconciliation were "race" and "ethnicity." As Noble writes, in the postrevolutionary period the objective was to synthesize the plurality of "racial identities that coexisted within the national boundaries" and to "offset multiplicity and diversity against a notion of singularity and coherence, using *indigenismo* as a unifying tool" (2000, 110). Rooted in nineteenth-century discourses and representations of the nation, *indigenismo* implied not a reinstatement of Indian culture, pre-Hispanic or otherwise, but rather a recoding of the historical, social, and racial categories Spanish, Indian, and mestizo. According to Noble, "As it had been in the preceding centuries, [*indigenismo* was] an elite discourse deployed in the name of a nation-state struggling to consolidate and legitimate its identity" (2006, 177).

In the colonial period mestizo identity—as depicted in the *casta* paintings—was a sign of illegitimacy and miscegenation. By the mid-nineteenth century, when more than half the population recognized itself as mestizo (including Afro-mestizo), and for most of the twentieth, the mestizo was considered the embodiment of a renewed national identity. In neoclassical art, as Magali M. Carrera notes, "Indian and *mestizo* bodies were revised and represented as national icons" (2005, 32). The once excluded and stigmatized figures appear in two important paintings exhibited in 1869: as an Indian woman in a reenactment of origins in *The Discovery of the Pulque* by José Obregón and as a mestiza in a depiction of independence, *The Allegory of the Constitution of 1857,* by Petronilo Monroy. This allegorical impulse persisted in the visual culture and discourse of the postrevolutionary period. A mythic image of the Indian was constructed that originated in the conquest rather than in precontact or modern history, and the mestizo was either rehabilitated for its potential as class and ethnicity to overcome the gulf between backwardness and modernity or integrated into national culture as the ideal, hybrid category that José Vasconcelos called "the cosmic race."

Given the diversity and complexity of Mexico, the task of creating consensus around a single category capable of defining the "essence" of national identity was complicated. As Mauricio Tenorio explains, if "no single image can depict the figure of the *indigenista*," the affirmation that "there is an authentic *indigenismo* and a false one" is not viable either (1995, 259, 261). The work of Diego Rivera offers examples of fluctuations in the treatment of Indian themes. The muralist approached the theme at first mostly in terms of the history of conquest. In a contemporary context—the murals at the Secretariat of Public Education, for example—he aligned the figuration of Indians with explicit official objectives: cultural when promoting folk and popular art expression; political when depicting the government-initiated literacy and land distribution campaigns. Allegory replaces realism in the later murals painted at the National School of Architecture in Chapingo (1926–1927). The art historian Dawn Ades considers the painting *Blood of the Revolutionary Martyrs Fertilizing the Earth* haunting, poignant, and, to a degree, critical. It renders the bodies of Emiliano Zapata and Otilio E. Montaño, in her words, "as though in triumphant contradiction of the reactionary vow during the revolution to 'exterminate the Zapatista seed so that it will not germinate again'" (1989, 165). Back in the Soviet Union in 1935, Eisenstein wrote about the work of the Mexican muralists. His description of this painting in the unfinished article written in 1935 titled "The Prometheus of Mexican Painting" is worth quoting: "From the red, bloody wrappings of the dead Zapata grow the strong plants of a future freedom" (1982, 227).

Out of the divergent views on the social and cultural place of indigenous sectors within nationalist discourse, competitive visual narratives emerged. These narratives took a variety of forms depending on whether they were articulated by the politicized vanguard or by artists at the margins of official modernism. In the latter, *indigenismo* is not separated from social issues. Poverty, rather than ethnicity, is the central theme of *The Peasant Mother* and *Proletarian Mother* painted by David Alfaro Siqueiros in 1929.[7] With its somber vision of the realities of exploitation and marginality of indigenous women, the Siqueiros imagery breaks with the idealized representations favored in prevailing discourse. The technology of modernization complements religious tradition in the depiction of the countryside in *Ladrillera* (1929) by Gabriel Fernández Ledesma. As Fausto Ramírez writes, the painting "seems to summarize in visual terms the ambiguous, contradictory vision of the country and the city that emerged in multiple manifestations of postrevolutionary culture in Mexico" (1999, 259).

The perspectives of the visual artists appear in the materials intended for the "Maguey" episode and are expanded through Eisenstein's representation of power and gender relations. The scenes of María's introduction to the landowner and the arrival of his daughter Sara are notable examples. Set in the courtyard, they reproduce the social ranking within the hacienda, showing the owner sitting at the top of the stairs that lead to an open hallway while his administrators and guests are grouped around tables set below on ground level. Medium and long shots reveal the marginalization of the women from what is a typical tableau of affluence and male privilege. María stands slightly to the side of the owner, her meek behavior and posture as she removes her *rebozo* establishing her lower rank in the social order. Even if the overconfident and boisterous Sara is squarely in the center, her back is turned to the camera as she runs to greet her father. Except for one close-up that shows her sitting on his lap, the back-view framing undermines her superiority and virtually excludes her from the plot in which María is the main character. Crucial to these scenes is the scrutinizing look of the owner and Señor Balderas, a guest also in *charro* attire who will subsequently rape María. The gaze dramatizes the libidinal dimension of power, and—as Robé writes—"suggests that their vision of María is all a part of the same gender (if not class) visual economy"(2006, 12).

The caricature-like physiognomy and posture of the rapist brings to

FIGURE 4.4.   Que Viva Mexico! *"Maguey"* episode, frame enlargement

mind a drawing by Orozco included in the English-language edition of Mariano Azuela's *The Underdogs* (1929), a novel that Eisenstein purchased shortly after he arrived in Mexico (De los Reyes, 2002, 133). It shows a revolutionary general in *charro* clothes holding a drink in one hand and a woman in the other. Every element of this image is overtly sexualized: the oversized hat, the raised arm propping up a rifle, the legs spread wide open, and even the backside of the woman sitting on the man's lap. Eisenstein's shots of the ranchero savoring the glass of pulque convey phallic dominance and the looming threat of violence. After close-ups of the brutish face and lascivious gaze, a medium shot of the reclined body and leg propped on a chair is—to use Robé's words—"a literal cock-shot of the rapist" (2006, 12). This image reveals that Orozco's influence was not limited to the "Soldadera" episode, as customarily claimed. With its emphasis on class and gender domination, the scene signals Eisenstein's affinity with the work of an artist who rejected mainstream *indigenismo* in favor of a demystifying representation of the revolution. Given that the Orozco image was used to illustrate the most important and also most critical novel about the revolution, its citation suggests Eisenstein's ambivalent posture on postrevolutionary historicism.

WITH CHABELA IN TETLAPAYAC: VERNACULAR IDIOMS AND GRAPHIC ARTS

Eisenstein conceived each of the six episodes (or "novellas") of his project as an homage to the major figures of Mexican art: the prologue to David Alfaro Siqueiros, "Sandunga" to Jean Charlot, "Maguey" to Diego Rivera, "Soldadera" to José Clemente Orozco (never filmed), and the epilogue to José Guadalupe Posada. "Fiesta" would have been dedicated to the Spanish painter Francisco de Goya. Yet the artists who were most receptive to his work, and arguably more influential, belonged to a new vanguard. Members of groups that embraced cosmopolitanism, they presented themselves as a countercurrent to the officially recognized muralist movement. Worth mentioning among them are Álvarez Bravo, Fernández Ledesma, María Izquierdo, Carlos Mérida, and Roberto Montenegro, all involved in the literary and art magazine *Contemporáneos* (1928–1931). In May 1931 this magazine published Eisenstein's article "Principles of Filmic Form" on his "montage of attractions" theory in a translation by Agustín Aragón Leiva. Also included in this issue were production stills of *Que Viva Mexico!* and the famous photograph of Eisenstein holding a sugar skull taken by the photographer and later cinematographer Agustín Jiménez (Rodríguez Álvarez, 2002, 74).

Eisenstein's contacts with the ¡30-30! Group were more direct and resulted in mutually productive exchanges that can be documented in the prodigious number of drawings he made in Mexico. This avant-garde group took the name of the firearm of choice during the revolution in order to challenge conservative teaching methods and academic ideas on art. All the members were, at one time, involved with the Popular Painting Centers that operated in Mexico City between 1927 and 1934, where they practiced a wide range of pictorial media and participated in the revival of engraving techniques. Isabel—or Chabela, as she was called by her friends—Villaseñor and Fernández Ledesma, both members of the ¡30-30! Group, were introduced to Eisenstein by Montenegro in the Secretariat of Education. In an unpublished typescript, Fernández Ledesma recounted that the Soviet filmmaker was so struck that "after talking for 10 minutes, he proposed to us that Chabela work in his film" (quoted in Figueroa, 1998, 34). The twenty-one-year-old artist, whose first solo show had opened to considerable notice in September 1930, reluctantly agreed to be the principal performer in what would become the most notorious episode of *Que Viva Mexico!*

The photographs taken at the Santiago de Tetlapayac hacienda, includ-

FIGURE 4.5. *"Chabela revolucionaria,"* 1931, *photograph attributed to Gabriel Fernández Ledesma. Courtesy of Olinca Fernández Ledesma Villaseñor, Guadalajara, Mexico*

ing those attributed to her partner and future husband, show Chabela in the peasant costume of the character she played. It is clear from these pictures that Eisenstein recognized in her the same striking mestiza features that her contemporaries who photographed her (before and afterward) saw. A portrait made in 1935 by Manuel Alvárez Bravo captures her exquisite features and turns her into an archetype of femininity. About this metamorphosis, the Mexican art historian and curator Judith Alanís Figueroa writes, "By accepting the challenge to participate as a protagonist in the film, Chabela gives birth to another Chabela who becomes the prototype of postrevolutionary *mexicanidad*" (1998, 36). Yet what is also striking is how her body posture and facial expressions reveal her physical and psychological discomfort. Although Villaseñor left no detailed account of her stay at the hacienda, there is evidence that it was not always pleasant. In a letter to Eisenstein dated July 7, she wrote about "the enormous hardship endured by having to live together with people who for me are disagreeable and untrustworthy" (quoted in De la Vega Alfaro, 1999a, n.p.). Among the predominantly male group of artists, bohemians, and intellectuals who visited the hacienda, the painter saw herself as an outsider. What the photographs show is an awareness of difference that, in my view, cast doubts on the efforts of inclusion by her partner, Fernández Ledesma, who photographed her with a rifle in hand and claimed she enjoyed entertaining the guests with her own *corridos* on days when rain interrupted the shooting (Figueroa, 1998, 35). (See figure 4.5.)

Among the thousands of drawings that Eisenstein made during the three-month stay at Tetlapayac, the twenty belonging to the Villaseñor–Fernández Ledesma couple depict Chabela as a saintly and protective figure.[8] As in the photographs by her contemporaries, she stands apart as a figure to be worshiped and—like the Virgin of Guadalupe—a symbol of comfort and mediation. In "Santa camaleoncita (figure 4.6)," she appears surrounded by musician Manuel Castro Padilla playing the harp, artist Fernández Ledesma in oversized glasses and a striped cap, and Grigory Alexandrov and Martín Hernández—who interpreted Sebastián—in large peon hats (see *S. M. Eisenstein: Dibujos inéditos*, 1978, n.p.). The title of this drawing, as De la Vega Alfaro points out, comes from the nickname "saintly little chameleon" that Eisenstein gave her when she tried to rescue the small chameleons that invaded the hacienda from the frenzied guests bent on wiping them out (1999a, n.p.). With its playful sense of humor, this drawing also introduces an element of cruelty that is absent from the photographs. Chabela is seen as a mocking figure hovering above a cloud from which a group of suffering males hang from ropes with their feet

FIGURE 4.6. *"Santa Camaleoncita," 1931, drawing by S. M. Eisenstein.* From S. M. Eisenstein: Dibujos inéditos

over burning oil lamps. The lanky figure on the right is that of Best Maugard, who was acting as official adviser. In other drawings, the painter is associated with the maguey. In an untitled drawing, the maguey is the altar on which she sits, like the ancient Otomí goddess Mayahuel, surrounded by her admirers, including a donkey and a chameleon who make an offering of their flaming hearts. There is a noticeable difference in the often-reproduced stills of the "Maguey" episode footage. Unlike the images of peasants nestled among the clawlike spikes of the maguey, there is no hint of eroticism or pathos. The razor-sharp thorns and the edges that curve inward as if in a protective gesture have disappeared. The smooth, flowerlike shape of the maguey suggests serenity and stands in sharp contrast to the serrated lines and sense of despair found in the Orozco drawings to which Eisenstein refers in the shoot-out scenes between peons and *hacendados* discussed in the next section.

The Tetlapayac drawings, together with the innumerable production stills, suggest "a trace of contact between the filmmaker and the subject represented" (Noble, 2006, 183). They prove that Eisenstein's views on Mexico were not merely an imaginary projection, and offer a rare glimpse of how Eisenstein dealt with the problems and frustrations that eventually led to the project's cancellation. In addition to their value as documents, these drawings "express the other way, at times satirical, ironic or sublime, in which Eisenstein contemplated the country, and contemplated himself through the characters and locations of the film" (De la Vega Alfaro, 1997, 87). Their significance also lies in their affinities with contemporary and historical printmaking practices in Mexico. They share the spontaneity and grotesque lyricism found in the graphic work of Villaseñor and Fernández Ledesma and evoke the popular broadsheets and prints of José Guadalupe Posada in the humorous rendering of maguey plants, wild and domestic animals, folk toys, musical instruments, winged figures, and peasant costumes. This primacy of vernacular motifs is suggestive of Eisenstein's assimilation of the iconographic and expressive elements of devotional images, satirical cartoons, domestic scenes, and still-life compositions so prominent in Mexican graphic arts. Ostensibly, he was drawn to the possibilities of this medium.

The drawings of Chabela in Tetlapayac are another instance of Eisenstein's identification with the practices of the Mexican vanguard that adopted lithography and engraving for social activist purposes. With the rediscovery of Posada in the 1920s, woodblocks and linoleum plates became in the hands of members of the ¡30-30! Group instruments aimed at stretching the boundaries of artistic idioms and folk expression. Attention reverted to easel paintings and graphic works that integrated vernacular forms and were created by young artists trained, like Villaseñor, in the Popular Painting Centers established with the aim of democratizing artistic creation. The involvement of Villaseñor in the "Maguey" episode suggests the value of looking beyond the influence of the famous artists and works of the Mexican Renaissance of the 1920s. While these practices have already been identified as having played a formative role in Eisenstein's aesthetics, they are only one factor among others in the construction and negotiation of the imagery of Mexico found in his project. The documentary evidence demonstrates the Soviet director's ability to accommodate and respond openly to changing conditions of visual production and expression in the early 1930s.

THE HACIENDA AND THE *Charro*: HISTORICITY AND CRITICAL PERSPECTIVE

The contract signed by Eisenstein stipulated that the Mexican Film Trust, the company set up by Sinclair and the project's investors, would have full ownership of the footage. So when the production was halted, and in order to recoup costs, Sinclair sold some of the footage and gave it to the documentary director Sol Lesser to edit. The result was a seventy-four-minute film titled *Thunder over Mexico* (1933). Promptly released, it caused enormous controversy in the United States and in Mexico (Robé, 2006, 3-6). In the latter, Lesser's film was characterized in a manifesto signed by artists and intellectuals as "one of the most brutal assaults on art and intellectual creation which have been known in history" (quoted in García-Romeu, 1998, 95). The writer, critic, and translator Aragón Leiva spurred the controversy and censored the producers. In an article published on September 11, 1932, in *El Nacional,* he asserted that Eisenstein's work "would be for Mexicans a revelation of their own country's most original features and perennial splendour" (n.p.). Already during the filming, the weekly *Universal Ilustrado* had printed frame enlargements and production stills in a series of articles aimed at promoting the film and signed by Adolfo Bustamante Fernández, a lawyer representing Sinclair's company in Mexico. He lauded Eisenstein because his project represented "a truly Mexican work of art, profoundly nationalist and beautiful" (1931, n.p.). Like most of his contemporaries, he considered the portrayal of Mexico and its people authentic because the director had chosen to use actual locations and genuine characters. Another factor was the director's stated intent to pay tribute to the country, to the inherent beauty of its landscapes and monuments and the diversity of its cultural and artistic wealth. As Noble notes, these articles about "Eisenstein's visit bestowed international prestige on Mexico and assured national cultural producers and audiences alike that the country's indigenous heritage was indeed a sight to be acknowledged as self, and imagined as an integral part of that self" (2006, 179).

The controversy about *Thunder over Mexico* and the combined circulation of visual materials intended for Eisenstein's *Que Viva Mexico!* contributed to the incorporation of this ill-fated project into debates on Mexicanness (García-Romeu, 1998, 95). Eisenstein's treatment of iconic images and visual themes was seen as counteracting both the stereotypical viewpoint of Hollywood cinema and the folkloristic imagery of local film productions. If nationalism was a determining factor in the Mexican reception of the project, the validation of the imagery came from its aesthetic proposals. In contrast to other foreign and Mexican photographers who integrated nationalist themes and motifs into their modernist repertory, Eisenstein's approach distinguished itself for the dramatic possibilities of composition and the symbolic resonances of images of pyramids and maguey plants, women of Tehuantepec and peasants of the highlands. For that reason, as García-Romeu writes, the imagery of *Que Viva Mexico!* "left an important mark on the iconography of what was 'Mexican'" (1998, 101). Nevertheless, as indicated above, the symbolic content recedes to a secondary level in the footage shot for the "Maguey" episode where the iconic motifs are recoded to represent labor and class exploitation. To expand this idea, and using as examples the scenes showing the peons' attempt to rescue Maria and its tragic aftermath, I examine how objects and figures belonging to the physical and human geography of the hacienda are used to counter the idealized depictions of the Mexican landscape and to expose the tensions at work in the revival of the *charro* as a nationalist icon.

The main location of the "Maguey" episode is the Santiago de Tetlapayac hacienda. Situated in the Apam highlands of the state of Hildalgo, this ancient estate, dating back to the time of the conquest, housed a pulque factory that was being converted at the time of filming into an agricultural co-op. It was the American-born painter and engraver Pablo O'Higgins who took Eisenstein to Tetlapayac for the first time. The director and his crew subsequently became frequent guests. They were joined by Mexican and foreign artists and writers; some simply went to visit, while others were directly involved in the production. The monumental building of the hacienda and the picturesque environment of maguey fields and volcanoes was a perfectly suited background for re-creating Mexico's violent history. "Aggressiveness, virility, arrogance and austerity" are the words Eisenstein used to explain the story of "Maguey," which revolves around the victimization and execution of three peons at the hands of a vengeful landowner (Eisenstein and Alexandroff [*sic*], 1992, 197).

Whether the scenes are shot inside or outside the building, architec-

FIGURE 4.7. Que Viva Mexico! *"Maguey" episode, frame enlargement*

tural and scenic elements are brought to bear on the drama being enacted. Examples can be found in the early stages of the peons' attempt to rescue María, where matching shots visualize their ineffectiveness and vulnerability. In one, a low-angle shot shows them standing on a heap of crushed stones, the ramparts behind them, and aiming at the ranchers who stand high above. In two others, high-angle shots from the *rancheros*' point of view show them dwarfed by an empty bullring and wall-enclosed interior yard as they run away. Similarly, the awe-inspiring scenery dominates just about every image in the extant footage of the gunfight, threatening to derail the narrative. Shifts in perspective function as a corrective to the spectacle, granting agency to individual protagonists, as in the back and frontal views of peons firing that convey their tenacity and Sebastián's delight at what he believes to be the posse's retreat. Also, analogies add pathos to what otherwise could be seen as an ordinary western-genre shoot-out. Examples are the overhead shots of Sara's white straw hat rolling down a slope bordered by *nopales* (prickly pear cactus) and the body of a murdered peon lying beneath the massive maguey plants. Missing is the idyllic view of the scenery that in earlier scenes evokes the Brehme and Weston photographs reproduced in *Picturesque Mexico* (1926) and *Idols behind Altars,* respectively.

FIGURE 4.8. *"Under the Maguey (Campo de batalla) (Battlefield?),"* 1926–1927, *José Clemente Orozco, pencil and ink, 33 x 45 cm signed,* Los Horrores de la Revolución. *Museo Carrillo Gil, Mexico City.* © *Clemente V. Orozco*

Together with the close-ups of *pencas* used as cartridge holders and slashed by bullets, these shots show nature as a site of death in a manner that is reminiscent of Orozco's series of drawings, *The Horrors of the Revolution*. Like the subsequent lithographic version known as *Mexico in Revolution,* this series of six drawings commissioned by Anita Brenner in 1926 adapts, as Anna Indych notes, "the monumentality of the [National Preparatory School] murals in a small-scale format" and "represents the sheer brutality and bloodshed" of the revolution (2001, 155, 156). No wonder, then, that this imagery appears repeatedly in films that either counter reified depictions of male heroism (*Let's Go with Pancho Villa!*) or expose graphically the materiality of death (*The Wild Bunch*). In Eisenstein's extant footage, torn maguey branches on which corpses rest signify the country's violent past. Other than recoding the most picturesque motif in nationalist and foreign representations of rural Mexico, the Orozco citation serves to rehistoricize devastation and carnage as an extension of, rather than a break from, the Porfiriate.

How the universe of the hacienda is reconfigured reveals a convergence between Eisenstein's own Marxist background and the political views prevalent among progressive Mexican artists and intellectuals. The setting and the *charro* character are associated with reactionary sectors and represented as remnants of a feudal and repressive society. In this sense, the sequences filmed in Tetlapayac are consistent with the narrative of the hacienda that was dominant in the immediate postrevolutionary period. The hacienda represented the ancien régime in need of being overturned by a mass movement to pave the way for the emergence of a new bourgeois state. Even if historically, as Juan Felipe Leal and Mario Huacuja Roundtree have argued, "the hacienda was never a static institution" (1982, 9–10) and combined diverse economic and social strategies, it was portrayed as an archaic, feudal, and autocratic form of domination based on indentured labor. As such, it was designated as a factor that retarded development and a propitious site of insurrection.

Eisenstein also includes iconic figures of the world of the hacienda: the *charro* who since the nineteenth century has been one of the most spectacular, prominent, and picturesque stereotypes of mestizo identity in Mexico. As a nationalist and social construct combining gender, class, and ethnicity to form a representative category of identity, the *charro* belongs to the distinct, at times contrasting, repertory of images and meanings that all social sectors in Mexico share. Whether associated with the *rurales* (the armed militia) and the landowning class of the Porfiriate or with the new middle-class elite that emerged after the revolution, the *charro* is part and parcel of the folklore of the mariachi in Mexican mass culture at home and abroad. As noted in the previous chapter, in the early years of the postrevolutionary period, *charro* identity (notwithstanding its opposing associations) was refashioned in accordance with the ideological aims of cultural nationalism. Pérez Monfort explains that in the 1920s members of the predominantly urban sector, engaged in the elaboration of nationalist stereotypes, rehabilitated his figure by calling on the image of the revolutionary they first saw when the Northern Division and the Army of the South entered Mexico City in 1914. For them, he writes, "Pancho Villa and Emiliano Zapata descended from the *charro* tradition. Their taste for horses, large sombreros and guns was proof of this" (1997, 148). The *charro* of hacienda culture replaced the peasant in gun belts and huaraches, and the stylized version of rural male dress and the horse-riding traditions of the Porfiriate were integrated into the nationalist spectacle.

An important factor in the representation of the *charro* as an agent of violence in the "Maguey" episode was an incident that occurred at Tetlapayac on June 18, 1931, forcing an interruption in the filming. Félix Olvera, who played the role of Felicito, accidentally killed his sister with a gun reportedly owned by Tissé (De la Vega Alfaro, 1993, 46).[9] The killing and its aftermath changed Eisenstein's views on the new postrevolutionary bourgeoisie. He was deeply affected by the behavior of his host, hacienda owner Julio Saldívar. The brutality of the pursuit and apprehension of the young man by the hacienda's employees revealed to Eisenstein that, as De la Vega Alfaro writes, "the Mexican Revolution had not altered many of the conditions that prevailed during the Porfiriate" (1993, 46). The director's shift in position is reflected in the scenes of the capture and punishment of Sebastián by means of the visual prominence given to the materials and practices of *charrería* tradition.[10] The close-ups of silver spurs, *chaparreras* (leather chaps), and *reatas* (maguey ropes) worn by the *charros* make explicit the masculine and class connotations of *charro* attire. The gendered meanings are expanded to reveal the sinister and deadly effects of these accessories in the scenes that show Sebastián and the peons being brought back to the hacienda and later taken to the maguey fields to be killed. What is more, the overdetermined meanings of *charrería* practices are destabilized. The techniques of cattle roping and the choreography of Arabian horse riding that turned *charro* dexterity into spectacle in the 1920s are used by Eisenstein to dramatize degradation and death. The sadistic villainy of the *charros* and horrendous agony of the peons is represented by alternating close-up shots of the legs of charging horses, their hoofs swirling up the dust, with low-angle shots of the terrified faces of the victims. In the scenes of Sebastián and the two other peons being lassoed with maguey ropes, dragged across the fields, and presented to the landowner, the symbolic power of the subjugated and objectified Indian body reinforces the associations made by postrevolutionary discourse between *charrería* and the culture of privilege and repression of the Porfiriate.

Even as Eisenstein was drafting the film script of *Que Viva Mexico!* in Tetlapayac, he understood the potential problems of depicting the part played by the *hacendado* class in the exploitation and repression of peasants. A record of this awareness is found in his introductory comments to what is generally called the film's scenario, which appeared first in 1932 in *Experimental Cinema* but is better known in the 1947 version reprinted in Seton's biography. The Soviet director commented on the need to gloss over specific scenes to placate the anxiety of Sinclair and the other investors about anything that could be construed as radical by the Mexican government. He remarks regarding the government reaction, "To our arguments that only a sufficient demonstration of the class struggle on the haciendas could explain and make understandable the revolution against Porfirio Díaz in 1910, we received the reply: 'But the hacendados and peons are above all Mexicans and it is not necessary to stress the antagonism between the different groups of the nation'" (1978, 504).

FIGURE 4.9. Que Viva Mexico! *"Maguey" episode, frame enlargement*

As the extant footage shows, Eisenstein had no intention of complying with the official view. Representation in the "Maguey" episode fractures the meanings that *charrería* acquired during the nationalist wars of the nineteenth century and exposes existing tensions between the historical patrimony and the political activism of the conservative sectors who set up the first *charro* federations in the 1920s. Although most of those involved "supported clandestinely *cristeros* [agents of the 1926–1929 counterrevolution] and opponents" of the revolution, they used the *charro* figure to legitimize their nationalism "in face of charges made by postrevolutionary governments that conservative landowners embraced foreign values and lacked patriotism" (Pérez Monfort, 1994a, 124). And as the official response quoted by Eisenstein demonstrates, the state drew on the federation's reinvention of the *charro* as a true Mexican hero to further its own agenda—that is, to rebuild the country's reputation for violence by blocking out any hint of class or ethnic conflicts. What emerges, then, from the extant footage of the "Maguey" episode is Eisenstein's critical perspective in the form of a historical recoding of romanticized depictions of the Mexican landscape and an ironic deployment of the *charro* and *charrería* imagery. He superimposes the diverse connotations and ideological emphasis of the iconic images and visual themes of Mexicanness constructed from the political retrieval of traditions that came to represent in the postrevolutionary discourse, and national imaginary, the homogeneity and essence of rural culture.

By drawing on recent Mexican historiography regarding Eisenstein's project, I have examined his contribution to regional filmmaking and his rapport with aesthetic shifts in Mexico. The multiple visual operations that coalesce in the extant footage of the "Maguey" episode demonstrate that Eisenstein was not an average cultural tourist. By setting the story against the backdrop of the hacienda, he complicated the place and meanings of iconic motifs in the nationalist scenario. He also went against the grain of postrevolutionary historicism by evoking Orozco's graphic work to represent the exploitation and class violence of the Porfiriate. While concurring with De los Reyes's view that accounts aimed at reconstructing Eisenstein's project contain equal parts evidence and speculation, I also believe that Eisenstein's representation of Mexico cannot be reduced to a single narrative (2001a, 173). The political positions and competing perspectives that emerge from the extant footage of the most notorious episodes of *Que Viva Mexico!* need to be negotiated by taking into account the ambiguities and contradictions that shape them. Evidence of the multivalent, transcultural features of modernism, they are made even more partial and incomplete not just because they belong to an unfinished work but also because what constitutes "Mexico" and the revolution will continue to be debated, revised, and contested.

Chapter 5

Reconfiguring the Revolution
CELEBRITY AND MELODRAMA

The golden age of Mexican cinema (1935-1950) coincides with the consolidation of the revolution that began with the election of Lázaro Cárdenas (1934-1940) and extended into the presidencies of Manuel Ávila Camacho (1940-1946) and Miguel Alemán (1946-1952.)[1] An important feature of this process was a redefined relationship between state and culture that consisted in the elaboration of policies aimed at sustaining nationalist discourses on modernization and the use of mass media to promote national unity, prosperity, and internationalism at home and abroad. The effect was a new renaissance in which cinema, music, architecture, and dance replaced muralism as vehicles of cultural development and prestige. Thus the 1940s mark a turning point in the "maturing of *mexicanidad*," a term that I borrow from Michael Nelson Miller's study of the cultural policies of the Ávila Camacho regime.

During his tenure, government funding of the cultural sector grew exponentially. For cinema, it meant the nationalization of the National Bank of Cinematography in 1947 and the implementation of a financing system based on private-public partnership to support producers and directors and expand the industrial infrastructure. Fundamental as well, Miller points out, was the "attempt on the part of the state to recreate a mass media–based cultural nationalism rooted in loyalty to Mexican personalities who embodied the experience of their history in the artifacts of their creativity" (1998, 1). Out of this strategy, a celebrity culture was born that included figures from the world of visual and performing arts, music, architecture, film, and broadcast radio. For cinema, it meant the creation of a star system. Actors became icons of identity and agents of change, and their interpretations turned them into carriers of moral values. On- and offscreen, they embodied style and modernity. Their publicity photographs printed in newspapers and magazines and close-ups in films projected glamour; their faces and poses enhanced by makeup and lighting confirmed that they were exceptional models of Mexican beauty, honor, and courage. Thus actors (and even some directors) became subjects of public adoration in Mexico and abroad, mostly in Latin America, where their films were also very popular. Their fame and cultural prestige was sanctioned through the awards they received from the Mexican Academy for the Cinematographic Arts and Sciences, established in 1946, and international film festivals. With the state favoring "films whose characters and characterizations embodied values and virtues consistent with those of the state," a new mythology was constructed (Miller, 1998, 87).

Thirty years after the revolution erupted, the social and political fabric of Mexico and its traditional institutions, family, religion, village, and region had been substantially transformed. As the country was becoming more urbanized, cinema more than any other media reflected the uncertainties brought about by change. From the films, as Monsiváis writes, audiences wanted "a glimpse of what was inevitably to come, lifestyles that frightened and fascinated them, and transgressions that made this patriarchal God-fearing country unrecognizable" (2004, 593). Jesús Martín-Barbero provides a complementary view. "In some ways," he states, "the people projected on to and recreated memories in films that simultaneously degraded and elevated them, capitalizing on their weaknesses and their search for new signs of identity" (1993, 168). Thus melodrama retained its primacy as a genre. It was an aesthetic and a sensibility capable of conveying what being Mexican and modern meant, offering guidelines of behavior and opinion, as well as a repertoire of gestures and idioms. No matter the theme or setting, its narrative and formal elements were refashioned to represent prevailing experiences and imaginary projections of nation and identity.

To the extent that melodrama adjusted its didactic dimension to the citizen- and nation-building agenda that the state had been implementing since the 1920s, the revolution made a comeback as a narrative backdrop. Notable were *Flor silvestre* (Wildflower) (1943), *Las abandonadas* (Abandoned Women) (1944), *Enamorada* (Woman in Love) (1946), and *Río Escondido* (Hidden River) (1947), all directed by Emilio "El Indio" Fernández and masterfully photographed by Gabriel Figueroa. By resorting to melodrama and its protocols to resolve class, gender, and ethnic differences, these films visualized landscapes and depicted characters as symbolic and gendered constructs of Mexican authenticity. With women as the protagonists, these films proposed different ways to represent and position women within official discourses on nation building and cultural authenticity. Charles Ramírez Berg has dubbed the system of representation resulting from the Fernández-Figueroa creative partnership, which started in 1943 and ended with *Una cita de amor* (Rendezvous with

FIGURE 5.1. Hidden River *(Emilio Fernández, 1947)*, *digitalized frame from the filmstrip collection of Gabriel Figueroa.* © *Gabriel Figueroa Flores, Mexico*

Love) (1956), the "cinematic invention of Mexico" (1994). In spite of numerous borrowings, he explains, they "did manage to establish a characteristic visual style that drew consciously on Mexican traditions" (1994, 21). Moreover, their works were suggestive of how Mexican cinema in general, and the films made by the director and cinematographer team in particular, "*adapted* as well as *adopted* the Hollywood model, giving the Hollywood paradigm a decidedly Mexican inflection" (1994, 13; original emphasis). For their part in the remaking of a modernist aesthetic, their films were—and remain—canonical works.

Of these films, the most overlooked is *Abandoned Women*. It is a story of shame, love, and maternal sacrifice set in Mexico City in which Dolores del Río plays a single mother who works as a prostitute to pay for her son's education and Pedro Armendáriz interprets a revolutionary general who falls in love with her. It expands the historicity and visual motifs of revolutionary melodrama. It is the first film in the director's long and distinguished career to use urban locations and deal with the figure of the prostitute. Portrayed at once as a victim and a catalyst of change—her sacrifice enables her son to succeed—the film reaffirms her place as "the icon of *mexicanidad* and of the urban experience of modernity" (De la Mora,

FIGURE 5.2. Abandoned Women, *film still. Courtesy of Filmoteca UNAM, Mexico*

2006, 67). The performances of Del Río and Armendáriz endow stereotypes of femininity and masculinity with a new look, turning the characters they portray into models of identity and agents of Mexico's renovated nationalism. It is this convergence of celebrity and melodrama that I consider below. *Abandoned Women* relocates and reconfigures the revolution by means of a series of repositioning strategies. It uses the city to visualize and dramatize the precarious place of women in the modernist scenario. Concurrently, it makes the most of star identification and melodramatic protocols to represent the tensions between social reality and discourse. At the end, the film reiterates the mythologizing postrevolutionary narrative. It glorifies sacrifices made in the name of progress and reveals that the female protagonist's suffering and heroism come at a cost: the denial of motherhood and the transference of ideals to the male child.

PLOTTING *Abandoned Women*

As noted above, the film reproduces the modernizing tendencies of cultural nationalism by incorporating the city and the prostitute into the representation of the revolution. Its expanded time frame—from 1914 to the 1940s—links symbolically the female protagonist to the nation: her transformations mirror cultural and social change; her sacrifice and her son's success reflect the progress-driven historicity of postrevolutionary discourse. Joanne Hershfield writes, "Thus, although it is not one of Fernández's explicitly 'Mexicanist' films, *Las abandonadas* does exemplify the director's troubled vision of the Mexican Revolution and its legacy" (2000, 64). Produced by Filmes Mundiales and shot at the CLASA studios in Mexico City between May and November 1944, *Abandoned Women* drew once more on the creative talent of the team made up by director Fernández, cinematographer Figueroa, novelist and screenwriter Mauricio Magdaleno, and editor Gloria Shoemann. The film benefited from a high budget, necessitated in part to cover staging costs and costumes; thirty of a total of one hundred costumes were created by the Hollywood designer Louis Royer for Dolores del Río (García Riera, 1987a, 63). The casting was aimed at capitalizing on the public success and cultural prestige attained by Armendáriz and Del Río after playing the leading couple in *Wildflower* and *María Candelaria* in 1943. The story conceived by Fernández and adapted by Magdaleno promised to find favor among audiences. It reworked elements from Hollywood-produced melodramas dealing with women who sacrifice all for their children, such as *The Sins of Madeleine Bodet* (Edwin Selwyn, 1931), *Madam X* (Sam Wood, 1937), and *Stella Dallas* (King Vidor, 1937.)[2] It gave a distinctly nationalist inflection to this theme by fusing into one character the mother and the prostitute—the emblematic figures of femininity in Mexican cinema since the introduction of sound in the 1930s. In this way, as Hershfield notes, the film "provided a different vision of femininity for [Del Río's] audience, one that offered up other possibilities of identification" (2000, 64).

The plot also made reference to the gangs of criminals disguised as soldiers that terrorized Mexico City in 1915 and 1916 and which had already been popularized in *El automóvil gris* (The Grey Automobile). This serial, directed by Enrique Rosas in 1919, and the sonorized feature-length version released in 1933 and 1937 re-created the criminal activities, capture, and execution by firing squad of a group that operated in 1916.[3] It is not clear whether allusions to incidents that—at least in the public imagination—linked delinquency to the military played a role in the denial of the exhibition permit. Yet press reports on the censorship board's ruling and statements by its director, Felipe Gregorio Castillo, pointed out that high-ranking officials in the Secretariat of National Defense considered the film offensive to the armed forces (García Riera, 1987a, 63). Authorization was granted only after the producers complied with the initial recommendation to specify the time frame of the story and to insert a scene in which the general, played by Armendáriz, is revealed to be an impostor (García Riera, 1987a, 67). The film was finally premiered at the Cinema Chapultepec in May 1945 to positive reviews. Audiences too responded well. Box-office profits announced in 1946 assuaged whatever concerns the producers may have had about the financial effects of the delayed opening (García Riera, 1987a, 63).

After the credit sequence, a title situates the story in "the turbulent Mexico of 1914." The plot is set in motion by a scene of a couple frolicking on a beach and a conversation during which Margarita Pérez (Del Río) can barely disguise her despair when Julio (Víctor Junco) tells her that he must leave. After parting at the train station, she goes home to announce her marriage to the man with whom she has eloped. Her joy turns to grief when she is confronted by Julio's wife and banished by her father. In Mexico City, she gives birth to a boy. Her friend Guadalupita (Lupe Inclán) cares for him while Margarita works as a prostitute. Out of shame, she excuses herself from being photographed with her son, Margarito (Joaquin Roche Jr.), during his fifth birthday party. At a party in a brothel run by a French woman (Maruja Grifell), she makes a grand entrance. Captivated by her beauty, the revolutionary general Juan Gómez (Armendáriz) proposes she become his mistress but virtually locks her up in an elegant house and charges his assistant, Gertrudis López (Alfonso Bedoya), to watch her every movement.

Margot—as she now calls herself—is happy but fearful of being abandoned if Juan finds out about her son. She accepts his marriage proposal only after he pledges to do everything so the boy can become a "great man." To celebrate, they attend a vaudeville show. As spectators aim their binoculars at the beautiful Margot, a group of men keep an eye on Juan. When they enter the upper-tier balcony to arrest him, Margot finds out from the policeman (Alejandro Cobo) that her lover is a member of the notorious "grey automobile" band. On the way out, Juan tries to escape and is killed. Court proceedings reveal that he was an impostor who adopted the identity and rank of an officer who died in battle, and Margot is sentenced for complicity to eight years in jail. Upon her release, she wants to reclaim her son. At first, she dismisses the arguments of the director (Arturo Soto Rangel) of the orphanage-school to leave the boy there, but relents after witnessing Margarito's (Jorge Landeta) leadership talents. Realizing that he is not aware of her identity, she tells him that his mother is dead. Unable to get a job, or to keep her promise to pay for the boy's education, she returns to the streets. Not able to earn enough money, the elderly prostitute resorts to stealing. When Margarito addresses the court, she is in the audience that applauds the lawyer's speech on motherhood and celebrates the acquittal of the abused woman he was defending. Outside the building, she is pushed by the jostling crowd and falls to the ground. Margarito helps her up and, thinking that she is a beggar, gives her a coin.

RELOCATING AND REGENDERING THE REVOLUTION

The image of Margarita kissing the coin and exclaiming "He is a great man" provoked the following comment by García Riera: "Audiences reduced to pulp leave the cinema happy" (1987a, 71). Even though not all moviegoers may have responded equally to this closing scene, its pathos and excess are consistent with melodramatic protocols. As Martín-Barbero notes, "The catharsis works by making the victim of tragedy a character whose weakness calls out for protection and inspires the protective feelings of the public, but whose virtue is a strength that causes admiration and calms the public" (1993, 117). Given that this character is an aging prostitute and the backdrop of her redemption is the exterior of a courthouse, the finale sustains in two ways the prevailing awareness in the 1940s of the import of the city. First, *Abandoned Women* aligned the representation of the experience of modernity—in all its uncertainty and confusion—to the increasingly popular urban film and proposed an alternative mode of historicizing the revolution. The customary plots and iconography of social inequity, class solidarity, and bravery are relocated and regendered. Haciendas, trains, and battlefields are glaringly absent, replaced by popular neighborhoods, city streets, public buildings, entertainment venues, and private dwellings. Now sacrifice and heroism belong to women struggling to survive in the face of impossible odds. Second, Margarita is also a rural migrant who, by her mere presence in the city, like the anonymous *soldaderas* before her, reclaims a place in a scenario from which she had been excluded. Her trajectory entails displacement and memory; it visualizes what leaving the countryside and arriving in the city meant for those who settled in urban areas since the revolution. As Segre indicates, demographic growth in the 1940s and 1950s changed the nature of urban representations. The depiction of Mexico City in painting, graphic arts, cinema, and photography, she writes, "assumes the form of

FIGURE 5.3. Abandoned Women, *film still. Courtesy of Filmoteca UNAM, Mexico*

a parable-like narrative oscillating between metropolitan initiation and vestigial ruralism" (2007, 126). Evidence of these narratives can be found in the imagery created by Figueroa in *Abandoned Women*.

An example is the long segment of Margarita's trip to Mexico City that is accompanied by a melancholy ballad performed on- and offscreen by a trio of musicians riding on an oxcart. It anticipates the now-canonical scenes of Rosaura's (María Félix) journey to assume a teaching job in an isolated village in *Hidden River*. From the initial to the last shot, in which she is seen covering her head with a *rebozo* and moving along a ridge respectively, the sky fills the frame to signal a merging of identity and land. The imagery points to the mutual influence of Eisenstein's formalism and modernist Mexican landscape painting, particularly the curvilinear perspective found in Gerardo Murillo's (best known as Dr. Atl) paintings of the volcanoes and valleys of Central Mexico that, in the words of Ramírez Berg, "more realistically approximated the act of seeing by the human eye" (1994, 16). In line with this modernist impulse to dramatize vision, the cinematography stylizes the swells of clouds, deciduous trees, and cacti growing on arid ground and the maguey fields and reconfigures the country's vast and forbidding landscape as a nationalist spectacle. It expands the iconic motifs of the oxcart led by a peasant and a *rebozo*-shrouded woman, replotting Mexico's indigenous heritage and peasant culture into a migration narrative. In the process, Margarita's escape from the rural world and the past is at once a journey into and homage to the natural beauty of Mexico's geography and an aesthetic reenactment of displacement.

Abandoned Women promotes modes of identification with the city shaped by the viewing habits and expectations of audiences for whom moviegoing was a chance to renew their sentimental attachment to the rural past and experience the glamour of the modern. Urban landscapes are impregnated with the ambience of village life, projecting the affection for the countryside that film viewers—many of whom were recent migrants—shared. Exteriors shot in the CLASA studios replicate rural locations; even the military barracks where Juan Gómez, his adjutant, Getrudis, and the revolutionary troops are stationed resembles a battlefield encampment. Mise-en-scène draws attention to architectural details and accentuates the rustic look of adobe walls, stone-paved roads, austere frontages, and narrow streets. Other than picturesque and permeated with nostalgia, set design is in line with modernist tendencies, wherein contrasting settings epitomize the promise and dangers of modernity.

Success and romance are staged in richly decorated sets. Luxurious costumes and props that seem to come straight out of Hollywood sustain the fantasy, even at the expense of historicity. Juan and Margot move about in horse-drawn carriages, despite his alleged links to the "grey automobile" gang, and cars appear in the film only after Margot leaves prison. If the absence of modern technologies introduced in the 1920s and integrated into the Mexican modernist vernacular in the 1930s appears anachronistic, the profusion of visual motifs of misery and exploitation sustains the complementary notion of the city as a cruel place. The archways of interior courtyards and the lampposts on neighborhood streets serve as a backdrop for the grueling and oppressive work of women who must either wash clothes or sell their bodies to survive. Whether shown in daylight or in night scenes, the actions and surroundings epitomize the underbelly of modern existence. Depth of field and chiaroscuro lighting construct, to use Segre's words, "horizons of despair" that symbolize the dark and hopeless universe inhabited by the disenfranchised (2007, 132).

PUBLIC AND PRIVATE SPACES

Abandoned Women resorts to discourses and modes of representation that naturalized women's exclusion from the public sphere. Actual locations are used to align modernity with the paternalist state and symbolically reinforce its role as protector of abandoned women. For Margot, the road to redemption starts at the orphanage-school and ends in front of a courthouse. In the first setting, she denies her past when she tells Margarito that his mother has died. In the second, she rejoices at her son's public success after his impassioned speech gets an abused woman acquitted. With Margot entrusting the director with her son's future, the orphanage-school is the site that legitimizes the citizenship- and nation-building agenda of postrevolutionary nationalism. Although she places her faith in the historical project to integrate the disenfranchised masses of peasants through education, she unknowingly pushes Margarito to reject his class origins by withholding the information that she is his mother. The courthouse is the place where the former orphan, now a successful lawyer, becomes a champion of vulnerable women. There injustices are rectified, and the melodramatic pleasure in the nobility of women's sacrifice is sanctioned. Suggestive is Margot's placement in the middle plane of the frame, first standing in front of the buildings slightly sideways to the crowd and then facing the crowd with her back turned to the camera because it excludes her from the triumphant celebration. With male characters being social agents and Margot reduced to being an eyewitness to change, these locations gender the modernized city as male and visualize women's precarious place in the modernist scenario.

Conversely, the domestic space is established as a site where women's desires as individuals and community find expression. Worth discussing are the two back-to-back scenes of Margarita celebrating her son's first and fifth birthdays in the company of her female friends. They visualize the character's transformation from lowly to high-priced prostitute but also reveal the personal cost and moral burden of being a prostitute and a mother. At the first party, prompted by her friend Ninón (Fanny Soler) to make a wish before blowing out the single candle on the cake, she says, "I wish my son grows to be . . . a great man; one of those who get their photographs in the newspapers." During the second, Margarita promises the boy that she will buy him a horse but only after having his picture taken. As the obsequious photographer readies his camera, he refers to the guests as "a true bouquet of flowers." What he sees is a portrait of middle-class propriety: a group of female friends, all in classy clothes and hats, and a

FIGURE 5.4. Abandoned Women, *frame enlargement*

charro-suited boy. When Ninón orders the women to stand aside ("And you know why!"), they do so reluctantly. As Margarita watches, her gaze reveals that she feels included in the remark. She excuses herself and joins her prostitute friends on the sidelines. By refusing to be photographed, she forfeits her social identity as a proud mother; by admitting her shame, she submits to public standards of morality that censure women for choices not of their own making.

Women's ability to rise above poverty is apparent in the differences between the shabby-looking brothel in the first birthday scene and the well-appointed *sala comedor* (living-dining room) in the second. As the Spanish-language name indicates, it is at once a place for the family to gather and display its prosperity and the public face of domestic life.[4] *Abandoned Women* draws attention to the normative meanings of the *sala comedor* only to reveal that affluent circumstances and fashionable appearance are not enough to disguise the shame of prostitution. In Margarita's household, and with Ninón as a father substitute, rituals are enacted and social norms enforced. The representation of relations among women emphasizes the pleasures they indulge while in the privacy of their homes, and it is aligned with their newly acquired status as consumers. Their co-

FIGURE 5.5.   Abandoned Women, *frame enlargement*

quettish gestures express how sophisticated they feel in their pretty suits and expensive jewelry.

Within this portrait of social mobility and female camaraderie, Guadalupita is the only discordant figure. Standing in the background, with her braided hair and traditional long skirt, she evokes the thousands of peasant women who migrated to the capital in this period and became domestic workers. While she embodies the dignity that the postrevolutionary state promised to restore to the indigenous and lower-class sectors of Mexico, Guadalupita is also the other to the "fallen woman." Her silence and modesty are in stark contrast to the incessant chatter and self-confidence of the prostitutes. However, when they comply with Ninón's order, Margarita and her friends become docile like Guadalupita. As the friends move away, a series of shots of the women looking at each other register embarrassment and vulnerability. In the close-ups of Margarita's face—her features partially shaded by the wide-brimmed hat—the downcast gaze signals worthlessness and self-loathing. If posing for the camera during the revolution was a gesture of self-affirmation, what this poignant moment captures is women's self-exclusion from representation. With Margarita, her friends, and Guadalupita as silent bystanders and the boy photographed standing alone on the top of the table, this scene anticipates the film's ending wherein historicity and agency belong to the male. As well, the birthday sequence destabilizes the modernist notion of the home as a shelter from the hostile world and reinforces women's unstable position in the urban environment.

STAR IMAGE AND PERFORMANCES OF IDENTITY

Abandoned Women reproduces the remaking of Dolores del Río into a Mexican star. It turns the transnational dimensions of the actor's off- and onscreen persona into spectacle and exemplifies to what extent, as López writes, "the process of image construction [was] an integral part of her characterizations" (1999, 30). Yet the role of Margarita/Margot Pérez required the then-forty-year-old actor to play a young woman, a mature courtesan, and an aging prostitute. For this performance, she was rewarded in 1946 with a second Ariel by the Mexican Academy for the Cinematographic Arts and Science. Explicit in these characterizations are the identities that were either fashioned for her by Hollywood studios starting in 1925 as a sexualized and racialized icon of exoticism or that she assumed upon returning to Mexico in 1942 as a model of beauty and cosmopolitan nationalism. The caricature by Audiffred printed on March 29, 1945, in *El Universal* (figure 5.6) captured the transnationalism of Del Río's off- and onscreen persona. Dressed in an evening gown with a wide-brimmed hat and fox stole, she holds a sign that reads *"Abandoned Women."* Next to her are four female figures, all very stylish were it not for the odd effect produced by having names written on their faces instead of features. While the drawing aligns the Mexican actor with other seduced and abandoned women of Hollywood melodrama, it identifies her as being exceptional. Her star image is one with the character she portrays in the film.

No other moment defines better the actor's transnational image than when she appears at the top of the wide staircase in a sequin-embroidered gown and wearing ornamental feathers in her hair (figure 5.7). She is the ultimate fetish object: the embodiment of desire. But there is more. Everything in the scene evokes the sophistication of Hollywood productions and glossy movie magazines. As Monsiváis notes, after her marriage to MGM art director Cedric Gibbons in 1930 Del Río experienced the celebrity lifestyle but also loathed being cast in decorative roles. In spite of that, he writes, "glamour endows Dolores with the aura of being a woman of her time—modern, blamelessly happy, and without prejudice—who embodied and offered the public the chic atmosphere and up-to-date taste

FIGURE 5.6.   Abandoned Women, *drawing by Audiffred,* El Universal *(Mexico City), March 29, 1945*

FIGURE 5.7.   Abandoned Women, *frame enlargement*

FIGURE 5.8. Abandoned Women, *frame enlargement*

which were lacking in Mexico" (1997, 78). The scene in the luxury brothel restages the public fascination with stars and signals the actor's rebirth as a screen goddess when an offscreen male voice announces Margot's entrance: "Oh, take a look at who's up there." In one fell swoop, the disjunction is erased between the image of dignified poverty in Del Río's previous films and the refinement found in publicity stills and society page pictorials in Mexico's daily press that displayed her wearing the latest fashion.

Moreover, spectator investment is shared equally between characters and viewers. It is rendered visually by placing prostitutes and revolutionary soldiers in groups, as if they were an internal audience, and finds expression when Armendáriz—the leading man and stand-in for the audience onscreen and in the cinema—says, "Come down.... Please.... I want to make sure you exist, that this is not a dream." Matching close-ups prolong the moment in which star image supersedes character, spectacle displaces plot. Figueroa's cinematography mediates the actors' transformation into icons. Soft-focus composition, filters, and key lighting accentuate the photogenic quality of their faces in a manner that explicitly evokes the glamour shot in film advertising and fashion. What each close-up shot shows—and what each actor performs for the camera—is an ideal of Mexican beauty. In contrast to the previous teaming up of the actors, *Abandoned Women* reframes this representation. By favoring cosmopolitanism and modernity, it privileges the Hispanic/mestizo elements of Mexican identity formations and neutralizes the indicators of rural class origins and indigenous ethnicity so prominent in *Wildflower* and *María Calendaria*.

While photography eroticizes both Del Río and Armendáriz, editing keeps them visually apart to guarantee their exceptionality as stars and their individuality as characters. In view of this, Armendáriz's performance as Juan Gómez in this scene is worth considering. It reaffirms the actor's reputation at home and abroad for being, to quote Monsiváis, "the finest version of Mexicanness, with his lusty voice, his dominant presence, his gait of a general on his way to battle and a face that could express anger as easily as adoration" (2004, 593). Since his debut in 1935, he had set himself apart for his ability to portray the honorable and brave hero, whether he was an Indian peasant, revolutionary, or middle-class urban male in *María Candelaria*, *Wildflower* (both directed by Fernández), and *Distinto amanecer* (A New Morning) (Julio Bracho, 1943), respectively. It reveals as well that representations of masculinity in Mexican films, or what Sergio de la Mora calls "styles of manliness," are unstable yet powerful symbols of national identification (2006, 3). His entry into the narrative may not be as spectacular, but his placement in the middle of the frame singles him out. Whether he stands in front of the stairs ordering his soldiers to have a good time or sits on a chaise flanked by two women, he commands notice. Low-angle shots enhance his stature; the formal military uniform and trademark baritone voice of his delivery underline his virility. Yet these masculine traits are put to the test by the over-the-top behavior of his character (he fires a gun in the air, seemingly to assert his authority) and starry-eyed look when he sees Margot standing at the top of the stairs. The acting out of sexual potency and facial expression conveying vulnerability feminize him. Armendáriz's portrayal of a male enraptured by female beauty unsettles the hypermasculine stereotype of the revolutionary.[5]

This is not the only instance in *Abandoned Women* where the production of identity is linked to spectacle. After Margot finally agrees to marry Juan, they decide to celebrate their last night as bachelors by going to the theater. With the couple's arrival, the attention of the bourgeois audience shifts away from the stage and the performance of vaudeville star María Conesa's signature song, "The White Kitten." The series of shots (some masked to replicate the view from binoculars) position the couple as the object and the male spectators as initiators of the gaze. As it turns out, spectatorship is disciplinary too. The detectives on the auditorium floor are there to arrest Juan. After entering the balcony, they point to Margot's jewelry as proof of his alleged involvement in the "grey automobile band" robberies. Juan is exposed and Margot humiliated; their transgression into high society is punished when he is killed and she is jailed. Even if this scene draws attention to the actors' onscreen identities as provisional, narrative rules require that their characters' overdetermined signifiers be maintained. As the judge explains during the trial, Juan is a fake: in the wake of a battle in the Coahuila state locality of Hondo he stole an officer's uniform from a corpse. The account is complemented by a flashback. Shown standing next to a horse and wearing the traditional *charro* costume, he is reinstated albeit fleetingly into the story line as an authentic revolutionary.

Two consecutive scenes represent the restoration of Del Río's onscreen identity as "the devastated and oppressed Long Suffering Woman" (Monsiváis, 1997, 81). The first is set in a prison. By means of a combination of backward-forward tracking shots, the elegant bereaved widow standing behind the bars disappears, gradually to be replaced by a modestly dressed yet dignified woman who walks out of the cell. The second scene takes place in a cemetery. It shows her in a low-angle shot silhouetted against the skyline and in close-up with her head leaning against a wooden cross that marks Juan's grave. How Margarita looks and what she says exemplify to what extent the filmic construction of female identity is subject to melodramatic imperatives. The solitary *rebozo*-clad figure recalls the film's early scenes; the dialogue verbalizes the character's acceptance of her female condition and destiny. As during her arduous trek to the city, the imagery denotes her vulnerability and misfortune, but it is first and foremost a repositioning strategy. Only as a humble woman can Margarita/Del Río become an icon of Mexicanness. Only in her dignified acquiescence can she become an actor in the postrevolutionary narrative. What is more, the cemetery scene contains an explicit citation of *María Candelaria*, specifically, the often-reproduced shot of her visit to Lorenzo Rafael (Armendáriz) in prison.

ABJECTION AND IDEALIZATION

Spectator investment in the renewed nationalist discourse proposed by Mexican melodrama was based on theatricality and modernization. Another device, Martín-Barbero notes, "was degradation. That is, in order for the people to recognize themselves, it was necessary to place nationhood within their reach" (1993, 167). Identification was premised at once on offering a forward-looking image of nation and on representing and providing narrative solutions to existing social realities. *Abandoned Women* attests to this protocol. It shows Margarita/Margot's transformation into a modern subject, and it dramatizes the experiences of hardship and exclusion shared by migrant women. For her ordeal to be resignified as bravery, her degradation must be absolute. The film's opening moments anticipate this operation. The credits are superimposed on a night shot of prostitutes gathered around a lamppost. In the center, an old woman sits at a table covered with a white cloth. On her right is a woman who is smoking, and on her left another leans against the wall. The hard-edged quality of the shot is achieved by lighting and the angled view of the sidewalk behind where other women stand. This image reappears shortly after the scene at Juan's grave site. Insert shots identify the woman on the left as Margarita. The camera tracks back when she removes the *rebozo* to show her in revealing clothes and garish makeup. With her shoulders thrown back and the sideways gaze, the body language is that of a seductress, the chewing gum adding vulgarity to what otherwise could be taken as a standard representation of the femme fatale. The middle-class man in a dark suit and light straw boater who turns around to look at and then walks back toward Margot infers with his action that she is deserving of his attention.

If this scene reveals the sexual economy of women's labor, it visualizes the narrow scope of viewer engagement with the depravity of prostitution and provokes questions about the film's discourse. By favoring the protracted gaze elicited by Margot's appearance in the luxury brothel over the transient gaze of the urban flâneur, the film sides with the idealized image of sex workers found in Mexican popular culture, specifically in vernacular poetry and music. The ever-popular *bolero*—those wistful ballads born in the 1930s from middle-class fascination with bohemia and life in working-class neighborhoods—turned brothels and cabarets into settings, and prostitutes and dancers into agents of romance. "The imaginings of hypocrisy," as Monsiváis notes in his essay on the legendary composer Agustín Lara, "engendered ideal prostitutes and dissipated the sordid and abject exploitation of thousands of women in filthy lodgings" (1977, 73). This mythology shapes the representation of the "fallen woman" as an ethereal, angel-like and asexual figure who, as the cultural historian puts it, "does not sell orgasms but supplications of love" (1997, 73). The shot of Margot/Del Río standing at the top of the stairs attests to the reconfiguration of the prostitute into an object of social fantasies. No wonder that is the most memorable and frequently reproduced image of *Abandoned Women*.

This figuration is consistent both with Fernández's belief in the didactic power of cinema and with his contradictory views on women in general and prostitutes in particular. Far from reducing them to simple stereotypes, as Tuñon writes, one of the director's "obsession[s] was to construct an ideal woman" (2000, 51). He created characters that personified female virtue, dignity, and obedience, even if some were unruly and dangerous. Regarding the prostitute, he stated: "she must be presented as a suffering woman, one who is atoning for her sins" (quoted in Tuñón, 2000, 52). That this principle did not extend into his private life is clear when he said, "In reality, certainly not! I'd be overjoyed if there were more whores around" (54). Be that as it may, Margarita/Margot embodies all these attributes. Whether she is a naive young woman or a suffering mother; a romantic courtesan or an abject prostitute, location, class, and age determine her subjectivity. Regardless of name and costume changes, she remains the devoted mother, at least in the film viewer's eyes since her successful son fails to recognize her.

By bringing together the iconic female figures of Mexican cinema into one character, she prefigures Violeta—the prostitute-mother of *Víctimas del pecado* (Victims of Sin) (Emilio Fernández, 1950). Yet this is only one of the features connecting *Abandoned Women* to the *cabaretera* film of the late 1940s and early 1950s. As Hershfield points out, this subcategory of the urban melodrama "emerged as a response to changes in social and economic roles for women and the resulting difficulty of incorporating these changes into patriarchal discourse about female sexuality" (1996, 77). Conventional scenarios focused on the suffering and exploitation of prostitutes by abusive pimps. The only affirmative instances in the otherwise tragic plot were their efforts to rise above the circumstances that got them there. In true melodramatic fashion, the female protagonists were granted some degree of autonomy (even a little happiness) and their sacrifices rewarded by means of cathartic endings. This genre adjusted the representation of sexual difference to the new realities of women as urban workers and consumers. The city became the stage for the visual production of femininity, with various public and private spaces (cabaret stages and dressing rooms) providing the backdrop against which tensions could be negotiated between women's histories and official discourse, that is to say, between their marginalization and the state policies designed to integrate them. Indeed, the name given to the *cabaretera* genre signifies the organic bond of setting and character. Within the dance hall—the symbolic site of sexual pleasure and transgression—the prostitute is "the emblematic social agent that embodies the anxieties, desires and contradictions generated by the transition from tradition to (post) modernity" (De la Mora, 2006, 25).

Under scrutiny, *Abandoned Women* reveals itself as a complex and idiosyncratic film. It projects an image of Mexico capable of accommodating modernity and tradition. It expands the time frame of films dealing with the revolution and relocates and transfers the reified themes of sacrifice and bravery onto the story of a woman. It ascertains the place of the city in Mexico's nationalist narrative. Public and private settings are at once stages to represent the promise and dangers of modernity and an opportunity for the filmgoing public to renew its sentimental attachment to the rural past and experience the glamour of the modern. Locations reaffirm to what extent female subjectivity is overdetermined. Margarita/Margot's sex work is incompatible with the normative meanings and protocols that govern social and cultural places.

The film resorts to spectacle and melodrama as guarantees of authenticity and vehicles to represent under what conditions the transformation of the modern subject is possible. From the perspective of iconography, it exposes the anachronisms of Mexico's renewed nationalism: its predisposition to celebrate progress and rescue popular memory. The fantasy of cosmopolitanism and nostalgia for the rural past coexist, albeit in a fluid manner. Celebrity informs the performances and characterizations of Del Río/Margarita and Armendáriz/Juan as gendered models and icons of nationalism. Yet their identities are unstable and subject to visual and narrative repositioning. Regarding the first, she embodies the contradictory views of Fernández on women, and her status as a heroine is contingent on the didactic dimensions of melodrama. Margarita/Margot's agency oscillates between shame and pride, denial and affirmation of who she is as a prostitute and a mother. Only by excluding herself from representation can she be restored as the ideal woman. *Abandoned Women,* then, sheds light on the ambivalence of image construction in the golden age. It ascertains the existence of social realities and cultural determinations that no imagery of glamour or narrative of redemption can fully wish away. Its emphasis on displacement and degradation reinforces the complicated process of historicizing in the postrevolutionary period. Last but not least, the city and the presence of the prostitute-mother of the emerging *cabaretera* film anticipate the decline of the revolutionary genre: its transformation into spectacle.

Chapter 6 | The Aesthetics of Spectacle

In the era of economic prosperity and development historians have termed the "Mexican miracle" (1940–1968), the state promoted history as a heritage and marketed culture and identity as a commodity. "The post-1950 period," Eric Zolov writes, "was the culminating moment in the refashioning of Mexican stereotypes of backwardness and danger" (2001, 235). In the process, cosmopolitan-folkloric discourses regained currency. As in the nineteenth century, modern and indigenous elements were brought together and placed at the service of a nationalist project aimed at rehabilitating Mexico's image abroad as well as reinforcing the official view of progress and growth at home. Even if the realities of underdevelopment risked derailing the state's agenda, the iconic images of picturesque Mexico were resignified, their negative implications cast aside, and foreigners and locals invited to partake in Mexico's authenticity. Cinema played a fundamental role because it could entice middle-class audiences with the promise of reliving the golden age at a time when the popularity of Hollywood films and the appearance of television in 1950 threatened the industry's existence. Big budgets and star power served to project the image of prosperity and glamour promoted by the state. In films dealing with the revolution, visual themes and characterizations were rebranded as fetish objects of Mexico's cinematic patrimony.

To what extent the tendency to "metamorphosize the historical moment into a nationalist spectacle," as Monsiváis notes, persisted is exemplified by *La escondida* (The Hidden Woman) (1995, 119). This color super-production directed by Roberto Galvadón in 1956 and starring María Félix signals a movement away from the didactic, citizen-building agenda of the Fernández-Figueroa film discussed in the previous chapter. The film repopularizes the revolution by relying on strategies that had proved successful: a talented creative team, a celebrity cast, a major literary work, and a stunning setting. With its citations of the "Maguey" episode in Eisenstein's unfinished project, the murals of Diego Rivera in the Secretariat of Public Education, and images composed by Figueroa for other films, it reframes visual motifs and themes within an aesthetic that privileges display, thus endowing nationalism with cultural prestige and commodity value.

Produced when Félix was forty years old, this film reconfirmed her place within the Mexican star system and revived her career as a "new mythical revolutionary heroine" (García and Aviña, 1997, 79). With the celebrated actor as the historicizing agent, Mexican history and identity are given a new look. Just returned from Europe, where she refashioned herself into a paragon of cosmopolitan glamour, Félix performs with great panache a peasant who forsakes her humble origins to become the mistress of a Federal general. Competently directed and masterfully photographed, she is a beautiful, determined, and proud woman who elicits either fascination or scorn from women and men irrespective of class. Because Gabriela is the last in the lineage of the romantic figures interpreted by Félix in the 1940s, this role is a farewell tribute to her earlier career. Armendáriz, who shares top billing and whose character and performance evoke his previous work in the films directed by Fernández, compounds the nostalgia factor. No wonder this film is viewed as the last attempt to restore cultural prestige to the revolution by drawing on the popular appeal of the golden age at a time when Mexican cinema was in decline.

Moreover, the film reaffirms the discourses that regained currency in the 1950s. It makes the most of the nationalist politics of representation that turned the revolution into a patrimony and commodity and which found a dramatic and visually compelling expression in Mexican muralism. What would a trip to Mexico be without seeing the officially commissioned wall paintings that adorn public buildings in the capital and other cities? Monumental, not only in scale and artistic achievement, the murals are heritage-as-tourist-attraction: a spectacular showcase of the country's past and culture. Foreign visitors have experienced them as a window into Mexico's otherness. In 1937 Katherine Anne Porter wrote, "For myself, and I believe I speak for great numbers, Mexico does not appear to me as it did before I saw Rivera's paintings of it" (quoted in Walker, 1978, 6). As reductive as it may be, this statement has proven extremely resilient. By positioning Rivera as a primary agent, it has reinforced views of Mexico as picturesque because it is based on an overvaluation of folkloric and decorative elements in the painter's murals. It has also found expression in Hollywood films on the revolution, mainly through citations, with those of Rivera's work far outweighing other artists.

Notable is the relative disregard for José Clemente Orozco, an artist who spoke against folkloric motifs and used painting critically to represent the tragedy and pathos of the revolution. These views led to public criticism of his 1923 murals at the Preparatory School, set off a lifelong enmity with Rivera, and diminished the popular acceptance of his work. Validation came in the 1950s when Orozco's position and practice found an echo among Mexicans and foreigners frustrated by the state's ongoing patronage of muralism and marketing of nationalist themes to sustain its populist agenda. The artist's bleak view was manifested occasionally in the cinema, mostly in the form of explicit citations in Eisenstein's project (see chap. 4) or in the work of the cinematographer Gabriel Figueroa. As noted earlier and as I argue below, the themes of corruption, betrayal, and victimization found in drawings that make up *The Horrors of the Revolution* series are evoked in *Let's Go with Pancho Villa!* (see chap. 3) and *The Wild Bunch* to visualize a critical position on the brutality of war.

When executive producer Phil Feldman agreed that *The Wild Bunch* would be shot in Mexico, Sam Peckinpah was thrilled. It meant returning to a place that had fascinated him since he attended summer school at the National Autonomous University in Mexico City in the late 1940s. Even though he went back numerous times, among them to film *Major Dundee* (1964) in the states of Durango and Morelos, this time he had a project that brought together his favorite stories: the western and the Mexican Revolution (Weddle, 1994, 71). However, he disregarded affirmative elements by centering the plot on a group of U.S. outlaws who cross into Mexico after a botched robbery and pay the ultimate price at the hands of a counterrevolutionary army unit. He represents the west as morally corrupt (its code of honor compromised by greed and violence), the revolution as repressive and vengeful (its ideals betrayed by vicious methods), and insinuates redemption and liberation symbolically in the film's cathartic finale.

A great deal has been written about *The Wild Bunch* as a morality tale, an allegory of the U.S. enterprise in Southeast Asia, and an ultra-violent spectacle. Due to its south-of-the-border setting, it has also elicited comments on its treatment of Mexico. For the most part, U.S. critics have tended to romanticize the director's view, as in the remark by Paul Schrader, "Sam Peckinpah's Mexico is a spiritual country similar to Ernest Hemingway's Spain, Jack London's Alaska, and Robert Stevenson's South Seas. It is a place where you go 'to get yourself straightened out'" (Bliss, 1994, 17). Others have looked at this issue politically. With the true revolutionary being the peasant-fighter (and not the vile counterrevolutionary), as Noël Carroll remarks, the film reaffirms both a "favourable view of the Mexican Revolution" and a sentimental inclination whereby "Americans want to believe that intervention is justified in support of social justice" (1998, 60, 61). Conversely, Mexicans have been predictably dismissive. They consider the climactic mass killing in the Federal camp offensive. In the portrayal of General Mapache (played by none other than Emilio Fernández), they see an extreme and objectionable parody. It compounds the western bandit, the demonized Huerta, and the pathetic figure of a sixty-four-year-old director-turned-actor notorious for his volatile personality and drinking.

Other reactions, more judicious, are noteworthy. Mexico, as Arthur G. Pettit notes, "serves as a vehicle for Peckinpah's moral pronouncements on sex, sadism, violence, law, crimes and social orders—especially social orders" (1980, 231). For the literary critic, Peckinpah's opinion on the revolution is represented symbolically as a clash between a cruel and a gentle Mexico, hence critical of the violence and suffering it generated. To elaborate on this view, I consider the multilayered features of the film's iconography, what Jim Kitses calls "its disturbing edge," in relation to spectatorship (2004, 216). Peckinpah re-creates ways of looking and seeing and reconfigures the imagery of death and victimization generated by Americans and Mexicans during the revolution and after (2004, 216). He does so in a manner that is more consistent with Orozco's fatalist vision than the objectified treatment in period U.S.-produced postcards aimed at satisfying public curiosity about violence in Mexico. But before dealing with this film, and in the next section, I discuss *The Hidden Woman*. By focusing on stardom, I address how the revolution was repopularized in the mid-1950s as spectacle and iconic images and visual themes were repackaged for mass consumption.

MEXICAN NATIONALISM AND COSMOPOLITAN GLAMOUR IN *The Hidden Woman*

In life as in death, María de los Ángeles Félix Güereña was a spectacle. The journalist César Güemes wrote in the Mexico City daily *La Jornada* on April 10, 2002, that the tribute held to mark the actor's passing two days earlier was the finale of "the mythology generated in the twentieth century by national cinema." The sight of the crowd gathered at the Palace of Fine Arts prompted the journalist to ask, "To whom did [they] come to say good-bye: to a way of comprehending the nation, a *self-made-woman* [in English] par excellence, a self-nourished myth or a tangible reality?" Instead of expressions of public sentiment, he saw monumentality: a melodramatic spectacle choreographed for live television. He reported that calla lilies and white rosebuds filled the stage where the casket was placed.

As the show went to air, a curtain was lifted to reveal an enormous photograph of a youthful Félix and from the loudspeakers her familiar voice commanded: "The moment has come." In this ritualized show of collective memory, presided over by Félix herself, the supporting roles were played by film clips and melodies that included *María Bonita,* written for her by composer (and third husband) Agustín Lara, and the traditional farewell song "Las golondrinas."

The symbolism of this tribute reflects her status as a nationalist icon of glamour. Whether playing fictional characters in forty-seven films or modeling for painters and photographers in French haute couture gowns, she projected sophistication and sex appeal.[1] These attributes made her into a goddess of the silver screen. As Julia Tuñón writes, she "filled the screen with her beauty and forceful presence" and was a "star who invoked the phenomenon of fetishism, imitation and admiration of the masses, the *diva* who was not asked to do a good deed but who represented, one way or another, herself" (1997, 480). She came to personify what her friend and admirer Monsiváis calls "the logic of *glamour*," the perfect balance between "the refined features and the personality of a woman who will not yield to anyone and the courtesan who uses each and every one"(1993, 12; original emphasis). Even when Félix courted controversy, she retained the admiration of her fans, because she managed public scandal and personal affront with self-assurance and grace. "When she returned to Mexico with the casket of [Jorge Negrete] her husband (deceased in Los Angeles), the widow was reproached for wearing pants. Painted by Diego Rivera in a see-through dress, everybody feels offended including herself" (Paranaguá, 2003, 110). In the mid-1950s and after her marriage to the Swiss entrepreneur Alexander Berger, every quarrel with those she deemed mediocre journalists was a professional triumph; she managed to turn insults into pronouncements about her wealth and fame. Impassioned responses to her stylish and photogenic features often diverted attention from her narrow range of acting abilities. Nothing contributed more to her star status and charisma than the camera. Gabriel Figueroa composed the most astounding images, including the signature close-up of her eyes from the film *Woman in Love* (1946), that adorns her official Web site.

If cinema made her famous, she was the agent of her own mythology. She became one with the characters she played. As Paco Ignacio Taibo I. explains, producers and scriptwriters "made films 'for María Félix.' In other words, for the María Félix she was assumed to be and the one she was creating with a discipline and wilfulness that astounded anyone who has looked into her life" (1985, 13). But no one expressed better what she

FIGURE 6.1. La cucaracha, *film still. Courtesy of Filmoteca UNAM, Mexico*

represented than herself. In a famous statement attributed to her, she asserted being "the triumphant Mexican, who doesn't get duped by anyone" (quoted in Tuñón, 1997, 480). This self-identification contributed to making her an agent of Mexican culture and nationalist mythology. Susan Dever describes this as a "transformative process" that "legitimates Félix's persona and establishes her as a cultural mediator whose discourses will be controlled by the kinds of roles she is permitted to play" (2003, 65). The actor reproduced this self-identification by way of characters that are self-confident, even arrogant. These figurations remain exceptional within the repertoire of Mexican stereotypes of femininity because she claimed them as her own.

Onscreen, Félix was (among others) an audacious, yet rightful woman such as the landowner's daughter Beatriz in *Woman in Love*, the rural teacher Rosaura in *Hidden River* (1947), and the Indian maiden in *Maclovia* (1948), all three films directed by Fernández. But her most memorable roles were those of the *devoradora*, a devourer of men and a Mexican version of the femme fatale. She was the social climber Teresa in *The Woman without a Soul* (La mujer sin alma) and the wronged and vengeful *Doña Bárbara*, both directed by De Fuentes in 1943. Although the moniker La Doña that came to signify her singularity is rooted in her role as Doña Bárbara, another germinal character was the *machorra* (a female version of the *macho*) she played in *La cucaracha* (Ismael Rodríguez, 1958). Since she repeated this part in *Juana Gallo* (Miguel Zacarías, 1959), *La bandida* (Roberto Rodríguez, 1962), *La valentina* (Rogelio A. González, 1965), and her last film, *La generala* (Juan Ibáñez, 1970), writers commenting on the final period of her career have privileged this stereotype over others. The most overlooked of all her characters is Gabriela in *The Hidden Woman*. As a peasant-turned-courtesan, her fate is predetermined. Taibo I. writes, "*La escondida* [the hidden woman] has to hide because she is 'a bad woman,'" and when she is killed, "we know that not only has the revolution triumphed, but also the prevailing morality" (1985, 193).

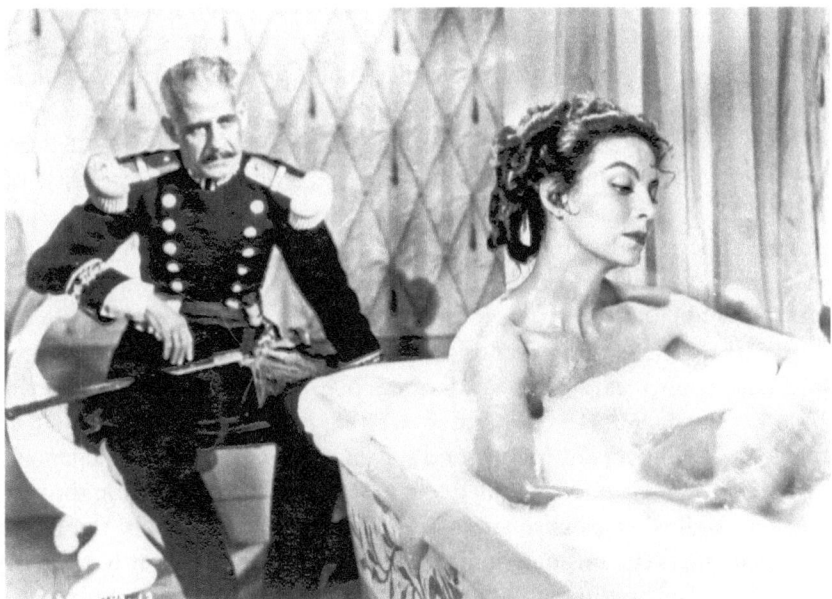

FIGURE 6.2. The Hidden Woman, *lobby card. Courtesy of Filmoteca UNAM, Mexico*

Cultural Reconversion and Authenticity

Filmed in the locality of Huamantla, Tlaxcala, and the Churubusco studios in fall 1955, *The Hidden Woman* intertwines the discourses of nationalism and stardom. Set in the years 1909–1912, the plot covers the fall of the Díaz regime and the campaign undertaken subsequently by Madero to halt the Zapatista insurgency in Tlaxcala, a small state southeast of Mexico City. As announced in the opening title, it reconstructs "a dramatic episode of those turbulent and confusing times. It's the story of a love that was dragged through the whirlwind of the revolution." The film is based on the eponymous novel published in 1948 by the Tlaxcala-born author and academic Miguel Nicolás Lira, which combines romance with "an intelligent description of the historical and social contradictions of Zapatismo in the Tlaxcala region" (De la Vega Alfaro, 2004, 60). In line with the literary work, the film's representation of the revolution is driven by social and political conflict, with Gabriela (Félix) and Felipe (Armendáriz) as the lovers torn between desire and social purpose, loyalty to and betrayal of each other and their class. However, the film's historicity is anchored in the use made of the actors who share top billing. Félix and Armendáriz reinforce the already overdetermined meanings of plot and imagery by inserting the cultural and ideological values of stardom into the film. The function of these two major figures of the Mexican star system exceeds the narrative. The actors return to roles they interpreted nine years earlier in *Woman in Love*, and become carriers of public memories.

During the tenure of Adolfo Ruíz Cortines (1952–1958), the Mexican film industry was showing unmistakable signs of "a structural crisis of quality" (De la Vega Alfaro, 1999b, 176). Strategies aimed at increasing production were detrimental because they were driven purely by commercial imperatives. Producers reduced budgets and unions invoked seniority to block access to new directors; and low-cost genre films with outdated aesthetics and populist plots became the norm. Yet these strategies only confirmed a state of affairs. Since 1947 Mexican cinema had been losing ground. Revenue and investment had decreased as a result of the combined effects of Hollywood's abrupt withdrawal of the financial and technical assistance provided to the Mexican industry during the war and the studios' aggressive strategies to reclaim their share of the Latin American markets. Prominent directors were affected differently by these conditions. For Emilio Fernández, they translated into an obsessive repetition of themes and characters that had brought him fame and success; for Roberto Galvadón, they enhanced his standing, so much so that "he was considered a worthy successor" to Fernández (De la Vega Alfaro, 1999b, 173).

Galvadón gained critical recognition at home and abroad for his ability to balance the industry-imposed need for profitability with the aesthetic standards demanded by quality cinema. He may have distinguished himself as a director of film noir–style urban melodramas, but he was equally adept in other genres. He used cinema to convey his own views by returning to themes that preoccupied him personally and which he regarded as being integral to Mexican society and culture because they reflected the national fixation with identity (Zúñiga, 1995, 195). One of these themes is otherness, and it appears in *La Otra* (The Other) (1946) and *La diosa arrodillada* (The Kneeling Goddess) (1947). These films revolve around women interpreted by Dolores del Río and María Félix respectively and draw on mirrors and doublings to situate the characters' identities within opposing structures of femininity and class. This duality is sustained by the deliberate casting of Del Río as identical twins and Félix as a model-turned-prostitute and the actors' identification as international stars and icons of *mexicanidad*. Even though melodrama requires that female characters pay for their transgressions, they are agents of a nationalist search-for-identity narrative. Galvadón revisits this theme in *The Hidden Woman*, this time to set in motion a process whereby Félix is reinstated as an embodiment of cultural authenticity.

Performing the Myth

Before discussing this matter, a plot summary is in order. Sitting in a train car that will take her back to Felipe, Gabriela remembers the past. The arrival of troops at the Vergel hacienda and the killing of a peon set the events that changed her life in motion. When Felipe decides to join the insurgency, he agrees to have Gabriela join him. Before leaving, the store manager, Ventura (Wally Barrón), accuses her of stealing in retaliation for having rejected his sexual advances. Felipe takes the blame. After Hortencia (Sara Guash) and Gabriela plead that he be spared from indentured labor, the hacienda owner, Don Esteban, orders conscription to be his punishment. On leave, Felipe returns to learn that Gabriela has left with her upper-class friend, Hortencia. He persuades his father, Agostino (Domingo Soler), and Máximo Tepal (Jorge Martínez de Hoyos) to take up arms against the government. During the investiture of the state governor, Felipe sees Gabriela standing on a balcony and realizes that she is the mistress of General Nemesio Garza (Andrés Soler). The revolutionaries stop a train on which Gabriela is traveling. Herrerías (Carlos Riquelme), who is being used to entrap Felipe, is forced to show himself and request the rebel's surrender, and he is killed by Garza. In the shoot-out, Felipe is captured and tied to a maguey. He rejects Gabriela's explanation by yelling, "Dirty bitch!" After the counterattack, revolutionaries are buried and soldiers executed and Felipe is told about Gabriela's whereabouts. Their violent confrontation ends with a passionate kiss. The regime of Díaz has fallen, and Felipe becomes a general. His romance with Gabriela is cut short when he is ordered to put down the Zapatista rebellion led by his fellow worker Máximo. Realizing the justness of his friend's cause and backed by his lover, he returns to Tlaxcala. The assault on a train ends the flashback. As the battle rages, he goes to find Gabriela, but it is too late: she has been hit in the forehead by a stray bullet.

In the late 1940s, and despite her success and fame, Félix sought to project herself beyond Mexico by working in Spain, Italy, and France (Paranaguá, 2003, 108). The supporting roles in *La corona negra* (The Black Crown) (Luis Saslavsky, 1950), *French Can-Can* (Jean Renoir, 1954), *La belle Otéro* (Richard Pottier, 1954), and *Les Héros sont fatigues* (Heroes and Sinners) (Yves Ciampi, 1955) provided the cachet of prestige but not the international recognition she craved. Nevertheless, as Taibo I. points out, "the French experience has transformed her in precise ways: the Parisian influence shows not only on her wardrobe but also her behavior" (1985, 189). *The Hidden Woman* is a homecoming of sorts: it is a return to a Mexican theme and to a character that had shaped Félix's personality on- and offscreen.[2] Whether or not, and under what conditions, the reinstatement of the Félix myth is successful is proposed in the film's initial train sequence.

By relying on the film viewers' foreknowledge, this sequence confirms visually the values and attributes of femininity associated with the star, in other words, what Richard Dyer calls the "perfect fit" of character and star (1991, 145). The diffuse lighting and soft focus close-up shots of Félix sitting at the window highlight her unique features: translucent skin, high cheekbones, lustrous lips, and sculpted eyebrows. Everything in these shots conveys elegance, not just the white scarf covering her head and the black coat she wears but also the grey, dark blue, and green gradations of the coach fixtures and scenery. With the lowering and lifting of the blind, the affective resonance of her face is transferred onto the character. These melodramatic gestures visualize Gabriela's urge to shut out the chaos of war and the memories of her past. After the train stops and human voices replace the grating sound of the wheels, Gabriela sees a young woman in

FIGURE 6.3. The Hidden Woman, *frame enlargement*

braids and wearing an embroidered blouse on the platform. The point-of-view shot and the reflection of Gabriela's face in the window generate a dual image that serves primarily as a plot device because it initiates the flashblack. Yet the matching shot of Gabriela, the vivacious young peasant who uses her charm to persuade passengers to buy the syrupy *aguamiel* drink she carries in a clay jar, is also a reminder of the actor's iconic identity. It encourages film viewers to recognize her as personifying at once cosmopolitan glamour and Mexican authenticity.

Since *The Hidden Woman* is a star vehicle, visual tropes are used strategically to fuse narrative agency, identity, and history into a single body. While the face of Félix/Gabriela reflected in the train window reinforces star/character identification in a reflexive manner, point-of-view shots and close-ups express the strength, pride, and sexuality of the women portrayed previously by the actor. In addition, the pairing of Gabriela and the unnamed *aguamiel* vendor evokes one of the central features of the Félix myth. The actor frequently performed the contrasting moral and social values of stereotypes in a single character, disrupting the normative mother/whore split. This alternative way of representing female stereotypes, or what Tuñón calls "disassociation as a contiguous mode" (1998,

97), is visualized in *The Hidden Woman* by means of the side-by-side placement of the courtesan and the peasant girl. To contain the threat posed by the visual separation of contrasting modes of femininity, the narrative must restore Félix's identity at once as an exceptional star and an embodiment of an authentic Mexico.

This realignment is contingent on the manner in which the train is used. Whether it is associated with Zapatismo or Gabriela, the function of the train is overdetermined by its significance in the historiography and mythology of the revolution. It is a setting in which the moral values of loyalty and betrayal associated with the revolution are put to the test. A case in point is the train attack that takes place halfway into the film and ends with Felipe's capture. In a scene set inside the train car, just before the assault, Gabriela talks to Hortencia about her inability to free herself from the past. Not just from Felipe, who haunts her "like a remorse, an accusation," but from the landscape. "It's this awful place," she says, looking out the window, "the loneliness you feel in the weight of the air and this never-ending landscape of magueys that makes me feel defeated." Just as this angry reaction to the place she has left behind is a denial of her roots, it verbalizes in melodramatic fashion her estrangement from the life-affirming bond of land and peasantry in postrevolutionary nationalist mythology. This bond is restored in a cathartic moment when violence compels Gabriela to side with the revolution. During the counterattack, she is horrified to find her friend dead. When she sees Garza firing the machine gun, she shoots him with the gun he gave her to avoid being captured alive. No longer a bystander, she may begin reclaiming her rightful place in the revolutionary scenario. In fact, her entry into this narrative is nothing short of spectacular. Framed in the coach's doorway of the coach, her body language is accentuated by the strobelike effect of the intermittent flashes of gunfire. The fierce and belligerent Félix/Gabriela becomes the melodramatic personification of competing desires, the actor in a drama in which private ambition and collective goals are at odds.

The Cultural Prestige of Citation

García Riera points out that *The Hidden Woman* contains some of the most accomplished and sophisticated images ever produced by Galvadón. Yet, he writes, the overall effect "is more celebrative and exhibitionist than dramatic or tragic" (1994c, 132–133). Visual production is anchored in artistic practices and viewing positions that acquired cultural prestige, celebrity status, and commodity value in the 1950s. The icons and themes associated

FIGURE 6.4. The Hidden Woman, *film still. Courtesy of Filmoteca UNAM, Mexico*

with national identity and history are given a new look, in keeping with the aesthetics of display in high-budget filmmaking and nationalist valorizations of authenticity. As noted, signs of identity designated authentic are those capable of reflecting in affirmative ways the idiosyncrasies of Mexican culture and politics, and as such worthy of being preserved. An example of this strategy is the early scene in which Don Esteban and his upper-class friends are arriving at the Vergel hacienda. At the sight of two peons accused of rebellion, their hands tied to their backs, being led by soldiers on horseback, a woman says, "Spectacles, like the one we have just seen, do not exist elsewhere in the world. Isn't it delicious that we still conserve customs that are so original?"

The ancient Hacienda San Francisco Soltepec (today known as Hacienda La Escondida) is the principal location of *The Hidden Woman*. Its rampartlike walls, ample buildings, and open courtyards are ideal not only for staging class and moral differences but also for visualizing the past as patrimony. Depth-of-field shooting in the pulque fabrication scenes, for instance, draws attention to the columns and archways supporting the colonial structure, the wooden casks containing the pulque, and the garlands adorning the altar of the Virgin of Guadalupe. The grand scale effect of the architectural and decorative details dwarfs the working peons. Even if the frame-within-the-frame design integrates different temporalities into a single shot and the chanting on the sound track validates the indigenous and mestizo heritage, ancient traditions and peasant labor are reduced to mere objects of a performance set on a monumental stage. In a later train scene in which Máximo explains to Felipe why he has decided to continue to fight the government, the compact grouping of figures, multiple plane composition, and monochromatic palette are an overt homage to Diego Rivera. The revolutionaries in white shirts and pants, gun belts, and wide-brimmed hats fill the frame. Those in the foreground with their backs turned to the camera replicate the internal audience disposition found in the murals, equating the film viewer's position to that of the tourist visiting the Secretariat of Public Education. One of the canonical works of postrevolutionary nationalism is offered as a big-budget historical drama for mass consumption.

A comparable overvaluation of photogenic elements occurs in the scenes showing the peasants of the Vergel mourning the death of Guadalupe (Manuel Vergara), the peon killed by soldiers. Except for the dramatic effect achieved by a crane shot slowly revealing a cross on the ground made out of stones, the use of chiaroscuro lighting and depth-of-field composition is purely ornamental. The interior shot places Gabriela and another woman, both wearing the traditional *rebozo*, on opposite sides of the frame in the foreground. With the doorway and the people gathered outside as the focal point, this shot is a quote-within-a-quote. In spite of inverting the angle and having the subjects face the camera, the shot evokes the burial in *Wildflower,* which is inspired in turn by an Orozco lithograph titled *Requiem* (1928.)[3] By relegating the corpse of Guadalupe, the subject of collective mourning, to the lower edges of the frame, affect is transferred onto the star.

This reflexive use of citation to authenticate star image can be found throughout the film. In an earlier scene, it is used to introduce the character played by Pedro Armendáriz. After Gabriela leaves the train station and is physically attacked by rival *aguamiel* vendors, she walks through the fields in search of her lover. She sees Felipe extracting *aguamiel* from the heart of a maguey with a large calabash. This shot is an explicit quote that combines a Brehme photograph from his book *Picturesque Mexico* (1926) and an extant shot of Eisenstein's "Maguey" episode in *Que Viva Mexico!* (1931).[4] Wearing a wide-brimmed straw hat, the front lifted to reveal his face, Armendáriz personifies the *tlachiquero,* the archetypal character of

FIGURE 6.5. Wildflower *(Emilio Fernández, 1943)*, digitalized frame from the filmstrip collection of Gabriel Figueroa. © Gabriel Figueroa Flores, Mexico

the hacienda tradition. Another citation from the "Maguey" episode can be found in the train attack segment. Having taken Felipe prisoner, Garza orders that he be tied to a maguey and left there to die. Beyond the pose, evoking that of Sebastián and his companions in the capture and torture scenes, the deportment and expression belong entirely to Armendáriz. Medium shots reveal the powerful affect of the actor's face, which, Monsiváis has written, "could express anger as easily as adoration" (2004, 593), and confirm his status as a romantic lead. All through the confrontation with Gabriela, the melodramatic performance and body language project an inimitable blend of pride, courage, and vulnerability. If in the shots of Eisenstein's unfinished project the male body becomes the object of desire, here Gabriela's gaze defuses the transgressive homoeroticism to reinstate the normative heterosexuality that enabled the actor (then forty-two years old) to be identified at home and abroad with Mexican nationalism.[5]

Felipe and Gabriela are invested with meanings that exceed their characters. In the climactic postal coach scene, the signature cinematography of Figueroa romanticizes sexual surrender, deflecting attention from the threat of violence. As Felipe searches for Gabriela, his rage is visualized as an out-of-control performance of masculinity that comes to an end when he slaps her. Alternating close-ups of his face and boots stepping on empty bullet casings destabilize the self-affirming virility of *machismo*, in effect emasculating the archetypal figuration of the revolutionary hero. Key lighting is used for Gabriela to glamorize her fear and vulnerability, turning her into an embodiment of desire. This erotically charged scene ends with a passionate kiss. Felipe is literally pushed out of the frame (and the narrative) by means of over-the-shoulders shots that make her ultra-feminine face the focal point of the image. As in the closing scene of the film, in which Felipe cradles her lifeless body in his arms, these magnificent close-ups replicate the iconic images of Armendáriz and Félix in *Woman in Love*. Their offscreen identities are repositioned in the film's symbolic system and melodramatically displayed as fetish objects of Mexico's cinematic patrimony.

Made during a period of prosperity and stability and when the golden age of Mexican cinema was drawing to a close, *The Hidden Woman* synthesizes the way in which the imagery of the Mexican Revolution was re-popularized as spectacle. In this regrettably overlooked film, big-budget production standards invest representation with the values of mass consumption. With Félix, as the historicizing agent, Mexican history and identity are visualized as patrimony to be displayed. Whether as a courtesan wearing urbane European-style outfits or a peasant dressed in the traditional *china poblana* clothes, her performance and character draw on the Félix myth. With Armedáriz in the supporting role, Félix reclaims ownership of her iconic off- and onscreen identity, at once as a Mexican and an international star and a personification of cosmopolitan glamour and Mexican authenticity.

SPECTATORSHIP AND VIOLENCE IN *The Wild Bunch* (SAM PECKINPAH, U.S., 1969)

On the morning of January 15, 1916, three men accused of stealing military supplies by Federal army officials loyal to Carranza were put in front of a firing squad in Ciudad Juárez. Among those who witnessed the execution were American civilians from El Paso who, for the past five years, had been assiduously looking across the border and watching the violence in Mexico. Also in attendance was Walter H. Horne, a photographer and entrepreneur who fabricated postcards and marketed them under the brand name Mexican War Photo Postcard Company. He faced Captain Javier J. Valle so that the men lined up in firing squad formation, the sentenced standing against the wall of the railroad station, and the curious

FIGURE 6.6. *"Triple Execution," postcard. W. H. Horne Collection. Courtesy of the Border Heritage Center, El Paso Public Library*

bystanders were in the viewing range of the camera. He recorded three times the moment in which the shots were fired, each time altering somewhat the angle and distance. After Francisco Rojas, Juan Aguilar, and José Moreno were killed, his employees circulated among the crowd, persuading people to place orders. "For twenty-five cents," the historians Paul J. Vanderwood and Frank N. Samponaro write, "the photographer guaranteed mail delivery within ten days, of three view cards of the execution" (1988, 68).

Known as "The Triple Execution," this postcard series turned a considerable profit for Horne's company. He reprinted it in summer 1916. His main customers were members of the U.S. Army stationed at the border in the wake of the Columbus, New Mexico, raid. Since then, and reproduced innumerable times, this series has become one of the most infamous picture postcards of the Mexican Revolution.[6] It carries on with the tradition of commercializing images of extreme violence and inhumanity that began with the Jimmy Hare photographs from the 1898 Cuban-Spanish-American war (Oles, 1993, 59). Along with other postcards that record the aftermath of executions, this series presents violent death as spectacle and constructs a compelling narrative about dying in Mexico. It freezes for posterity the various phases of the incident: the crowd arriving, the soldiers firing, and physicians examining the corpses. Those watching, then and now, are drawn into the impending sense of dread and the revulsion of witnessing death and its aftermath.

The Wild Bunch restages this experience in the final shoot-out between a gang of U.S. outlaws and a group of Mexican army regulars in the fictional town of Agua Verde. Notorious for its graphic representation of carnage (the production crew labeled it the "battle of bloody porch"), this ten-minute sequence revealed cinema's potential to visualize death and Peckinpah's ability to push its representation to its ultimate consequences. In what follows, I reflect on the questions provoked by the analogies between "The Triple Execution" and the film and the impact of the hyperstylized aesthetics of death on the film's view on the revolution. But first, and by means of selected segments, I look at spectatorship as a visual theme aimed at historicizing the revolution and endowing Mexican characters with narrative agency. Next, I consider how settings and iconography sustain divergent, yet complementary, modes of visualizing Mexico as both primitive and brutal.

As Stephen Prince notes, "*The Wild Bunch* deals with flawed heroes caught in a period of transition" (1999, 23). Its plot revolves around a band of outlaws who cross the border into Mexico. Pike Bishop (William Holden), Dutch (Ernest Borgnine), Angel (Jaime Sánchez), the Gorch Brothers—Lyle (Warren Oates) and Tector (Ben Johnson)—and Buck (Rayford Barnes) ride into San Rafael to rob a bank. Ambushed by bounty hunters led by former band member Deke Thornton (Robert Ryan), they shoot their way out of the small Texas town, leaving behind a trail of death and destruction. In Mexico, they meet up with Sykes (Edmond O'Brien). After discovering metal washers instead of silver in the bank bags, they head to Angel's village where Don José (Chano Urueta) tells them about a Federal army raid and the murder of Angel's father. After a moving farewell by the villagers, the bunch rides into the headquarters of General Mapache (Emilio Fernández) in Agua Verde. To restore their fortunes, they agree to steal guns from a U.S. Army ammunition train. The bunch outwits Thornton and his inept men again, first during the robbery and later on the bridge that takes them back to Mexico.

On the way to deliver the weapons, they are intercepted by Herrera (Alfonso Arau), one of Mapache's officers, and escorted back to Agua Verde. Pike explains that the location of the cases will be disclosed gradually and only upon payment. Everything goes well until Mapache finds out that a case has been given to the revolutionaries and Angel is arrested. With Thornton closing in, the bunch returns to Agua Verde, where a wild party is being held. They see Angel being dragged behind Mapache's car. When the general refuses to hand over Angel, they seek out the camp prostitutes. Pike summons Dutch and the Gorch brothers to rescue the young man by simply saying, "Let's go!" After Lyle says, "Why not?" they walk side by side to confront Mapache. Instead of handing over Angel, the general slits the man's throat and is instantly killed by Pike. A moment of silence precedes the gruesome slaughter of most of Mapache's army, including the German advisers, and the death of the Americans. As the Mexican survivors leave the compound, the bounty hunters arrive to claim the bodies of the bunch. Thornton decides to stay behind. Sykes and Don José find him at the gate and invite him to ride with them to fight alongside the Mexican revolutionaries.

By all accounts, the adventure Peckinpah promised to actors and crew surpassed all expectations. Once the production of *The Wild Bunch* moved to Mexico, all those involved faced artistic and technical challenges that eventually became part of the film's lore.[7] From March 25 to June 27, 1968, the director, production managers, actors, and technicians traveled around the state of Coahuila, starting in Parras de la Fuente where the bank robbery scenes were filmed. All were consumed by the intense schedule and by Peckinpah's tendency to improvise. His obsessive attention to detail carried on into editing and postproduction, pushing the film's editor, Lou Lombardo, and studio personnel to innovate montage, sound, and music mixing techniques. At the end of the day, the finished product thrilled everyone who participated. Not even the polarized responses of preview audiences in May 1969 deterred studio production head Ken Wyman and executive producer Phil Feldman from supporting the film (Weddle, 1994, 363). Nevertheless, *The Wild Bunch* became a casualty of competing views about its distribution, of exhibitors' negative responses to its 143-minute duration, and studio concerns about slow financial returns. After the press screenings and initial New York opening in June 1969, the order to remove 15 to 20 minutes was given by Ted Ashley, who took over as studio head after the dissolution of the Warner Brothers–Seven Arts partnership. Feldman implemented these cuts without Peckinpah's authorization (Seydor, 1994a, 51).

Historicity and Spectatorship

Among the flashbacks and other scenes that were eliminated and reintegrated in 1995 for the film's rerelease was the only one dealing explicitly with the revolution and the only one not featuring the U.S. characters.[8] Known as "Mapache under attack," this sequence is set in Las Trancas railroad station where Mapache's troops have gone to wait for news of the arms robbery.[9] It draws attention to the multiple mediations at work in the recording and re-creation of the revolution as a visual event. Of particular interest is the use of period imagery to signal viewer investment and fascination with spectacle by making Mexican characters its agents. In the initial moments, insert shots of individuals alternate with wide crane shots of the arid landscape and the provisional encampment on the rails. While the opening shot of a *soldadera* singing a *corrido* surrounded by musicians on the back platform of a train car with its vignette-like framing evokes the numerous group portraits found in the Casasola Archive, that of a boy dressed in a military uniform reacting to the battle dramatizes vision as a motif. He is shown inside the telegraph office, kneeling on a table and looking intently out the window at the cavalry charge and the clouds of dust from the explosions. The juxtaposition of motifs found in the archive and subjective shots implicates film audiences as agents (not just accomplices) in visual production.

Details about the film's preproduction and production phases indicate a conscious effort on the part of Peckinpah to get acquainted with period imagery. He consulted in 1967 the vast collection of photographs and films in the Paramount research department while turning William Douglas Langford's biography of Villa into a screenplay titled *Villa Rides!*[10] Actor Yul Brynner disliked the script, and producer Ted Hamilton (who hired Peckinpah) agreed to get another writer and bring in Buzz Kulik to direct. Peckinpah recalled comments made by the actor after reading the script that he "knew nothing about Mexico" (Weddle, 1994, 298). For *The Wild Bunch* the director and cinematographer Lucien Ballard screened U.S.- and Mexican-produced newsreels. "What they noticed in all of them," Seydor writes, "was a prevailing flatness of perspective, and they carefully chose a selection of telephoto lenses to replicate that flatness" (1994a, 140). The director may have also seen *Memories of a Mexican* (the documentary by Carmen Toscano de Moreno released in 1950; see chap. 1) upon Wallon Green's advice passed on to him by Roy Sickner (Seydor, 1999, 43).

When Peckinpah turned Green's early treatment of Sickner's story into a screenplay, he added the "Mapache under attack" sequence because he "was not about to make a film set in that period without an appearance by Villa" (Seydor, 1999, 59). Yet the leader is physically absent. Allusions in the dialogue, and the visual ones described below, point to the myth of the revolution and Villa as being one and the same. Battle shots depict the renowned superiority of the Dorados, and the compressed depth of field achieved by using telephoto lenses intensifies the awesome effect of Villista combat tactics. Amid the chaos of the retreat, Mapache raises his

FIGURE 6.7. The Wild Bunch, *frame enlargement*

binoculars and sees a group of revolutionaries on horseback waiting by the rails. This masked, grainy, and almost monochrome shot is remarkable. Its spectral qualities dramatize the extent to which Villa haunts the cinematic imagination, as an indispensable fetish object of revolutionary mythology.

During the attack earlier, and as gun shells explode around him, Mapache issues orders to keep fighting. After delivering the telegram with Pike's message about the arms robbery, the young boy salutes the general and acknowledges his hero's courage. The scene adds a human dimension to what is mainly an action-driven sequence. Peckinpah saw its removal as "an absolute disgrace." "[It is] possibly one of the best moments in the entire film," he said. "It made the point that I tried to make with the entire film, that the Mexicans were no worse than William Holden's bunch" (Harmetz, 1994, 171). Whether the director's intent to restore the balance between characters is fully realized or not, the focal point of this scene is the interaction between the starry-eyed boy soldier and the gruff Mapache. How they react to each other and the affect conveyed by their intersecting gazes unsettles the stereotype of the counterrevolutionary. The child's posture, straight and proud of being noticed, replicates that of the numerous anonymous boy soldiers who posed for photographers. This gesture of self-affirmation turns him into an actor in a broader narrative, one that Monsiváis recognizes in the Casasola Archive. This is what he says: "Without any reserve or the slightest modesty, [the common fighting people] write their own story under the inquisitive gaze of others" (1984, 50). To the boy's military salute, Mapache responds with a smile. The low-angle shot registers an expressive shift, moderating the hypermasculine

FIGURE 6.8. The Wild Bunch, *frame enlargement*

FIGURE 6.9. *Emilio Fernández as "Rodrigo Torres" in* Wildflower *(1943), digitalized frame from the filmstrip collection of Gabriel Figueroa.* © *Gabriel Figueroa Flores, Mexico*

performance of Fernández, which evokes the character of Rodrigo Torres that he interpreted in his own film, *Wildflower*. It salvages (albeit briefly) the stereotype of brutish decadence of the character modeled on the historical Victoriano Huerta, who personified, for Mexicans and Americans, treachery and deceit (Pick, 2000, 8–10).

Nowhere is the dramatization of the gaze as a visual motif and vehicle to validate the narrative agency of Mexican characters more significant than in the "Sadness and Celebration" and "Farewell to the bunch (La Golondrina)" segments. While the imagery is consistent with the theme of nostalgia in Peckinpah's westerns, spectatorship is the prime element because it assigns the role of humanizing the bunch to the people in Angel's village. The conversation scene between Pike and Don José exemplifies that the villagers are knowledgeable and responsive. When Pike notices ("Now I find that hard to believe") the Gorsch brothers engaged in a game of cat's cradle with Rocío (Elizabeth Dupeyron), Don José says, "We all dream of being a child again. . . . Even the worst of us. . . . Perhaps the worst most of all." Each statement is complemented by insert shots that depict respectively the brothers' gentleness, Pike's amusement, and Angel's seething rage and convey the village elder's ability to see beyond the surface.

This theme is reinforced in the farewell scene. It begins with the dissolve from Pike's face (as he observes a joyful group of children watching couples dance) to the two rows of peasants waving good-bye. As the bunch rides out, the camera singles out Pike, Dutch, Lyle, and Angel to register their gratitude for the displays of affection of which they are recipients. Don José is shown twice, leaning against a tree trunk with his arms crossed across the chest. The dignified serenity that comes across when he salutes first Pike and then Angel mirrors that of the men, women, and children singing "La golondrina," a plaintive ballad that has been part of the Mexican musical repertoire since the nineteenth century. The effect is profoundly melancholy. It is achieved in part by matching the slow pace of the tracking shots to the tempo of the song, thus enhancing the lyrical qualities that the smoke wafting among the ancient cottonwood trees gives to the mise-en-scène. Indeed, Peckinpah instructed that the song be played during the filming of this scene (Weddle, 1994, 341).

There is more to this idyllic scene than Peckinpah's predilection for processions and on-set improvisation. Shot in a day, it links symbolically Mexico and the outlaws. It ritualizes the encounter between different, if not incompatible, histories and cultures. Its aesthetics bring to mind the multiple pictorial and photographic renderings of rural culture and experience found in foreign and nationalist representations of Mexico and its revolution. What is more, the affect generated by the exchange of gazes is crucial to the story and its resolution. This is what Peckinpah said about the film: "*The Wild Bunch* is simply what happens when killers go to Mexico"; and the scene: "If you can ride out with them there, and feel it; you can die with them and feel it."[11]

Another improvised scene known as "Let's go; why not?" takes place in

168 | CONSTRUCTING THE IMAGE OF THE MEXICAN REVOLUTION

FIGURE 6.10. The Wild Bunch, *frame enlargement*

Agua Verde and shows Pike, Dutch, and the Gorch brothers on their way to confront Mapache.[12] Here the iconography of the Mexican Revolution and the western film genre overlap. How Mexicans become witnesses to the gunfighters' ritual walk out is recorded in *The Wild Bunch: An Album in Montage* (1995). To illustrate Cliff Coleman's testimony on the filming of this scene, the documentary incorporates black-and-white silent 16 mm footage shot by an unnamed cameraperson that was found in the Warner Brothers vaults by producer Nick Redman and director-writer Paul Seydor (Weddle, 1994, 340–341). On the same day of the shoot, Peckinpah decided to lengthen the scene. Instead of two separate actions (the men getting their guns and entering the courtyard), he opted for an extended take of their walk and charged assistant directors Cliff Coleman and Jesús Marín to choreograph it. Using the smoke-stained outbuildings and dilapidated adobe walls as backdrop, they placed groups of musicians and soldiers, old men, *soldaderas,* women, and children in the background, foreground, and outer edges of the shot. The group portrait composition evokes period imagery and positions the people watching the outlaws as an internal audience. Just as in the farewell scene, the other becomes the observer rather than the observed, and the outsider becomes the object of the gaze rather than its subject. Like the peasants in Angel's village, Mapache's followers are the narrative agents of what Prince calls the film's "mythography." Their gaze assigns a point of view that is this time Mexican rather than American "to validate the idea of a vanished West and a frontier that no longer exists, save symbolically for these wild gringos, in Mexico" (1999, 23).

The Visual Production of Violence

How settings and iconography are used in *The Wild Bunch* sustains the divergent, yet complementary, ways of representing Mexico. On the advice of location scout Chalo Gonzales, uncle of Peckinpah's second wife, Begonia Palacios, Peckinpah chose locations in the state of Coahuila mostly around the small town of Parras de la Fuente on the Saltillo-to-Torreón rail line (Weddle, 1994, 322). He was so taken by the pastoral mood of Rincón del Montero that he lived there throughout most of the filming and made it the set for Angel's village. He was also fascinated by the ruins of the Hacienda Ciénaga del Carmen, using them as a spectacular setting for Agua Verde, even though it lacked water and electricity and required a forty-five-minute drive by car from Parras de la Fuente on a narrow and unpaved desert road (Weddle, 1994, 324–325). He treated each site figuratively, judiciously selecting the architectural and landscape features to visualize, as Pettit wrote, "two rival Mexicos" (1980, 231–232). With its verdant landscape and serene atmosphere, the village and peasant community stand for a primitive Mexico; the collapsing structures and inhospitable environment of the hacienda and the Federalist troops and their German military allies in Mapache's stronghold, for a brutal one.

Yet the meanings of the primitive/brutal dichotomy are complicated through visual analogies. Notable are the parallel scenes dealing with the bunch's arrival in Angel's village and Mapache's camp. Shot in the hacienda location, with the outlying buildings as a backdrop, these scenes disrupt idealized views on rural culture and position Americans as outsiders. Crosscutting of shots of Pike and his men riding into Angel's village and villagers peeking warily from behind the adobe walls and mobile framing in the Agua Verde scenes mimics the outlaw's scrutinizing gaze. In the village, only Dutch's curt comment over the initial reverse zoom shot of a mangy dog in the village—"Won't find very much around here. That damn Huerta's scraped it clean"—expresses some awareness of the devastating effects of the civil war. If here spectatorship serves to represent human suffering, in the other scene it favors historicity over plot. The men may be looking for signs of Thornton and the bounty hunters. Instead, they become mediating agents for the film's representation of daily life in the counterrevolutionary encampment.

Citations reveal the constructed nature of the dichotomy. The reverse zoom shot of a breastfeeding baby cuddled up against the cartridge belts that crisscross her mother's chest is poignant and provocative because it fuses the *soldadera* of period photography and the Virgin with child of

Christian painting. This strategy is repeated in the scenes that follow Angel's murder of Teresa (Sonia Amelio), the young woman he hoped to marry before she left the village and became Mapache's mistress. Distraught and drunk, the general orders the grieving women to leave the room. As the body is carried out, the group walks in front of the table where members of the bunch and the German military adviser Frederick Mohr (Fernando Wagner) are conferring about the robbery of the U.S. ammunition train. This time, the mise-en-scène brings to mind the modernist sensibility of the Fernández-Figueroa films. Witnessed by the U.S. outlaws, the solemn mourning ritual is a gendered expression of the endurance of popular tradition and religious sentiment.

In the "Machine Gun Mayhem" segment, shifts in affect destabilize the safe/hostile structure of the dichotomy. Shock supplants laughter when Mapache, unaware that the weapon needs to be mounted, unleashes a barrage of bullets and wreaks havoc on the festivities. With officers and German advisers standing on the gazebo and looking down, the spatial arrangement evokes the aesthetics of display and spectatorship found in the Porfiriate imagery of the Casasola Archive and extant period film footage. As the machine gun becomes a lethal weapon, the sight of people ducking for cover turns into a *danse macabre* wherein people are the casualties of the unsavory alliance of inept locals and arrogant foreigners. A similar effect is created in the "Dragged in the Dust" segment. Absurdity is replaced by revulsion when the bunch sees Angel being pulled by a shiny red touring car around the compound. The open-top vehicle on which Mapache made a spectacular entrance becomes an instrument of torture. Although the machine gun and the car symbolize the destructive power of technology, these scenes reinforce a key element in the film's configuration of Mexico. During Angel's ordeal, shots of jeering children expose the cruel nature of a world that, at first sight, seemed nonthreatening to the bunch and, by extension, to the viewing audiences. Just as in the opening scenes in which children gleefully watch a scorpion tormented by ants, this horrific image reinforces visually "a structure in which innocence and cruelty, laughter and barbarity, idealism and blood-lust, exist side by side" (Kitses, 2004, 218).

The unsettling effect of the Agua Verde sequences colored Mexican reactions to the film during the production and on its limited release in 1973. Luis Reyes de la Maza, who was charged with overseeing the production on behalf of the Dirección Cinematográfica, the official Mexican film agency, signaled its potential for negative interpretation. In his autobiography, the writer expressed disgust with the portrayal of a debauched and vicious Federalist army. Not even Fernández's argument about the analogies with the vilified Huertistas swayed his opinion (García Riera, 1988, 166-167). Exhibited in a movie house in the fashionable Mexico City neighborhood of Polanco, the film garnered little attention even after the re-release of the restored version in 1999. Few critics were willing to look beyond the stereotypical characters and violence to reflect on the complex layering and treatment of visual themes. Only the comment by García Riera stands out. He writes, "Peckinpah did not pretend to explain Mexico; instead, he was able to record gestures, attitudes, and all kinds of details defining a national ambience and mode of being" (1988, 165).

Death and Spectacle: The "Battle of Bloody Porch"

Death is undoubtedly the most ubiquitous visual theme of the Mexican Revolution. Whether it is a predictable outcome of armed conflict or a melodramatic gesture of bravery and self-sacrifice, death always requires agents and eyewitnesses to naturalize its overdetermined meanings. The audience dramatizes the fascination with death that Mexicans and foreigners alike associate with the Mexican ethos and the brutality of the revolution. No other film, in my view, represents this fascination more affectingly than *The Wild Bunch*. It is not surprising, then, that the ultraviolent massacre prior to the film's conclusion has elicited so much commentary. Scholars agree that the "battle of bloody porch" set the standards for cinematic violence in Hollywood films of the 1960s and beyond. They have remarked on its technical and artistic mastery: the montage technique combining variable speed shots, amplified sound, and multiple lines of action. They have also noted the paradox between the aesthetics of spectacle and the director's position that viewers need to "see how brutalizing and horrible [violence] really is" (quoted in Prince, 1998, 228). Indeed, Devin McKinney calls it "one of the most famously contradictory sequences in any film, the one that horrifies as it thrills, disgusts as it delights, inspires anger as much as approbation" (1999, 181). By and large, these same scholars have understood this final segment of the film as a critical intervention into the nature of violence in American society, be it the mythical West or the tumultuous decade of the 1960s, with its race riots, political assassinations, and the Vietnam war. Others have linked the explosive and cathartic ending to themes of heroism and glory in the epic tradition: "It is in the very graphic depiction of violence that these themes find their artistic validity, their complexity and irony" (Seydor 1994b, 128).

The impact on the representation of Mexico has largely gone unnoticed, except for an alternative view that sees the violence as evidence of the director's politics. If Mapache and his German advisers stand for the betrayal of the revolution, as Pettit wrote, by "killing the Mapachistas, Peckinpah argues that he is ridding Mexico of a blot on the revolution. It is what the Mapachistas stood for and what they wrought that was the great tragedy of the Mexican Revolution" (1980, 234). The Agua Verde location symbolizes this tragedy. The ruins of the Hacienda Ciénaga del Carmen typify the destructive power of war: its elevated aqueduct, courtyard, collapsing walls, and uneven ground an ideal backdrop to stage the breakdown of gender, class, and military hierarchies. The mise-en-scène reveals the ultimate consequences of the tragedy that was the revolution: it visualizes mayhem and slaughter by means of cinematic techniques aimed at intensifying violence and destabilizing viewer identification.

By historicizing the revolution as counterrevolution and exposing its viciousness and victimization, *The Wild Bunch* distances itself from the aesthetic and rhetorical baggage of official nationalism. Peckinpah breaks away from the narrative and visual themes that idealize death as glorious sacrifice, thus enabling the association with Orozco's work. The Agua Verde massacre and its apocalyptic aftermath expose the unforgiving and implacable hold of violence on the human and social body. Its materiality and finality are depicted without compromise: bodies are jolted by the impact of bullets and blown apart by explosions, blood gushes from wounds, debris flies through the air, women and children are shocked into killing, and men welcome death with hysterical laughter. The austere landscape, almost monochromatic coloring, and asymmetrical group compositions are reminiscent of the misery and devastation imagery of *The Horrors of the Revolution* (see chap. 4). In this series of ink drawings made during his first sojourn in New York, Orozco adopts a bleak and critical position. There is no sentimentality or heroism in the images of discarded corpses in a maguey field ("Under the Maguey," aka "Campo de batalla/Battlefield") and grotesque nudes in front of a blown-up train ("Tren dinamitado"), only emptiness and horror.

Above and beyond this association, Peckinpah draws on the wider field of visual culture. Hence I return to a remark made in the opening of this section, that is, to the analogies between the Agua Verde massacre and "The Triple Execution" postcards first produced and marketed in 1916. Horne's photographs visualize death as spectacle. Fixed camera position and long-shot framing place the eyewitnesses and consumers as observers.

FIGURE 6.11. The Wild Bunch, *frame enlargement*

This sense of detachment reinforces negative perceptions about border towns and objectifies violence. Conversely, the multiple and colliding perspectives in *The Wild Bunch* draw attention to viewer investment in the spectacle of violence. With bystanders who become killers and killers who become victims, the final shoot-out exposes the fascination and revulsion of violence that the postcard conceals. Notable are the extended cutaways that punctuate the bloodshed scenes. Shot mostly in close-up, they show women and children hiding under tables watching the slaughter. Unlike the irislike shot of Thornton looking through binoculars as Mapache's followers are killed in the patio, these inserts signal that there is no secure place from which to watch. Shock is countered by compassion as the fearful expressions of these "ordinary people forced to observe" register to what extent they are accustomed to violence (Sharrett, 1999, 97).

A similar effect is achieved in the gruesome aftermath. The mobile camera (and musical accompaniment) implicates the viewer in the spectacle of death but arouses empathy as well by mimicking the slow movement of women, children, and old men among the corpses scattered in the ruins, and later the procession of survivors leaving the compound. Panning shots counter the objectification of the postcards, specifically the one that shows a doctor inspecting the bodies of the executed. What is more, the survivors' presence interferes with citation. In the scene of Coffer (Strother Martin) and T. C. (L. Q. Jones) picking valuables off the cadavers, other meanings are insinuated. Vultures perched on the outer walls—their wings spread ominously—link symbolically nature's most efficient scavengers and the bounty hunters. At this point, as Christopher Sharrett writes, "we are reminded that Harrigan [the railroad owner bankrolling the bounty hunters], Mapache, Pike, and Thornton are all predators, and that the victimization of people is central to this story and the frontier experience" (1999, 91–92).

At once memorable and troubling, these images are symptomatic of the way in which death is experienced visually, as spectacle. By making affectivity a component, the most exploitative features of the U.S.-produced postcards are undermined. With brutality and victimization as the primary visual themes in the Agua Verde sequences, Peckinpah offers a view on the revolution at odds with the heroism and sacrifice narratives promoted by the postrevolutionary Mexican state. Having said that, *The Wild Bunch* ends with a celebratory image, with a back shot of the bunch riding out of Angel's village presented as a Panavision anamorphic image that recedes within the original frame. This repetition is crucial, not only for the plot as the director stated. It reinstates mythmaking, with the U.S. outlaws as its subjects. After all, Pike and his men take a last stand not out of solidarity with Angel. As men for whom violence is a way of life, death is a heroic gesture. With generic imperatives determining the film's resolution, the Mexican Revolution is discarded just like the corpses that lie abandoned among the ruins of Agua Verde.

Admittedly, this conclusion did nothing to assuage ingrained anxieties (justified, for sure) in Mexico about demeaning stereotypes and reductive treatments of the revolution in Hollywood films. It is symptomatic, as well, of the ambiguities that arise from the troubled history of U.S.-Mexico relations, and which not even Peckinpah—a self-professed admirer of the country, its people, culture, and history—was able to overcome. His film shares in the long-established idea of Mexico as other. Yet he negotiates difference by using spectatorship reflexively to replicate historical ways of looking and seeing, to destabilize the visual themes associated with the primitive-brutal duality, and to articulate a vision of the revolution that is at once personal and critical, notwithstanding the ultra-violent aesthetics of death and victimization. These are the reasons that *The Wild Bunch* is an exceptional film among all the westerns set in Mexico. Spectatorship signals viewer investment and fascination with the revolution as spectacle by making Mexican characters its agents and complicates the primitive-brutal duality that has shaped U.S. representations of Mexico as other. The multilayered and, as a rule, unsettling imagery exposes the viciousness generated by the revolution, bringing its representation closer to Orozco's drawings than to the U.S.-made postcards that turned death into mass commodity. In this way, the film breaks away from narrative and visual themes that idealize death as glorious sacrifice, even if in the end it gives in to the mythologizing tendencies of the western genre.

Whether valorized for its ability to capture the "look" of a period or construct viewing positions from which the past can be resignified, spectacle is the driving force behind representation in historical films. Its function is primarily visual: its features (architecture, landscape, and heroic actions) and protocols (iconography, staging, and performance) lend an aura of authenticity to anecdotes and agents. In this chapter I have reconsidered the persistence of spectacle in films dealing with the revolution, that is, how historicity in *The Hidden Woman* is consistent with discourses aimed at preserving the past as heritage and how the gaze is used reflexively in *The Wild Bunch* to complicate the primitive/brutal dichotomy associated with U.S. representations of Mexico and the revolution.

Chapter 7

Competing Narratives and Converging Visions

In fall 1913, coverage of events in Mexico increased in the United States, with special attention to Pancho Villa and his Chihuahua campaign. As Mark Cronlund Anderson notes, the media's fascination was due to the leader's military deeds and the success of his agents in promoting his agenda (2000, 47). Journalists traveled to the border to report on the fighting between revolutionary troops and the Federal army. Among them was John Reed, who had been hired by Carl Covey, editor of *Metropolitan* magazine on the advice of the veteran journalist Lincoln Steffens. To increase his income as a freelancer, the twenty-six-year-old Portland-born and Harvard-educated writer offered to send news features to the New York *World* (Rosenstone, 1975, 151). Response to these articles was positive, not just among socialist and reformist intellectuals. President Woodrow Wilson appears to have been equally impressed and issued an invitation to the journalist to discuss Villa. With the liberal media following suit, these reports shifted public opinion in favor of the revolutionary leader, in spite of the denigrating views circulated in the Hearst-controlled press (Katz, 1998, 321, 323). By describing Villa and his followers as a social movement and explaining its origins, Reed's articles provided a corrective to the photographers' and newsreel cameramen's coverage of the Mexican war that reinforced historical attitudes by visualizing Mexico as a backward and violent country.

At this time, as Britton points out, revolution was an unfamiliar concept in the United States. "In this sense," he writes, "commentary on Mexico was a kind of pioneering venture for U.S. observers, their first experience with a revolutionary movement outside the more familiar territory of North America and Europe"(1995, 13). While not advancing knowledge, Reed's dispatches—and the materials subsequently assembled in his book *Insurgent Mexico* (1914)—offered the public a compelling account of his encounter with the people and the country. The book, as Christopher P. Wilson notes, "presents itself both as a critique of conventional reporting and an affirmation of solidarity with Villa's cause" (1993, 339). Reed's reporting was different, in spite of its predictable sense of adventure and romantic outlook. Unlike others who had not set foot in Mexico, Reed made several trips during which he endured the hardships of a military campaign waged in the desert and witnessed combat and its horrendous outcome. He showed particular interest in the common soldiers—he called them La Tropa—and was sympathetic to their motives for joining and fascinated by the tactics they believed would ensure their cause's triumph. This is not to say that Reed ignored Villa. In effect, he embraced the myth more than the person and commented on the special relationship he developed with the leader.[1] He was equally fascinated by the landscape, describing the barren scenery in vivid detail, as well as the emotions it provoked in him. A sunset in the Mapimi desert in northern Chihuahua inspired the well-known statement, "It was a land to love—this Mexico—a land to fight for" (1969, 57).

After a near-fatal experience during the battle of La Cadena, as Wilson writes, "Reed's persona and practice deviated more decisively from conventional war correspondence idioms" (1993, 351). He disparaged the attitudes of U.S. soldiers of fortune and fellow journalists. He found the first "hard, cold misfits in a passionate country, despising the cause for which they were fighting and sneering at the gaiety of the irrepressible Mexicans" (1993, 160). He disputed notions of the heroics and thrill of war that were part of war correspondents' culture since Richard Harding Davis's coverage of the Boer wars in South Africa (1880–1881, 1899–1902) and the Spanish-American War in Cuba (1899).[2] Reed wrote, "A battle is the most boring thing in the world if it lasts any length of time. It is all the same" (1969, 253).

The historian and biographer Robert A. Rosenstone calls *Insurgent Mexico* "a book for the eye, a vast panorama like one of the great murals of the Mexican painters, full of color, motion and the life-death struggle of a people" (1975, 157). In spite of this opinion of the visual qualities of Reed's work, it took almost six decades to be adapted to the screen by the Mexican director Paul Leduc.[3] *Reed: Insurgent Mexico* (1971) represents the journalist's political awakening while demystifying the revolution. It maintains the vignette-like structure and style of Reed's account by blending documentary and fictional devices. It adopts his point of view to represent his encounter with combatants and leaders, reconstruct the everyday experiences of the civil war, and stress the war's confusion and chaos. If the book can be viewed as a coming-of-age story, as Rosenstone writes, "what is subtext in his pages becomes the organizing theme of the film" (2006, 100). In this way, the film reinscribes the perspective of a foreigner and draws attention to the multiple mediations at work in the representations of the Mexican Revolution. It adopts a revisionist position to represent this momentous event as a sum total of its narratives, of its competing and diverging meanings. While this approach is consistent with revisionist Mexican historiography, Leduc also draws on the aesthetic and political agenda of 1960s Cuban and New Latin American cinemas.

Another film that reconstructs the life and experiences of foreigner visitors is *Tina in Mexico,* an eighty-minute experimental fiction film shot entirely on location that was written and directed by the Canadian filmmaker and feminist scholar Brenda Longfellow in 2002. As the title suggests, it deals with the 1923–1930 period during which Modotti, an Italian American photographer and Communist militant, lived in that country. It shares the intellectual and artistic inclinations of Leduc's work and the aim of reconstructing an individual's encounter with Mexico as a journey of self-discovery. By revisiting her participation in the emergence of modernism in the postrevolutionary period, *Tina in Mexico* proposes another way to look at Modotti. It explores issues raised by women's art and feminist aesthetics, bringing to light the multiple layers of context and mediations found in her practice. A complementary feature of the film's historicism is Longfellow's own position as a foreigner. As argued below, this awareness manifests itself reflexively by pointing to identity and difference as visual and narrative constructs.

"From 1920 to 1927," Delpar writes, "cultural relations between the United States and Mexico unfolded against a backdrop of apparently revolutionary change in Mexico and frequent periods of tension between the two governments" (1992, 15). Cross-border traffic included Mexican laborers and other migrants affected by economic and political instability and American intellectuals, activists, and artists eager to witness, explain, and participate in a social and political experiment perceived as being historically significant. No matter if they wrote, painted, or photographed Mexico, as Britton notes, the work of Americans who crossed the border captured the imagination of the public because it combined "tropical exoticism with revolutionary excitement" (1995, 8). By the time they arrived, the state had placed education and culture at the top of its national reconciliation agenda. With regional conflicts periodically erupting in violence, the government of Álvaro Obregón (1920–1924) set out to pacify the countryside and implement a politics of consensus aimed at integrating the various factions. A new kind of nationalism emerged that found expression in all visual and performing arts, either permanently on the walls of public buildings or ephemerally on city streets during civic festivities. About the murals commissioned by Education Secretary José Vasconcelos, the art historian Karen Cordero Reiman remarks, "The various strategies for the creation of a 'Mexican' art were thus put at the service of the process of legitimation of the post-revolutionary regime, and openly adopted a propagandistic function: to conform a vision of modern Mexico and propose a visual discourse that would unify the different sectors fragmented by the civil war" (1995, 21).

American artists visiting Mexico City flooded to see painters and their assistants, all dressed in overalls, laboring on top of scaffolds. Among them were Edward Weston and Tina Modotti. On his visit in August 1923, the renowned photographer noted in his *Daybooks,* "The murals of Diego Rivera have raised a storm of protests from the conservatives, but the work goes on. I cannot imagine his having the opportunity to start such paintings in any American municipal building" ([1961] 1973, 17). Four years later, to supplement her income, Modotti agreed to take pictures of Rivera's monumental project at the Secretariat of Public Education and the Orozco frescoes at the Preparatory School (Albers, 1999, 165–166). In spite of her friendship and admiration for these artists, Modotti found inspiration in groups and practices that represented an alternative to the overt didacticism of the muralists.

What drew Modotti to Mexico was the diversity of its art, past and present, and the debates about the role of art in the production of identity and nation. Cultural nationalism was an important theme. By and large, artists set out "to identif[y] and recove[r] the components of the American past. Others hoped to create and promote a distinctively American art, literature and music that would be organically related to the life of the people" (Delpar, 1992, 9). Those who went to Mexico found propitious ground to further their interest in folk and indigenous arts and saw primitivism as an antidote to the dehumanizing trends of modernization. Those who rejected the exploitative conditions of capitalism partook in discussions about art and social change. And all were attracted to the bohemian lifestyle that Mexico could offer.

Whether these artists produced a substantial body of work or played a part in the cultural dynamics of the time, the extent of their engagement is ultimately measured by their position within the historiography of Mexican modernism. Weston's arrival in 1923 is understood as a turning point in modern Mexican photography because his work anticipated a break with the pictorialist sensibility prevalent at the time.[4] But it is Modotti, his companion and later assistant, whose identity as a photographer is organically linked to the country. This appropriation is what makes her, with Eisenstein, an exceptional foreigner. Because she immersed herself in the artistic milieu and experienced radicalism firsthand, her work is seen to blend the aesthetic aims of modernism and the political aims of the revolution. These are the themes explored in *Tina in Mexico,* and in my commentary below. What interests me is how film represents the photographer's engagement in the politics and culture of the time and what position Longfellow takes in regard to the manner in which Modotti was turned into a Mexican photographer.

STORIES AND EXPERIENCES OF WAR IN
Reed: Insurgent Mexico

John Reed begins his narrative about the Mexican Revolution by describing the landscape around Ojinaga where the Federal army, led by General Salvador Mercado, was forced to retreat after being defeated in Chihuahua by Villa's troops. He writes, "At Presidio, on the American side of the border, one could climb on the flat mud roof of the Post Office and look across the mile or so of low scrub growing in the sand to the shallow, yellow stream; and beyond to the low *mesa* where the town was, sticking sharply up out of a scorched desert, ringed round with bare, savage mountains" (1969, 1). And this is how he ends his account of what happened a month later: "Then Villa, at the head of his army, appeared over a rise of the desert. The Federals resisted a respectable length of time—just two hours, or, to be exact, until Villa himself galloped right up to the muzzles of the guns—and then poured across the river in wild rout, were herded in a vast corral by the American soldiers, and afterward imprisoned in a barbed-wire stockade at Fort Bliss, Texas. By that time I was already far down in Mexico, riding across the desert with a hundred ragged Constitutionalist troopers on my way to the front" (1969, 9).[5]

These passages from the first chapter of *Insurgent Mexico* summarize Reed's various positions as spectator, reporter, and camp follower of a war that spread from the inhospitable northern deserts to the vast valleys of Central Mexico. He understood the revolution as a struggle for land waged by disenfranchised peasants and hacienda laborers. How the Greenwich Village bohemian and aspiring-writer-turned-war-correspondent saw the country and how people he encountered saw him is the subject matter of *Reed: Insurgent Mexico.* By filming in 1971 the story of an American who went to write about the first popular uprising of the twentieth century, Leduc turns his back on normative modes of representing the revolution.

Instead of relying on epic spectacle, heroic figuration, and melodrama, he validates the stories, subjectivities, and sentiments concealed behind official history.

The film is structured in two distinctive parts. The first is set in the early months in 1914 and details Reed's (Claudio Obregón) journey through the deserts of Durango with the advance guard of Villa's Northern Division commanded by General Tomás Urbina (Eduardo López Rojas). It emphasizes subjectivity by re-creating anecdotes about the journalist's interactions with officers and soldiers and shows the welcoming responses of Fidencio Soto (Carlos Castañon) and Longino Güereca (Hugo Velázquez) and the belligerence of Julián Reyes (Juan Ángel Martínez), who suspects him of being a counterrevolutionary spy. It deals with Reed's self-doubts and his responses to the dangers and hardships of war during the Villista retreat at La Cadena. The second part reconstructs Reed's interviews with Venustiano Carranza (Enrique Alatorre) in Nogales and Pancho Villa (Eraclio Zepeda) in Chihuahua. It depicts Reed's political awakening during his trip on the trains carrying the Villa troops to Torreón in March 1914. It shows him working alongside the soldiers, coming face-to-face with the thrill and pain of combat, exchanging views with a Mexican journalist and freelance photographer (Luis Suárez and Héctor García) on what it means to be a reporter, and attending a discussion between Villa and General Ángeles (Carlos Fernández del Real) on the imminent U.S. invasion of Veracruz. The film ends with a gesture that symbolizes Reed's commitment to the revolution. When the revolutionaries enter the deserted city of Gómez Palacio, he breaks a store window to take a camera that will replace the one he lost in La Cadena.

Having portrayed Reed as a character overwhelmed by the events, *Reed: Insurgent Mexico* culminates with an affirmation of agency. With this gesture, the journalist asserts control over his destiny. Indeed, the symbolism of this scene has not eluded those who have commented on the film. After remarking that it is a fictional incident, Rosenstone writes, "Clearly, it is the director's attempt to create a visual metaphor that expresses Reed's commitment to the revolution, as well as foreshadowing future actions which would not transfer well to the screen" (2006, 100). The Mexican film critic José de la Colina broadens the metaphor by noting that this moment "signifies also that something has been broken, has been opened, for Mexican cinema" (1972, n.p.). It is this view of the film — as a turning point — that I consider here. I use selected sequences to comment on how Reed's relationship with Mexican characters and his transformation from witness to participant are represented. Incorporated are remarks on the film's aesthetic operations: how the stylized mise-en-scène and textured sound track are used to reveal the quotidian and trauma of war. Finally, I explain how Leduc's film evokes the work of the early image makers of the revolution to reveal the stories and experiences concealed behind official historiography.

The filming of *Reed: Insurgent Mexico* began in November 1970 and ended in February 1971. It involved travel to ten locations in the states of Puebla and México, as well as shooting at the Churubusco Studios in Mexico City (García Riera, 1994d, 156; Gómez, 2003, 138). In charge were independent producers Salvador López (who facilitated access to the studios), Luis Barranco, and Bertha Navarro. All endorsed Leduc's decision to work outside the industrial structures. Most of the cast and crew were young and unaffiliated with unions. A few had professional credentials. They were either actors of the famed Teatro Universitario, such as Claudio Obregón, Ernesto Gómez Cruz, Eduardo López Rojas, and Juan Angel Martínez, or filmmakers such as director Carlos Castañon, Greek-born cinematographer Alexis Grivas, and editors Rafael Castañedo and Giovanni Korporaal. Some were active in other areas of cultural practice, such as Eraclio Zepeda, poet; Enrique Alatorre, stage actor; Hugo Velázquez, ceramist; Héctor García, photographer; and Luis Suárez, journalist. Others were either friends of the director or residents of the towns where the film was shot.

Working with a small budget and crew and using black-and-white 16 mm film stock was consistent with Leduc's training at the Institut des Hautes Études Cinématographiques (IDHEC) in Paris and his early documentary work and creative goals. As he noted, "The industry would not have appreciated these procedures. In my view, any one of the established producers would have believed that to recuperate their investment, the film needed to have all the requisites of grand spectacle (color, wide-screen, top-ranked players). Being made at the margins of the industry has given the film a different look, which is what I was interested in achieving" (quoted in *Esto,* 1971, n.p.). Given that Mexican film critics saw standard practices within the national industry as rigid and mainstream cinema as artistically bankrupt, they singled out *Reed: Insurgent Mexico* as a new beginning and hailed its innovative style and approach.

Indeed, times were good, and—as Daniel Maciel notes—"a second Golden Age seemed possible" (1999, 202). Cinema was an important component of the "democratic aperture" agenda of President Luis Echeverría (1970–1976). Reformist policies, including amendments to censorship, and substantial increases in state funding were intended to revitalize the industry. These measures were in line with the state's aim to restore its legitimacy by reintegrating intellectuals and artists who overtly contested the authoritarian rule of the Institutional Revolutionary Party (PRI). Driven by populist rhetoric rather than ideology, this strategy brought about accommodation, not radical change. Notwithstanding the official endorsement of director-driven projects and socially relevant themes, filmmakers and producers were forced to negotiate—not always effectively—the tensions resulting from what was only a pretense of liberalization and customary modes of institutional control (Maciel, 1999, 203). Not even Leduc was immune. It was one thing to make a film outside the established structures, another to ensure that it would be widely released. President Echeverría facilitated access to the Banco Cinematográfico, whose director was his brother, Rodolfo. With this backing, Leduc obtained exhibition approval, funding to legalize the film's status with the unions, and produce a 35 mm sepia-tinted print.

Official certification also guaranteed international exposure: *Reed: Insurgent Mexico* was screened at the Berlin, Cannes, and Pesaro festivals in 1972, awarded the Georges Sadoul Prize in 1973 for best foreign film exhibited in France, and showcased in a Mexican cinema retrospective that circulated worldwide in 1974. Validation took the form of largely favorable critical responses at home and abroad. Mexican critics saw it as a landmark film: a starting point for a truly independent national cinema and a work of historical retrieval. In his brief review in the daily *Universal Excelsior* on January 29, 1973, during the film's commercial run at the recently reopened Gabriel Figueroa movie house, Tomás Perez Turrent commented on its ability to "recuperate the immediacy and truth of the days of the revolution, bring them back to life in all their freshness, and restore the dimension that necessary, everyday actions must have had" (n.p.). In the view of the French critic Tristan Renaud, Reed was not quite a hero but "becomes through his struggles the conscience, the morality of the revolution, and as for the revolution, it appears to our eyes as incoherent, fragmentary, a process" (1974, 122). There were also some reproaches. As the U.S. film critics Judith Hess and John Hess put it, "There is no sustained political analysis—events are arranged as to give a picture of Reed's development, not the nature of the Revolution" (1974, 8).

Among all the accolades and criticisms, one feature was overlooked: the film's affiliation with Cuban revolutionary cinema and the oppositional practices that emerged in Latin America during the 1960s. *Reed: Insurgent Mexico* appropriated production and stylistic approaches aimed at altering existing patterns of cinematic culture. Through the interplay of documentary and fiction, the film generated new forms of address and spectator investment, managing to recuperate the historical legacy and international projection of the revolution.

Encounters across Generations and Cultures

Another fact that went unnoticed was the part the film played in reviving interest in Reed's work in Mexico. As Renato Leduc—a renowned journalist and poet, also the director's uncle—noted in the preface to the International Publishers 1969 edition, limited exposure to *Insurgent Mexico* was due to a tardy Spanish-language translation in 1954 and official attitudes. "Given the touchy sensibilities of the men who came to the top in the Mexican Revolution," he wrote, "it is easy to understand why they would not tolerate readily the raw-flesh descriptions by a foreigner of the miseries suffered by the peons who formed the core of their armies, of the ruthless cruelty and immorality flaunted by some of the leaders" (1969, xii–xiii). Leduc starts his preface with an anecdote about how, after coming across a copy of the book, he realized that the radical author of *Ten Days That Shook the World* (the eyewitness account of the Russian Revolution published in 1919) was none other than "Johnny, Juanito, the smiling pug-nosed gringo" reporter he met when he was a young telegraph clerk in Chihuahua (1969, xii). The writer's discovery and his delight in identifying the places and people described in Reed's book are also found in the film. Like his uncle, Paul Leduc treats the book as a compelling chronicle of war and a recollection of a cross-cultural encounter.

Deliberate or not, these parallels inform the film's historicity. This is what De la Colina writes: "The film sets up a dual reflection: that of John Reed on revolutionary action; that of a contemporary filmmaker on John Reed. That's why one can say that Leduc films the revolution in two periods, as a conversation between two moments in time" (1972, n.p.). *Reed: Insurgent Mexico* is intended for young audiences, mainly the left-wing activists radicalized in the student movement. It is an invitation extended by one of their peers—Leduc was then twenty-eight years old—to gain access to the multiple stories hidden behind official history. Above all, the journalist is a catalyst that enables a whole new generation to rediscover what drove Mexico's youth to take part in a struggle for social justice, to endure the hardships and disappointments of a protracted war.

The film's position manifests itself in two ways: by casting Claudio Obregón in the lead role and linking the character's agency and subjectivity to the Mexican protagonists. Reed is Mexicanized through language and

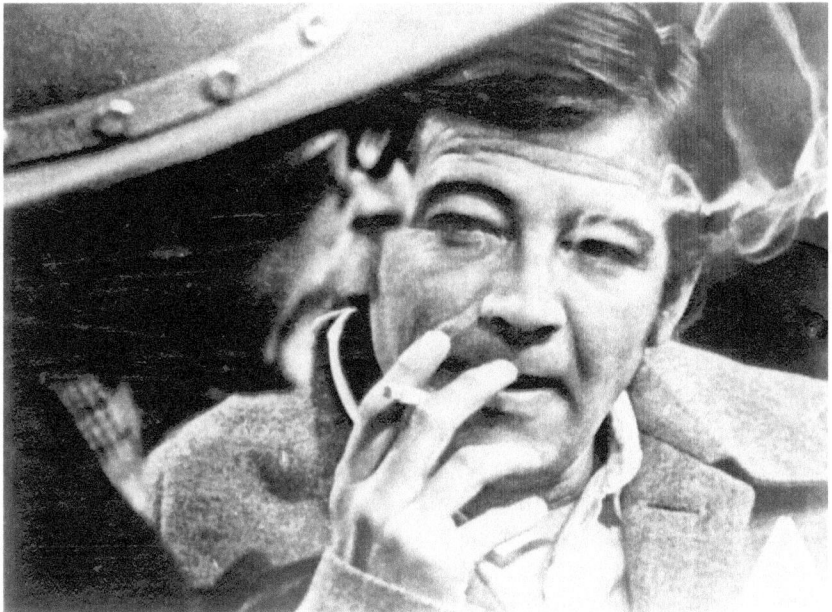

FIGURE 7.1. Reed: Insurgent Mexico, *film still. Courtesy of Filmoteca UNAM*

acting wherein local inflections and vernacular idioms are delivered effortlessly, and minimalist actions and gestures project a sense of spontaneity. Numerous, often extended dialogue scenes depict the bonds between Reed and the revolutionaries. Whether these exchanges occur in mundane situations or follow dramatic events, they show a self-conscious and apprehensive Reed, troubled by his own doubts and by what he witnesses. While these scenes signal shifts in the character's identity and political awareness, they also give voice to the identities, experiences, and ideals—some naive and violent but all resilient in their resolve—of the men of the Northern Division. How their motivations, prejudices, hopes, and fears are represented is exemplified in the matching sequences of Reed's initial meeting and then lunch with Villista officers.[6]

The first sequence starts when Reed, press credentials in hand, arrives at the headquarters of General Urbina in Las Nieves and is introduced to the chiefs of staff. After explaining that he wants to accompany the troops in order to write articles for his newspaper, he asks the officers for their opinions on the revolution. Camera placement, movement, and framing register the tensions at work in this encounter. Even if the 360-degree panning shot around the room establishes initially Reed's point of view, he is visually marginalized. When he asks, "And what is liberty?" and Julián

Reyes replies, "If you don't know, then, what are you doing here?" the camera stays on the officer to expose his belligerence toward the journalist and his questions. It remains stationary, too, as Longino Güereca speaks about the future—"When we win this revolution, we will have a government of men, not one that is run by the rich"—and remembers Madero. By relegating Reed to the edge of the frame in the first instance and offscreen in the second, the camera draws attention to a collective agency.

These themes are expanded in the second sequence. To be admitted into the revolutionary brotherhood, Reed must submit to Mexican hospitality protocols. First, he accepts the invitation to stay, even though he is impatient to join Villa's drive from Chihuahua to Torreón, and agrees to take a photograph of Urbina (more on that scene later). In doing so, the journalist recognizes the general's leadership and generosity. Next and over a meal, Reed comes face-to-face with the kindness of Fidencio and Longino, who share with him their plans for the future, and the antipathy of Julián, who suspects him of spying. The hostile exchange ends with the ultimate dare. When Reed agrees to drink *sotol* (a maguey-based liquor produced in the northern states of Durango, Chihuahua, and Zacatecas), he signals his acceptance of male codes and social conventions.

Self-identification with La Tropa is an important component of *Insurgent Mexico*. According to Rosenstone, anecdotes about sharing bottles of *sotol* reflect the effect that Mexico had on Reed. "There, among the ragged troops of revolutionary armies," the historian and biographer writes, "Jack underwent many experiences that could be summed up in the glorious feeling that he was truly one of *los hombres*" (1975, 150). Be that as it may, Leduc proposes an alternative view in an extended nine-minute scene especially created for the film. It is a conversation between Reed and Longino that occurs at night in La Zarca. After Julián confronts Reed at a party and grills him again about his intentions, Longino leads Reed away for a chat and drink around a fire. Troubled by the man's belligerence and insults, Reed admits that even as a child he preferred to walk away from a fight. Not even his friend's reassurance that he is not a coward can temper his anxiety and guilt.

Here the film steps away from *Insurgent Mexico* and into biography to link the historical figure and the fictional character. The dialogue alludes to Reed's imprisonment in summer 1913 when he reported on the silk workers' strike in Paterson, New Jersey, and his feelings of inadequacy for not being like his father, who had sacrificed all in the name of political activism. The mise-en-scène destabilizes the hypermasculine revolutionary stereotype by pointing to ways in which characters negotiate manliness.

Identification results from the actors' side-by-side placement and continuous shooting without cuts. Tight medium-shot framing, fixed camera position, and minimal lighting add a sense of intimacy to their exchange and accentuate Reed's vulnerability as he talks about the fear of dying that reduced him to being a spectator rather than an actor in the workers' struggle and the guilt of running away to Mexico instead of fighting in his own country. Longino is shown as a nonjudgmental and caring peer who appreciates Reed's intention—"You joined *la bola* to tell the truth and that's good, no?"—and suggests that the mission would make his father proud. Just before their conversation ends, he calls Reed his brother, his *compadre*. By valuing his friend's courage ("You're the manliest gringo around!") and solidarity, the Mexican soldier becomes the agent of Reed's integration into the revolutionary family.

Whether dictated by the constraints of low-budget production or assumed as a stylistic device, the use of sequence shots in these scenes exemplifies the film's approach. Continuous shooting without cuts challenges actors to get it right and lends emotional authenticity to their performance by drawing the viewer into the characters' hesitations or self-confidence and promoting identification with their shortcomings and motivations. Also reproduced in these scenes are the attitudes found in the testimonies of foreigners who went to Mexico in this period. Anecdotes about mistrust followed by appreciation are common. Foreigners told about being accused of spying for a rival army and used the stories of being accepted to prove their bravery and honesty. Rare are the expressions of solidarity with the combatants found in Reed's narrative, and on which Leduc draws to validate their agency.

At times, the director chooses silence. Examples of this strategy are the cemetery scenes discussed (see below) and the sequence of Reed's reencounter with a *soldadera* (Lynn Tilley.)[7] After crossing the gate of the Santo Domingo hacienda in the company of other survivors of the La Cadena battle, she asks if he recognizes her as his dancing partner at La Zarca and if she can spend the night with him. In the next scene, the woman gets ready for bed. Even with her back turned to the camera, her face blurred by the grimy mirror, she embodies serenity. The slow gestures as she moves around the room dignify her to Reed. He watches intently and tenderly as she removes her hat, bullet belt, and dress and turns out the lamps. Melancholy is the pervading affect here and is intimated by the low lighting and visual design of the scene. While the irislike masking with which it begins and ends recalls silent cinema, this vignette also pays tribute to the women who joined the war. It turns her silence into a moving affirmation of self to destabilize the *soldadera* images found in *Insurgent Mexico* and in Mexican cinema where she is either idealized to sustain Reed's self-image and reputation as a womanizer or masculinized to reproduce the raucous and vindictive character made popular by María Félix in *La cucaracha*. Instead Leduc portrays her as an agent of her own story, using Reed's gaze to elicit empathy with her fate as a woman who, after losing her man in battle, becomes the mistress of a captain.

If *Reed: Insurgent Mexico* rectifies the exclusion of the common soldiers from the revolutionary scenario, it also reveals the journalist's fascination with their leader. His role as an agent in the construction and circulation of Villa's legend is detailed in a lengthy interview segment.[8] After the burial of Abraham González, who had been assassinated on Huerta's orders, Reed walks into a bakery where he watches soldiers in bullet belts performing various tasks. Villa strolls in and listens to their grievance ("This is not a work for soldiers"). His reply is an endorsement of employment. "A soldier in peacetime should work," he says. "If he is idle, he'll only think about how to stir up trouble." Only then, Reed approaches. Skeptical at first, Villa agrees to speak to the journalist and invites him to share a meal.

Structured around a series of shots and countershots, the interview highlights Villa's ability to use anecdotes to communicate. He talks candidly about war strategy ("It would be a lie if I told you that I studied these things. But, when it comes to knowing where to fight, I see with precision") and responds to Reed's questions on the Hague convention protocols ("War is a serious thing. You can't make rules for it, as in a card game"). Reed also inquires about the Benton affair. The reticent Villa answers, "If you want to know about this, ask my chief Mr. Carranza. He is the proper person to talk to foreign powers." About his friend and mentor González, he says, "His death was a very bad thing for the revolution, a loss to us all. . . . I owe much to him. He made many things clear to me. And if I didn't understand, it was my own fault." Eraclio Zepeda plays the part of Villa brilliantly, endowing the character with the same attributes that turned the popular leader into an international celebrity. Yet the acting reveals the constructed nature of Villa's persona: the self-conscious body language and easygoing delivery, the down-to-earth charm and shrewd personality he cultivated. Here Reed's views converge with Leduc's representation. Regardless of factual errors, the portrait of the revolutionary in *Insurgent Mexico* details personality traits found in most period chronicles: his sharp intellect, sense of humor, and cruelty. What the director highlights are Villa's pragmatism and lack of personal ambition, in other words, the qualities Reed recognized but others ignored in favor of folktale embellishment.

From Observer to Participant

To what extent camaraderie and full membership are compromised by the harsh realities of war is made clear in the long La Cadena segment. In Renato Leduc's words, Reed "received his baptism of fire" during this battle, in which the Villistas led by Colonel Petronilo Hernández were overwhelmed by the Federal troops of Benjamín Argumedo (1969, xxi).[9] By reconstructing this incident, *Reed: Insurgent Mexico* works against the grain of reified representations of the revolution as a heroic spectacle. The segment begins when Reed is ordered to stay behind at the hacienda where the troops are camped. After watching soldiers on horseback and on foot move out, and unable to stop a galloping horse, he kicks a cooking pot in frustration. A bullet hitting the adobe wall and a bomb exploding in the field end his aimless pacing. Told by the retreating riders that they have been beaten, he starts running. When the teacher in civilian clothes next to him is hit, Reed finds himself alone and without his camera. During his flight in the desert, deep focus compositions, horizontal camera movements, and brisk cutting capture the chaos. Shots of lone figures on foot alternate with shots of groups on horseback, stirring up clouds of dust in the barren landscape; the scenery of scrawny trees and rock-strewn ground reinforcing their vulnerability and isolation.

All reviewers of *Reed: Insurgent Mexico* share the opinion advanced by Michael Goodwin that the film "shows the Mexican Revolution in a way it's never been shown before" (1974, 31). To explain this difference, the film's treatment has been often, and misguidedly, characterized as documentary. Although in this segment Leduc uses techniques (long takes, wide-angle lenses, and hand-held camera) and effects (immediacy and detachment) commonly associated with the cinema verité mode, he combines them with elements of fictional filmmaking. This mixing of modes can be found in the revolutionary and oppositional cinemas of Cuba and Latin America, notably in films such as *Los inundados* (Fernando Birri, Argentina, 1962), *Memorias del subdesarrollo* (Memories of Underdevelopment) (Tomás Gutiérrez Alea, Cuba, 1968), and *El chacal del Nahueltoro* (The Jackal of Nahueltoro) (Miguel Littín, Chile, 1969). Ana López writes that this strategy "generate[s] new modes of consciousness for the spectator" and "sets up a dialectical relationship between identification and distance" (1990, 409). The result is a poetic, critical, and reflexive realism capable of deconstructing rather than simply reflecting reality.

By drawing on this approach, Leduc makes the most of the visual properties of black-and-white film and blends synchronous and sound effects to create a dynamically textured sound track, without having to resort to a music score and period songs. With the distortions in image quality that result when 16 mm stock is blown up to 35 mm, these elements point to the mediated nature of filmic representation, that is, its capacity to expand the perceptual field of human and social experience. In the shots of Reed running alongside the teacher, for instance, the horizontal panning produces an effect of linearity and boundless space that suggests, as García Riera writes, "the sense and weight of death" (1994d, 159). Previously seen addressing a group of peasant-soldiers, the teacher is the personification of pragmatism ("Revolutions are ungrateful," he responds when questioned by Reed). When the slight man, recognizable by his black hat and suit, falls down, his body left behind in the field, so does the belief in a better future. Throughout Reed's run, the most effective element is sound. As the noise of hoofs and the distant din of firing are replaced by the sound of footsteps hitting the stony ground and labored breathing, attention shifts away from the action and danger is experienced in all its physicality. In the next scene, sound is more than a mood-setting device. A man appears in the distance, as Reed rests against a dilapidated wall in a cemetery. He gets up, walks to the entrance, and sees a corpse draped over the back of a horse and an old soldier digging. At the journalist's approach, the one-eyed man raises his head to stare blankly back. The creaking of a wooden door and scraping of stones reinforce symbolically the character's uncanny encounter with death.

Reed: Insurgent Mexico dispenses with depictions of actual fighting. As in the above-considered scenes, the protracted attack on Gómez Palacio (near the end of the film) represents the devastating impact of warfare. It starts with Reed wandering on a windswept and deserted plain—first in the company of two men and then alone—and seeing the wounded and dead being carried away. The grainy texture of the shots, compounded by the effect of the camera gliding along the ground in low-angle position, draws attention to the clouds of dust stirred up by the howling wind and the imprints left by weather, horses, and machines. The imagery evokes Reed's account of this battle in *Insurgent Mexico*. "It was an incredible dream," he wrote, "through which the grotesque procession of wounded filtered like ghosts in the dust" (1969, 215). Reed's walk ends at the edge

FIGURE 7.2. Reed: Insurgent Mexico, *lobby card. Courtesy of Filmoteca UNAM*

of an arroyo. He stops when a male voice shouts that the man lying in front of him is dead. Next he is shown under a wooden bridge, sharing a cigarette with several boys and responding to their questions and then fabricating bombs in the dark as they wait to be summoned to combat. The minimalist style draws attention to the quotidian of war. In the night scenes, camera position and key lighting block out the surrounding landscape to intensify the sensation of boredom conveyed in the shot of the boy who kills time by burning a spider web attached to the spiky edges of a maguey leaf. The down-to-earth attitudes of the soldiers reveal a disdain for death or simply a lack of purpose. By granting expressive power to ordinary gestures, war is resignified. Silence and apathy replace—at least momentarily—the sound and fury of battle.

Leduc's film reclaims the cultural legacy of the revolution by evoking the work of its early image makers. While it adopts a position that is at once detached and invested in bearing witness, it resorts to a foreigner's gaze to mediate the events and their aftermath. It revalorizes visual themes and motifs as constituent of popular memory rather than as icons turned stereotypes and cultural commodities. Scenes of Reed taking pictures, for instance, recuperate the diverse modes of visual production of the period. When he aims his camera at an old soldier who sits in front of a crum-

FIGURE 7.3. Reed: Insurgent Mexico, *film still. Courtesy of Filmoteca UNAM*

bling wall in the early part of the film, and later at General Urbina and his family, the film reproduces the mutually shared conviction of the power of the image.[10] The voyeuristic predisposition in the first scene is counterbalanced in the second by subjective investment. Agency does not belong to Reed but to the general. He orders his aides to bring his horse, dogs, and phonograph, decides on the placement of his mother and mistress, dons his medal-adorned jacket and sword, and writes his name on a wooden plank so that "they will know" who is in the picture. That the group portrait has become the film's best-known image is not surprising. It is the culmination of a narrative concealed behind the numerous period photographs that became, for better or worse, an emblematic and obligatory component of cinematic re-creations of the revolution.

At the time in which *Reed: Insurgent Mexico* was produced, an expanded version of *The Graphic History of the Mexican Revolution* was available in five volumes published by Editorial Trilla in 1960. With pictures selected by Gustavo Casasola from the extensive archive of his father, Agustín Víctor, the updated edition of this illustrated chronicle consisted primarily of snapshots of notable politicians and prominent figures in the business world. Still, a few photographs of the revolution were included. As in the 1940 version, these images are used arbitrarily and without proper credits. Fanciful captions misrepresent the content, at times making erroneous attributions. Notable is the use of the Mutual Film Company's film still of Villa at the Ojinaga battle to illustrate the victory in Torreón. Another example is the pictures of Federal troops embarking at the Buenavista train station in Mexico City that were designated iconic images of the revolution. "It is ironic that they have assumed this role," the archivist and historian Ignacio Gutiérrez Ruvacalba writes, "for the soldiers and *soldaderas* (the women who accompanied the combatants) all belonged to an army in which they had been forced to fight by the Huertista levy" (1996, 193).

Evocations of the archive in Leduc's film propose a different reading. The scenes of the Villa army boarding the train in Chihuahua replicate the imagery of collective mobilization found in the extant Toscano footage of Madero's triumphant trek from the U.S. border to Mexico City and the Abitía films and postcards of the Obregón campaign. Multiple points of view capture the magnitude of the spectacle: the overhead shots of the crowd and the tight framing individualize the sense of excitement shared by the Villistas. In this way, Leduc reappropriates meanings that, over the years as a result of mass reproduction and recurring citation in films dealing with the revolution, had been ossified by discourse. So when Reed is

FIGURE 7.4. Reed: Insurgent Mexico, *lobby card. Courtesy of Filmoteca UNAM*

shown inside a cramped railcar, surveying the space and the people who occupy it, he plays the customary part of spectator. While the insert shots of children playing and a soldier eating reproduce the multiple portrayals of daily life on the trains, Reed's smile moderates the detached perspective found in the archival imagery. The posture, his back resting against the sacks of provisions, likens him to his traveling companions. When an older woman takes a tortilla from her basket and hands it to him, bonds are cemented that cut across cultural and class differences.

This theme reappears in the nocturnal scenes that follow. Reed is a member of a crew repairing the rails blown up by the Federal army (fig. 7.4). Shots detail the backbreaking labor and single out the women and children who are there. Sitting on the rails or standing, they complete the tableau of teamwork and human resilience. Placed in the foreground of the shots, the women act as witnesses to Reed's transformation from observer to participant. The torch light adds a haunting quality to these images, which in turn weakens the iconic status of the period photographs. These scenes grant figurative agency to the anonymous women, children, and men who rode the trains and the soldiers who worked the tracks, yet are a poignant reminder that irruption of the masses into history was temporary. If Leduc's imagery recontextualizes the numerous group and individual portraits of the Casasola Archive, it also operates as countermemory. To the extent that the film is concerned with subjectivity and memory, it reinserts the popular sectors that made the revolution into representation and reactivates the awareness of their suppression from official history.

To conclude, *Reed: Insurgent Mexico* is a revisionist and innovative work whose power to demystify far outweighs its technical imperfections. As Jorge Ayala Blanco suggests, the sequence of the soldier who scorches a spider's web with his cigarette is an allegory of the film's objectives: to burn, demolish, and break the "web" of images and discourses that have shrouded the image of what once was the revolution and the individuals who fought in it (1986, 89). Leduc draws a compelling portrait of Reed's Mexican adventure. He depicts the journalist as an intellectual radicalized by popular struggle who relinquishes his role as a witness to become a participant, and reveals the part he played in the construction and circulation of the Villa legend.

From the initial scenes in El Paso in which Reed is seen walking amid the crowd of refugees that streams across the border, the film works against the grain of reified representations of the revolution. It avoids spectacle and melodrama to draw attention to the social and human cost of the conflict. It adopts a detached yet intensely observant perspective to represent the journalist's encounter with Mexico. As noted sequence shots promote identification and show how positions are at once affirmed and disclaimed, antagonisms are exposed and negotiated. Formalist strategies are used to visualize the quotidian of war and its ravaging effects on the landscape and the people. Last but not least, the film evokes the work of photographers and cameramen who recorded the revolution to grant narrative and figurative agency to the men, women, and children who participated. In doing so, *Reed: Insurgent Mexico* reclaims the stories hidden behind official appropriations of the archive. It breathes new life into the imagery of an event that cinema had reduced to a picturesque spectacle filled with clichéd tales of bravery and stereotypical characters.

A MEXICAN PHOTOGRAPHER? DEFINITELY! DIFFERENTLY? *Tina in Mexico*

As the year 1929 was coming to a close and for two weeks, December 2 to December 14, photographs by Tina Modotti were exhibited in the vestibule of Mexico's National Library. The significance of this show cannot be underestimated. Held two months before she was deported from Mexico, it included some forty-three items representing the various genres in which she worked during her brief yet prolific career.[11] The Mexican muralist, painter, and fellow Communist David Alfaro Siqueiros proclaimed it "the first revolutionary photographic exhibition in Mexico." (He used this phrase as the title for his closing day address.) The journalist and critic Baltasar Dormundo who had lobbied the rector of the National Autonomous University of Mexico, Ignacio García Téllez, to sponsor the show supported this view but went further. Writing in *El Universal* on December 16, Dormundo declared, "Each [photograph] captures the revolutionary spirit of Mexico, with its pain and hunger, its anguish and wrath, with the almost religious ideology of the campesinos who could not read but carried a .30-.30 [rifle] and went to fight for land. Each photograph is Mexico, our most painful falters, our most recent sacrifices, our rectifications, our purest insistence for social justice" (quoted in Nieto Sotelo and Lozano Álvarez, 2000, 139).

What these remarks suggest is an appropriation of Modotti as a Mexican photographer. They reflect not just the attitude of Mexican artists and critics but also that of Modotti herself. How she came to embrace Mexico, with all its foibles and merits, is precisely the topic of *Tina in Mexico*. After a short preamble set in California, the film presents her trip to and arrival in Mexico with Weston in 1923, their romantic and professional relationship, friendships with local and foreign artists, travels to various regions, their estrangement, and Weston's return to the United States in 1925. It shows Modotti's apprenticeship and development as a photographer, her emotional life and political activism, including her affair with the Cuban Communist Julio Antonio Mella, which ended abruptly in 1929 with his murder. Modotti was deported one year later when she was accused of being involved in a conspiracy to assassinate President Pascual Ortíz Rubio. Her return to Mexico in 1939, her work on behalf of the Mexican Communist Party, and her death in 1942 are treated briefly at the end of the film.[12]

"Tomorrow they will put me on a boat bound for fascist Europe, wrenching me from the only place that has ever felt like home," a disembodied woman's voice says over shots of a moonlit sky crisscrossed by drifting clouds and framed by the silhouette of treetops. In the background, a melody composed by Bob Derkach and interpreted on the guitar by Robert Piltch complements the melancholy narration. A dissolve to a close-up of Tina, eyes closed and hands moving slowly across her face, ascertains the ownership of the voice. This initial narration closes with the words, "Mexico will always claim me no matter where I go. I'll lie here and wait for the sun. With my eyes closed the past surges up like the ash from Popocatepetl," accompanied by a shot of the sun rising above a mountain chain. Every element alerts the viewer to the film as a cinematic and narrative construct. Alternation and discontinuity predominate: first in the barely noticeable change from color to black-and-white stock and then by having two actors play Tina. Allegra Fulton, a Canadian, provides the offscreen voice, and Tania Cabagne Ibarra, a Mexican, performs in front of the camera.[13]

This credit sequence establishes that *Tina in Mexico* is not just another artist biography. It is a remarkable and profoundly moving film that deals with the difficulties raised by what Noble terms "the wholesale 'Mexicanization' of Modotti" (2000, xxiii). In its form and approach, this work is poles apart from *Frida,* the U.S.-produced film by Julie Taymor and Salma Hayek on Frida Kahlo released in 2002.[14] Rather than adjust the narrative to fit romanticized notions of female creativity and reduce the representation of Mexico to cultural clichés and overdetermined figurations of otherness, Longfellow opts for a minimalist style that is at once lyrical and austere, detached and invested in, yet cautious of the lure of the exotic. *Tina in Mexico* is a reflexive fiction driven by historicity. It engages with the growing body of work on Modotti by means of either direct citations or references to extant biographies and critical commentaries. It addresses

FIGURE 7.5. Tina in Mexico, *frame enlargement*

prevailing assumptions and, at times, even moves beyond them to suggest alternative ways to look at the photographer's life and work.

By the time Longfellow initiated the production of her film, the work of historical retrieval—rediscovering her life and admitting her work into the modernist canon—had already been done, thanks to curators, scholars, and writers in Mexico, the United States, and Europe. Prints purchased by museums, numerous shows, and record-setting prices at auctions are evidence of institutional approval. Yet the institutionalization of female artists is fraught with danger. A case in point is Frida Kahlo. Although Modotti has so far largely escaped the excesses of Fridamania, she also has been the subject of reification. An instance of this process, as Noble comments, is the importance given to location, period, and gender in the sale at Sotheby's of *Roses, Mexico* (1924) in 1991, and the use made of this image by its new owner, the San Francisco–based designer Susie Tomkins, as a hand tag for her line of Esprit sportswear (2000, 29). In one fell swoop, Mexico, the 1920s, and the photographer became, as she writes, "a commodity in a marketplace that ascribes value to images made by 'exotic' women in 'exotic' locations. This commodification of Modotti is a form of colonization that makes it difficult to plot either Modotti or

Mexico onto the cultural map as anything other than paradigms of exotic otherness" (2000, 29).

In light of these remarks, I believe it is legitimate to ask, what position does Longfellow take in regard to the manner in which Modotti has been constructed? I attempt to provide answers to this question in what follows. By means of two parallel modeling scenes, I consider how the film uses reflexivity to counteract the objectifying gaze in the nude photographs of Modotti taken by Weston. Next I comment on the film's representation of Modotti's engagement with iconic themes of *mexicanidad* and her views on photography as a radical practice. A discussion of Longfellow's treatment of the exotic is followed by an analysis of the segment that reconstructs Modotti's only exhibition of her work in Mexico, held in 1929.

Weston's Tina: From Artist's Model to Feminist Subject

I begin with a segment in the early part of *Tina in Mexico*. The action is set in 1923 and alternates between Edward (Carlos Hieber) standing on the rooftop with his camera and Tina lying naked on the veranda below to re-create the modeling session that produced *Tina on the Azotea* (1924). This is probably one of the most famous nude photographs of Modotti and was included in Weston's first Mexican exhibition, held at Aztec Land, a store that catered mainly to foreign visitors by selling books, handicrafts, and tourist guides. Cinematic devices are deployed strategically. Enhanced ambient sound effects and interior monologues reveal the characters' subjectivity, their mood and thoughts. The voices belong to the actors Karl Pruner and Allegra Fulton. Framing, dissolves, slow motion, editing, and masking are used to draw attention to the camera, disrupting the voyeuristic structures of the gaze and exposing the investment of the apparatus and of spectatorship in visual production.

If this scene visualizes the proprietary meanings of the artist's gaze found in Western representations of the female nude, it is also suggestive of Susan Sontag's remarks on documentary photography: "A photograph is not just the result of an encounter between an event and a photographer; picture-taking is an event in itself, and one with ever more peremptory rights—to interfere with, to invade, or to ignore whatever is going on" (1977, 11). By fictionalizing the photo session, Longfellow depicts the moment in which the subject becomes an object of representation and imagines the stories and subjectivities concealed behind the actual pictures. By using the distinctive features of the location to set Tina physi-

FIGURE 7.6. Tina in Mexico, *frame enlargement*

cally and emotionally apart from Edward's actions and practice, the director constructs a space, albeit imaginary, for her character to ascertain her individuality and to express herself. The dissolve from an incandescent shot of the sky reveals Tina naked, in medium shot with her back to the camera. The slow downward pan replicates her lethargic movements as she brings her arms forward and turns on her back; the sizzling noise and luminous midday lighting match perception and memory ("The sun is so hot at noon—fifteen minutes and you lose boundaries, melt into the dust and adobe. Just like Italy when I was a child"). Over the full frontal nude shots, Tina reclaims her agency by refusing to yield to Edward's desire to turn her body into a canvas for his experiments with light and texture. She says, "He doesn't know how much I am giving to him now, the arch of my back, my head turned to the light, breath held while he ticks off the seconds."

This scene places vision at the center of the narrative, if only to counteract its mastery. Black frames, dissolves, and inversions disrupt the objectifying gaze of the still and film cameras. After the initial shots of Edward standing next to his camera and getting ready to take pictures, only low-angle shots of the tripod and the legs and shadow of a male figure connote

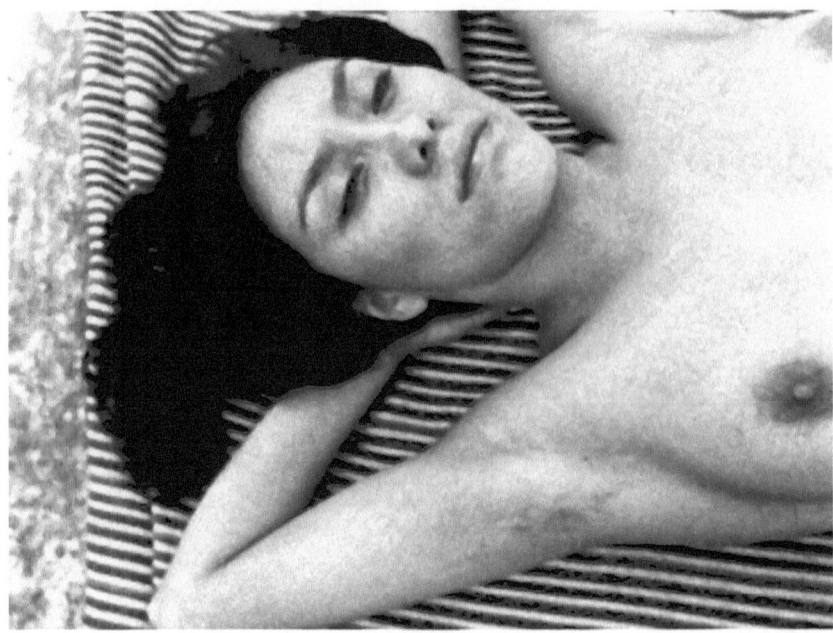

FIGURE 7.7. Tina in Mexico, *frame enlargement*

his presence, thus fracturing the dual function of the artist as owner and producer of the image (see figure 7.6). Over an upside-down image of Tina lying on a striped serape first and the actual Weston photograph after, Edward assumes the role of narrative agent of a process wherein the lover becomes an object, a photographic print to be exhibited and consumed. He says, "I held my breath while developing. The shadows are sharp and well defined. A good contrast between the flesh and blanket. The platinum paper makes printing slow and tedious but gives the final print very rich tones. Have to finish all printing before our first public show."

These aesthetic features are found later in the film, in a matching scene set in 1925 when the Weston-Modotti relationship was faltering. It fictionalizes the taking of Weston's photograph titled *Nude: Tina* (1924) to represent Tina's feelings of alienation and her awareness of what she has become to her lover. She says, "I wanted to give him so much. Is this all we share? The thin skin of emulsion as ephemeral as light?" The stark, grainy, and high-contrast shots, tight framing, and camera movement reveal what the photograph must contain to make the nude socially acceptable. These devices emphasize the materiality of Tina's body, the unshaved armpits and blemishes on the actor's skin. Reframing grants visual power to the female body, albeit briefly, to enable an interchange between viewer and image and to counter the objectification found in the Weston photograph. As the live action dissolves into the actual photographs of *Tina on the Azotea* and *Nude: Tina* at the end of these two scenes, another narrative has come to light: the politics of feminism. To reclaim Modotti as a subject means to draw attention, as Noble writes, to "the complex and charged relationship that Modotti enjoys in the visual realm" (2000, 4). This is precisely what Longfellow achieves in her re-creation of the modeling sessions. Cinematic devices are used critically to counter the objectifying gaze of the Weston photographs, and the fetishism of the body associated with the female nude, and to expose the investment of the apparatus and spectatorship in visual production.

Tina: Cultural Tourist and Political Activist

To this point, the film adheres quite closely to the chronology of Modotti's life; it matches reconstruction scenes to the period in which the photographs were produced. This pattern is broken in the segment that deals with the years 1927–1929 and focuses on Tina's work as an artist and Communist militant. By deferring to a later segment the relationship with Mella and his murder, her practice takes on an affirmative dimension. She is depicted as being invested in and responsive to her subjects, not traumatized by loss and the public vilification of which she was the victim after the shooting death of her lover. The segment consists of scenes that show Tina's trips with the American anthropologist and publisher Frances Toor to the Isthmus of Tehuantepec to shoot photographs for *Mexican Folkways* and with the muralist and painter Xavier Guerrero to attend a Party congress in Xalapa, her job at the Communist newspaper *El Machete*, and briefly her collaboration with Rivera and Orozco to photograph their murals and paintings.[15] Except for a brief interjection by Anita Brenner (Tanja Jacobs), the narrative agency belongs exclusively to Tina/Modotti. Her voice-over accompanies slide show–type montage sequences of her photographs of indigenous women and rural and urban peasant workers. Among those showcased are *Woman of Tehuantepec Carrying Xecapixtle* (1929), *The Hands Off Nicaragua Committee* (1928), "*A proud little agrarista*," *Mexican Peasant Boy* (c. 1927), *Street Scene outside a Pulquería* (1928), and *Mexican Peasants Reading "El Machete"* (1928).

Tinisima is a novelized biography written by the Mexican feminist, novelist, and cultural critic Elena Poniatowska. The short section on Tina's return from Juchitán ends as follows: "'How did you end in this country?'

Na'Chiña asked her. Tina remembers the question and closes her eyes; she feels that she has lost something along the way and begins to spin out her memories, some aloud, some to herself. There, before her, stands Na'Chiña: her interlocutor and unlikely accomplice" (1995, 53). Although Poniatowska and Longfellow use the Tehuantepec trip to invite the reader and viewer to assume the role of "interlocutor and accomplice," they do so differently. For the novelist, it is a springboard to chronicle Tina's early years in California and Mexico. For the filmmaker, it is a catalyst for representing the tensions at work in the photographer's investment in *mexicanidad*, the various—at times antagonistic—positions and practices around the question of what is Mexican that became the driving force behind postrevolutionary cultural nationalism in the 1920s.

The Tehuantepec segment brings up the issues of resistance and appropriation, if only to reimagine the self-other relationship. Tina is established in the opening as a cultural tourist who is responsive to and knowledgeable about the place this region occupies in the Mexican imaginary. Over tracking landscape shots, she says, "I close my eyes and move backwards in time, before Cortez, back to the heart of Diego's Mexico, the land of Zapotec, Mixteca and Chichimecas." Yet her account of taking pictures undermines the nativist fantasy. "Each time," she says later over a slide show–type montage of Modotti photographs, "I have to rush to find my frame and exposure. No time to do a calculation. I'll just average at f11. Suddenly they spot me—a strange creature under a dark cloth and they speed by, like birds in flight." Once again, the photographer-subject relationship is put to the test: Tina's fascination is at odds with the women's behavior. Although Modotti's *Women in the Marketplace* series records scenes of street life and everyday activities and focuses on the graceful posture and sprightly walk of the women of Juchitán, the women are shown either with their backs to the camera or interacting with each other. The story-behind-the-pictures approach in these scenes points to the dissonance between an idealized view and the practicalities of working in the field, in other words, between the Tehuana as a gendered icon of authenticity in the practices of *mexicanidad* and the women's refusal to submit to the camera's objectifying gaze.

Tina's remark—"I promise to send photographs. They promise to make me into a real woman"—is followed by the often-reproduced self-portrait from 1929. It shows her in a *huipil* (embroidered short-sleeved blouse) and long multilayered ruffled skirt, the traditional dress worn by the women of this region in the state of Oaxaca. Modotti biographer Patricia Albers calls this picture "a spiritual passport, and a talisman of her love for the

Mexican people" (1999, 224). Placed here, at the end of the montage of portraits, this image reveals Tina's self-identification with Mexico as a performance of feminine identity in which the women of Tehuantepec, like the fictional character of Na'Chiña in Poniatowska's novel, are the interlocutors and accomplices.

Two themes dominate in the Xalapa and *El Machete* scenes: Tina's position as a political tourist and Modotti's views on photography as a radical medium. The standard device of documentary exposition (matching voice-over and actual photographs) is used to visualize these themes. Photographs in the Xalapa scene are arranged according to scale (from long to medium and close-up) and move from shots of the assembly to group and individual portraits to signal a shift from a detached to an invested point of view. Over the pictures of men, women, and children standing in line and facing the camera, Tina says, "They are more curious than shy, a lady photographer wearing pants, smoking like a fiend! I crouch in the shadows while they arrange their serapes and look directly into the camera." Thus the moment in which histories and subjectivities meet is re-created. It is the awareness of difference that enables an exchange. This idea is represented by means of Modotti's well-known photograph *"A proud little agrarista," Mexican Peasant Boy* in which affect is poignantly conveyed and historicized. To pose for the camera is an affirmative gesture of identity, as evidenced in the innumerable pictures of peasant-soldiers taken during the revolution. What is more, this image evokes an experience Modotti shared with other female photographers in Mexico, one that Poniatowska describes: "To take a photograph is to create a bond" (1990, 55).

The *El Machete* scenes represent how artistic and political consciousness overlapped and found expression in Modotti's photographs. Over a group of pictures that include the photomontage *Poverty and Elegance* (1928) and *Hands Resting on Tool* (1926), Tina says, "I believe photography has the most radical potential. Precisely because it can only be produced in the present and because it is based on what exists before the camera, photography cannot avoid life, in all its harshness and chaos." This montage reasserts Modotti's modernism as being at once an aesthetic gesture and an activist intervention. If composition, texture, and framing resonate with formalism, the themes expose in a compelling way the contradictions between the realities of everyday life and the reified discourse on modernity promoted by the postrevolutionary state. The images printed in the Communist newspaper, as Mraz notes, "are probably the first examples of published photographs that questioned the new Mexican order" (1997a, 1086). By rearranging into a discrete segment the photographs of Tehuana women and indigenous rural and urban workers taken at different points in time, the film rehistoricizes Tina's self-identification with Mexico in terms of gender and class. In doing so, it politicizes Modotti's identity and practice.

Negotiations and Constructions of Difference

In the decades following the revolution, the nationalist Mexican intelligentsia played host to the international avant-garde. Britton provides a glimpse of this encounter when he describes a "wild party" hosted by Weston and Modotti in December 1925.

> In attendance was a collection of artists, art critics and writers dominated by Diego Rivera, the mountainous, free-willed Marxist, with his strikingly beautiful, unpredictably assertive wife, Lupe. Rivera loomed over the group not only by his artistic eminence but also by his imposing six-foot, three-hundred-pound frame. Three of his admirers (at least in the 1920s) were there: Jean Charlot, a sensitive young artist enamored of Mexican themes; Carleton Beals, a loquacious journalist with a misdirected inclination towards poetry; and Anita Brenner, a precocious Mexican-born writer and art critic. All of them were lively conversationalists with literary ambitions. Manuel Hernández Galván, a radical Mexican politician with a talent for playing guitar and singing, performed for the group. Frances Toor was not as garrulous as the others, but her rejection of bourgeois values and dedication to Indian culture gave her acceptance among the bohemians. ([1961] 1973, 50)

Tina in Mexico evokes this get-together in a party sequence that begins with a medium shot of Weston. It shows him with his back to the camera, smoking. The accompanying voice-over says, "The mist is lifting off the volcanoes in the distance. The sages predict that Popocatepetl will erupt in the next week. Too bad it cannot be postponed till the 31st, our New Year's Eve party. We might dance to our doom." With Tina's disembodied voice describing and a traditional mariachi ensemble providing the musical accompaniment, the sequence proposes a notion of authenticity that is based on visualizing rather than objectifying difference. Except for a short insert (a black-and-white photograph of a couple in cross-dressing costumes), no attempt is made to re-create the artist's account ("Everyone feasted on Lupe's delicious *chiles en nogada*. I smoked Edward's pipe while he wore garters and an old dress of mine with pink pointed buttons for nipples. He flirted shamelessly with Nahui [Olin], and ran through the full repertoire of a female coquette. Lupe was enraged and told him he was *sin verguenza,* without shame"). Instead, the scene shows *Los mariachis de oro* performing in the garden below and the guests lingering on and tossing coins from the open second-floor gallery. If the switch from the black-and-white images of Weston to vivid color (the volcano and party shots) is consistent with the predisposition for the picturesque found in foreign-made films, camera positions and editing produce variable modes of spectatorship. Reverse high-angle and low-angle shots destabilize the gaze, with guests and musicians being at once subjects and objects, and construct a fragmented view of the setting and action. What the effect of these devices conveys is Longfellow's attitude toward the exotic as a mode of representation waiting to be deconstructed.

Her critical awareness and sensibility converge with those of Modotti in an earlier sequence about a trip she took with Weston in February 1924 that ends with a photograph titled *Nopales, Mexico, ca. 1925.* Guitar music complements Tina's statement—"I want to see for myself what is happening in the countryside"—and description—"Arriving at a village, we found it barricaded awaiting a raid. Two days before [Adolfo] de la Huerta had attacked and taken away some thirty horses. Now on the roof, behind sandbags, soldiers leaned on their rifles. We wished them courage and left quickly." The next scene begins with static black-and-white shots of a man walking toward the camera, wisps of clouds in the sky and a hill in the distance, being replaced by color images of the same landscape. As a slow pan sideways reveals the chassis of a parked car, the perspective narrows. Over a dissolve back to black-and-white, from a soft to deep focus shot of the prickly pear cactus growing on the arid ground, Tina says, "I managed a quick composition of the *nopal.* I believe that I am starting to see in monochrome, and not be blinded by the colors that surround us." With the gaze as the primary motif, these scenes inscribe the multiple mediations at work in representation: the picture-seeking traveler and photographic technology. While movement mimics how the observant photographer scans the environment, variable focal distances and stock changes reproduce how the camera operates and what it registers. The freeze frame on Modotti's photograph with which this sequence ends is, in my view, far less meaningful than the process that is being visualized; in other words, the merging of subjectivities—those of the photographer and filmmaker—dazzled yet struggling to overcome the lure of the exotic.

To finish, I comment on the segment dealing with the first show entirely devoted to Modotti's work and the only one held during her lifetime. It starts with an intertitle and a period photograph of Modotti standing in front of some of the works in the exhibition. It includes two sections that draw attention to public constructions of Tina, as a thoroughly modern woman and as a photographer sensitive to the Mexican ethos. A different character narrates each section: the press coverage scene by a male announcer and the montage of Modotti's photographs by Diego. Raoul Bhaneja and Arturo Fresolone play the journalist and Diego Rivera, respectively. The montage includes the following photographs: *Mother and Child, Tehuantepec* (c. 1929), and *An Aztec Baby* and *An Aztec Mother* (c. 1926–1927.)

To represent the press coverage of the show, Longfellow creates a filmed reportage scene. In it, she simulates the stylistic elements and format associated with silent newsreels and present-day television, down to the flickering grainy image and standard shots of the interviewee in her home. There is even the ubiquitous walk toward the camera that shows Tina, camera in hand, coming down a staircase. The announcer's commentary establishes her as being attractive—"Suddenly we found ourselves before a beautiful suffragette, that among suffragettes may be the only one that is beautiful and kind"—and modern—she "smokes one of her favorite *Buen Tono* cigarettes." He mediates her thoughts on photography and Mexico—"She tells us she hates retouching, likes big cities, and loves all things Mexican"—and wraps up with his own opinions—"We are enthused by the composition of heads which file before our eyes, lacking those poses so manipulated by vulgar photographers." Diego is more specific in his opinion. Though he invokes Weston and Weston's alleged influence on Modotti's work, he sees hers as superior—"more abstract, more intellectual, more ethereal"—and admires her capacity for capturing "the essence of Mexico, to see beneath its cruel externals."

By exposing the rhetoric of femininity and influence, this segment draws attention to the collusion of patriarchal and art historical discourses in the construction of the female artist as a historical persona. Yet the actor's performance and the photographs get in the way to contest the objectification of Tina and the essentialist valorization of Modotti's work. Tina faces the camera with confidence; her body language and above all her gaze are assertive. In the pictures that accompany Diego's description, the focal point is entirely on the mother-child interaction; intimacy is represented primarily as a tactile experience. *An Aztec Baby* and *An Aztec Mother* suggest a different way to visualize the female body, drawing the viewer to experience it as tangible and corporeal. Thus, image-sound counterpoint generates a competing narrative, one that reinscribes Tina into history as a feminist subject.

FIGURE 7.8. Tina in Mexico, *frame enlargement*

Tina in Mexico, then, moves beyond normative assumptions to suggest alternative ways to look at Modotti's life and work. It represents her as a thoroughly modern woman, a photographer and a Communist militant, revealing a subjectivity deeply affected by Mexican culture and politics, one that responds to national myths and becomes its subject. It is at once a poetic and a complex film. It uses archival footage, dramatic reenactments, stylized citations, and compelling voice-over narration to turn a historical figure into a film character, to reconfigure Tina's subjectivity and politicize her practice. These cinematic devices serve to reimagine the stories and subjectivities behind the pictures—those of Modotti taken by Weston and those taken by Modotti during the five years in which she worked as a photographer. More important, Longfellow adopts a feminist position, using aesthetic strategies critically to draw attention to what is at stake in feminist representation and to implicate the viewer in visual production. While reinstating the artist's narrative and visual agency, the filmmaker reveals the part played by apparatus-mediated vision and discourse in the construction of Modotti's Mexican identity.

In this chapter I have examined two films dealing with foreigners in Mexico who were transformed during their visits and whose work focused on politics, social relations, and daily life to reinterpret Mexico. These films are, in my view, an appropriate way to conclude this book. Each suggests the value of reexamining periods that have come to represent the most intense—even conflictive—moments of Mexico-U.S. relations. *Reed: Insurgent Mexico* reconstructs the brief yet lasting effect of the encounter between Mexicans and Americans who crossed the border to report on, photograph, and film the revolution. *Tina in Mexico* reexamines the participation of foreign and local artists in the vast creative enterprise known as the "Mexican renaissance," the modernist practices that merged with nationalism to reinterpret the revolution. Both are experimental and innovative works that represent the realities and mythologies of the Mexican Revolution, all the while acknowledging its construction. The first adopts a Mexican perspective to revisit John Reed's journalistic account and propose a reengagement with the cultural legacy of the revolution. The second assumes a feminist point of view to explore the complexities at work in the remaking of Mexico's identity in the postrevolutionary period and the appropriation of Tina Modotti as a Mexican photographer.

Conclusion
THOUGHTS ON WORKING WITH THE ARCHIVE

Beyond any clichés summoned by films using as a visual and narrative backdrop the events that took place and the actors who participated in Mexico during the period 1910–1917, the revolution was a defining historical moment. It has shaped the modern identity of the country for Mexicans and foreigners alike and has informed to this day the ideology of Mexican nationalism, even as modernist concepts of nationhood are being challenged by globalization. The revolution captured the imaginations of progressive intellectuals and artists in Mexico and elsewhere and sparked their militancy and creativity. Whether their fascination was shaped by direct contact or mediated by representation, they were energized by the nationalist and modernist impulses of the revolution. In due course, they became the protagonists and interlocutors of a dialogue across cultures that endowed the visual archive with a transnational genealogy. To the extent that most appropriated the meanings of the revolution and interiorized its experiences, the narratives and images they produced, primarily in the ensuing decades, affected the ways in which the Mexican Revolution was and is arguably still represented. Thus the revolution is an accumulation of images and myths that make up Mexico's nationalist and modernist narrative.

The political incidents and military milestones, achievements or failings of larger-than-life heroes, and acts of bravery and violence by and against ordinary people that marked the years 1910–1917 inform *la Revolución,* a master narrative meticulously and selectively reconstructed in the 1920s and celebrated in the 1930s. As the historian Thomas Benjamin explains, "Contemporaries told stories, drew comparisons, and made arguments about recent events in particular ways to justify their actions, to condemn their enemies, to win converts and to do much more. Their talking, singing, drawing, painting, and writing invented *la Revolución:* a name transformed into what appeared to be a natural and self-evident part of reality and history" (2000, 14). Clearly more than a narrative, because it was painted, photographed, and filmed by Mexicans and foreigners, the revolution is an extensive archive whose substance, meaning, and pleasure depend on the mutual bearing of visual and mass media on the multiple ways in which history and culture are experienced. What follows is meant as a brief summary of the issues discussed in this book, with emphasis on pervasive themes and modes of representing Mexico and historicizing the revolution.

Reaching into the past to reflect the present of a nation and an identity in the making, the visual archive of the revolution has been disseminated in multiple forms. Consisting of period images that have been used to document, celebrate, and mythologize episodes, actors, and settings, it has been evoked and reinterpreted in fiction films. Alongside the images of trains moving people and military equipment across deserts and valleys, rotting corpses and buildings in ruins, are numerous pictures of anonymous peasant soldiers, *soldaderas,* and children, renowned military and political figures. Whether they are wearing bullet belts across their chests or field uniforms and urban clothes, all look directly at the viewer. The assertive gestures of identity and historical agency in these individual and group portraits exemplify to what extent visual production was a collective process in which producers, subjects, and consumers were equally implicated.

In this sense, the visual archive of the revolution is more than a historical record. Its symbolic, rhetorical, and affective power resides in the ability to represent the revolution as an event and a discourse. Integral to this power is an awareness of the role of media in conveying the social and cultural dynamics generated by incidents and actors. Yet, as Monsiváis points out in regard to the photographs in the Casasola Archive, this imagery is "more than a lesson in history, is (obviously) a visual experience, not a class in national politics. As we do from the films *Memorias de un mexicano* of Salvador Toscano, *Epopeyas de la revolución* of Gustavo Carrero, and Fernando de Fuentes's *El compadre Mendoza* and *¡Vámonos con Pancho Villa!* ... we want primary data: we want to understand how—depending on the prevailing cultural scheme of things—the faces of our nation conceal and reveal, and the extent to which we have given up or condemned the gestures and deeds that swept away a whole political, economic and social structure" (1984, 15).

Of all the themes of the archive, the most ubiquitous is Villa. At once a historical actor and a cinematic construct, he is the embodiment of the Mexican Revolution. Whether he appears on camera as the actual Villa or is interpreted by actors, his character personifies one of the most overdetermined features of the revolutionary genre: the collusion of mythmaking and historicity. Even when absent from the screen, as in *Wild Bunch*, where he turns up in the guise of the famed Dorados corps of the Northern Division, he is an agent of the film's discourse. By virtue of this overt reference, the film reinforces the enduring appeal of Mexico in the U.S. cultural imaginary, signaling to what extent the visual themes of the revolution overlap with the iconography of masculinity and nation making in the western genre.

For this reason, it would be useful to reconsider *Revolución o la sombra de Pancho Villa* (Manuel Contreras Torres, 1931). As the title of this early Mexican sound feature suggests, the revolutionary leader appears literally as a shadow. His silhouette on the wall and a close-up of his boots and riding crop serve to visualize the awe- and fear-filled responses he elicited from followers and foes. When he is actually seen, he materializes as the historical Villa in a brief shot showing him at the Ojinaga battle in 1914. Taken from the newsreel produced by the Mutual Film Company, this image is included in a four-minute montage combining extant Mexican and U.S. period footage. Amid picturesque images of hacienda and camp life and predictable situations involving gracious *chinas* and opportunistic *hacendados,* brave *charros* and their folksy sidekicks, this sequence stands out. It signals the film's historicizing intent—to enlist the archive as an illustrative device to depict Villa's military campaigns: the Zacatecas victory in 1914 and the Celaya defeat in 1916 at the hands of Obregón's army. Period materials are used too as insert shots in battle scenes, presumably to bypass the budgetary expense and technical problems of filming reenactments. Be that as it may, the archive grants authenticity to what is otherwise a conventional melodrama, just as the Villa citation in *The Wild Bunch* validates what would have merely been the usual plotting of the western.

Likewise, *Viva Zapata!* (Elia Kazan, 1952), a film still viewed in Mexico and elsewhere as the most serious Hollywood attempt to deal with the revolution, draws on the Casasola photographs for legitimacy and inserts an ideological narrative into the archive. It quotes the picture of Pancho Villa and Emiliano Zapata taken during the occupation of the capital by the revolutionary armies in December 1914 and incorporates the story behind the image into its discourse. By re-creating the leaders' encounter at the National Palace, it uses Villa's invitation to Zapata to take a seat beside him to be photographed and Zapata's initial refusal to sit on the presidential chair to visualize the corrupting potential of power. The making of what is arguably one of the best-known and iconic images of the revolution becomes an indictment of populism—read: communism. Based on a screenplay by John Steinbeck, directed by a notorious anti-Communist, and produced in the midst of the Cold War, *Viva Zapata!* is less a film about Mexico than about U.S. democracy. With the charismatic Marlon Brando in the lead role, Zapata was reconfigured as a tragic American hero; his radical posture on agrarian reform and defense of Indian community land rights ignored by portraying him as an idealist, victimized and betrayed by authoritarianism and political opportunism. Having been vetoed by the Syndicate of Film Technicians and Workers, headed by Gabriel Figueroa, Kazan was unable to film in Mexico and opted instead for locations in and around Roma, Texas. He made the most of the architectural landmarks and the countryside scenery of this small town on the Rio Grande across from Ciudad Miguel Alemán (Tamaulipas), founded in the eighteenth century by Mexican ranchers, to replicate the look and feel of the period. As a result, the visual design of the film favors the picturesque by blending themes and motifs inspired equally by U.S. and Mexican modes of representing rural culture.

For left-leaning and liberal writers such as Sinclair and Steinbeck, as for radicals such as Reed and Modotti earlier, the appeal of the revolution was initially fueled by geographic proximity and ideology, then by the improvement of U.S.-Mexico relations that produced what Delpar has aptly called "the enormous vogue for things Mexican." Intellectuals and artists profited from policies of political and cultural cooperation in the 1920s and 1930s and participated in equal measure in the construction of Mexico's postrevolutionary identity. Central to this process was the recuperation, translation, and commodification of iconic images of nation, mainly those associated with the land and its people.

This appropriation of elements considered "typical" and "authentic" on both sides of the border complicates the issue of what constitutes "Mexico" in Hollywood films dealing with the revolution. The prevalence of contrasting, at times concurrent, visual themes that designate Mexico as being at once primitive and brutal, which can be found in *Viva Villa!* and *The Wild Bunch,* for example, can be traced back to the Mexican-American War. To the extent that this dichotomy has historically informed American perceptions and representations of their southern neighbor, it reappears in the imagery generated in the 1910–1917 period, in the reports of the diplomats, political activists, and journalists and in the pictures taken by cameramen and photographers that circulated in newsreels, fiction films, and postcards. If these U.S. visitors and image makers shaped foreign attitudes about the revolution, they also became its earliest historiographers. Unable to make sense of the chaotic events and shifting military and political alliances, they reverted to the bandit and greaser types popularized in pulp fiction since 1847. It is from this standpoint that I regard the Villa-Mutual contract as symptomatic of the manner in which prevailing views about Mexico collided with—by and large to the detriment of—the cultural, social, and political dynamics of the revolution.

To become collective memory, before endless repetition in films and other media turned the period imagery into fetishized commodity, the visual archive of the revolution was put at the service of nationalism and given a pedagogical mission. In line with the nation-building agenda of the Mexican state, incidents were resignified and characters reconfigured to represent reconciliation and embody revolutionary ideals. Aimed at reifying the heroism of the masses or valorizing the Indian and the mestizo as models of identity, the archive was assigned the same task as that given to the murals by Education Secretary José Vasconcelos in the 1920s: to integrate multiple subjectivities and experiences into a single identity and history. This imagery appealed to tradition and "to myths and ideas already formulated during the wars of independence. Here was the origin of the prevalent 'indigenismo' and the exaltation of insurgents. In this instance the revolution represented a revival and a revaluation of fading traditions and repudiation of the liberal positivist epoch" (Rochfort, 1991, 15).

Consequently, another prevailing theme in the revolutionary genre is Mexico's rural culture. It became fashionable on both sides of the border because it validated vernacular culture and boosted nostalgia for a less threatening time. The exclusion of indicators of urban experience and modernity in national and foreign-made films is the result of the reification of traditions originating in the country's indigenous, colonial, and rural past. In the 1930s and 1940s, political debates on art and mass culture and cultural nationalism were factors in the recoding of signifiers of nation, most of which had been constructed in the nineteenth century and adopted by visual and mass media in the next, often by blending autochthonous and foreign elements. Celebrations of folklore, ethnicity, and rural culture in Mexican films were aimed at rectifying the racist stereotypes and the faux-folkloric inventions of Hollywood cinema. However, as Segre remarks, Hollywood "fashioned or recycled stereotypes (despite the scrutiny of the Mexican censors) that became familiar incarnations to the growing, cinema-going audience of the pervasive *mexicanidad* of political and cultural rhetoric" (2007, 90).

A distinctive feature of films made in the 1930s dealing with the revolution is the reconversion of visual themes and motifs associated with picturesque modes of representing Mexico. Influenced by European romanticism and its nostalgic predilection for the primitive, the picturesque was popularized in Mexico by way of illustrated albums, notably the travel albums *Voyage pittoresque et archéologique dans la partie plus intéressante du Mexique* (Paris, 1836) and *Monumentos de Méjico tomados del natural y litografiados por Pedro Gualdi, pintor de perspectivas* (Mexico, 1841), by Karl Nebel and Pietro Gualdi respectively, and the graphic compilation *Los mexicanos pintados por sí mismos* (Mexicans Painted by Themselves) (1853-1855) (Segre, 2007, 37-39). The latter was fundamental in the making and dissemination of *costumbrista* (literary and pictorial depiction of customs and character types) iconography. While the intent of this and similar works was "to reclaim local culture from the perceived condescension of foreign commentaries," Segre explains, "their iconography was neither formally naïve nor narrowly propagandistic but inflected with a developed critical awareness" (2007, 41). Visual production in Mexican cinema exhibits a similar approach. Of note is the systematic inclusion of musical interludes featuring well-known performers in the films of the early 1930s. Their renditions of *corridos,* folk songs, or ballads in camp life scenes serve to showcase rural culture. Still regarded at the time as a novelty, sound was put at the service of historicity. The theatrical mise-en-scène evokes the *cuadro de costumbres,* integrating into the revolutionary scenario the festive mood and enjoyment of the familiar found in the domestic and street life vignettes painted by José Agustín Arrieta (1802-1874) and the *charrería* scenes of Ernesto Icaza y Sánchez (1866-1935).

Whereas the cinematic translation of nineteenth-century portrayals of everyday life aims mostly, as in the past, at idealizing tradition and depicting national unity, this imagery has at times been used critically. *El compadre Mendoza* (Fernando de Fuentes, 1933), for instance, draws on the figurative and narrative motifs of Mexican genre painting to reveal the ambiguities of the social and affective structures of rural life. By focusing on moral crisis and betrayal, it subverts two persistent views of the revolution: as a rupture with the positivism of the Porfiriate and as a cataclysm generated by a primeval social force (*la bola*). Visualizations of the picturesque, including in the musical scene in this film, underscore class difference and conflict in a manner that is similar to the use of *charrería* in *Let's Go with Pancho Villa!* In conjunction with Orozco's graphic work, as in the extant footage of the "Maguey" episode in *Que Viva Mexico!* the *charro* iconography counteracts idyllic visions of Mexico and the new social contract promoted by postrevolutionary historiography.

With its distinctive fusion of local and foreign idioms, Mexican modernism is heavily invested in the rural. It is a seminal signifier of authenticity and a theme whose normative meanings are either memorialized in officially commissioned art forms or put to the test in the practices of a radical avant-garde. These features explain the affinities between visual arts and cinema and are the result—as noted about the Soviet director's unfinished project—of a series of conversations across cultures. No other film, in my view, exemplifies this notion better than *The Fugitive* (John Ford, 1947). Directed by an American, photographed by a Mexican, and based on a novel by an Englishman, the film reveals the tensions, and incompatibilities, within modernism. The cinematographer, Gabriel Figueroa, reinvents the rural Mexico that Graham Greene depicted as miserable, uncultured, and fanatical in his travel account *Another Mexico* (aka *The Lawless Roads*, 1939) and novel *The Power and the Glory* (1940).

The literary critic Ronald Walker explains that the work of British writers set in Mexico reveals a subjectivity deeply affected by the country: one that responds to national myths and becomes its subject and expresses itself in a simultaneous attraction and hostility. What he calls "the mystique of Mexico" is the fascination with a place and an ethos that contain all the necessary ingredients—history, landscape, violence, and native cultures—to make it "a veritable treasure of the exotic" (1978, 2). How Figueroa negotiates this paradox is worth considering. His imagery grants symbolic meanings to the characters and landscapes they inhabit. Expressionist lighting and minimalist deep-focus compositions highlight the intangible to turn the story of a wayward Catholic priest into a parable of faith, martyrdom, and renewal. The result is a visual construction of the primitive that evokes at once the selective processes of identity construction in Mexico in the 1930s and 1940s and those that have romanticized Mexico's peasant culture in foreign representations.

To the extent that Figueroa's signature style brings together the avant-garde impulse of Eisenstein's aesthetics with the commercial imperatives of mainstream filmmaking, his collaboration with Ford is indicative of the cinematographer's position as an agent of the genealogical lines that converge in the 1950s and 1960s. As noted above in regard to the Kazan and Peckinpah films, the visual archive is appropriated and reconfigured in accordance with historical, political, and cultural agendas. Whether used as citations or recoded, the iconic themes and motifs point to the collusion of historicity and mythmaking, endow the imagery of the revolution with patrimonial, ideological, and commodity value, and reinforce the transnational dynamics of the archive.

Exchange and translation are also key elements in the fashioning of what film scholars and commentators have designated the classical

Mexican style and associated with the work of the Fernández-Figueroa team. The impulse to dignify the revolution manifests itself in their now-canonical films by way of the didacticism proper to melodrama, the emblematic characters and the compositional symmetries and tonal contrasts in the visuals. The austere quality of the imagery stems from the graphic arts, an expression that inspired Figueroa because, as Segre notes, "its simplified and stylized compositions, the apocalyptic binarism of black and white, seemed to offer an antidote to the mystifications of 'local colour' and the foreign distortions of the picturesque" (2007, 94). The visual themes and motifs that emerged from this search for a "truly" national aesthetic came to represent "Mexico" and enhanced the cultural standing of cinema, notwithstanding Rivera's public criticism of the cinematographer's techniques (Segre, 2007, 109–110). Inferior imitations turned this iconography into stereotypes, revealing its shortcomings but hindering a better appreciation of its complexity. As my remarks suggest, the urban locations in *Abandoned Women* provoke questions about what happens when social realities make untenable the primacy of the rural in the revolutionary scenario.

As state discourse transformed the revolution into an overarching narrative of nation and modernity, the Mexican film industry capitalized on the nostalgia for the golden age and the commodity value of folklore. To guarantee its survival in the face of foreign competition and the rise of television in the 1950s, producers sought to revitalize the revolutionary genre by recurring to formulaic big-budget color productions, screen celebrities, and historical locations. The folklorized-to-death spectacles of the 1960s Mexican cinema, as Monsiváis writes, changed a "historical movement into a spectacle filled with trains, *soldaderas,* executions, horse cavalcades, cannons, [and] admirable deaths on the portals of Progress" (1995, 119). This trend toward spectacle notwithstanding, Mexican cinema has time and again represented the disruptive effects of the revolution on the social and cultural fabric. The existence of such films points to the matter of competing narratives and alternative modes of visualizing the revolutionary theme.

The women who rode the trains, cooked the food, and comforted the soldiers, and fought and died for the revolution are the protagonists of *La negra Angustias* (Matilde Landeta, Mexico, 1949) and *La soldadera* (José Bolaños, Mexico, 1966). In both films, the archetypal figure of Mexican wars is deconstructed. Whether she is an Afro-*mestiza* colonel or a fair-skinned bride-to-be, she is revealed as a gendered and racialized visual construct around which meanings of female identity are fought and negotiated. As in the numerous photographs in the Casasola Archive, she drifts precariously between legend and history, as a spectacle of femininity or a frail, yet unruly and resistant agent of her own destiny. Whether considered as antidotes to *La cucaracha* or *Like Water for Chocolate*, these films signal a break with the ethnicity-, gender-, and class-inflected representations of the revolutionary genre.

Coinciding with the revisionist enterprise of Mexican historiography, recent films have deployed the visual archive of the revolution critically and rearranged its meanings. At stake is the uneasy and shifting relationship between representation and discourse, whereby the potentially radical meanings of period imagery—co-opted by the postrevolutionary Mexican state to conform to its mythologizing project—remain open to reappropriation by cinema. If *Reed: Insurgent Mexico* is an example, to paraphrase Ayala Blanco, that the revolution still deserves a vignette, it anticipates the reflexive disposition found in *Tina in Mexico* and *The Lost Reels of Pancho Villa*. Formalist strategies in these films shed light on the complexities of visual production and the negotiations at work in historicizing the archive. Moreover, these films revalidate the significance of the Mexican Revolution for the history of visual culture. The revolution not only became an early example of the convergence of film and politics, profit, and journalism; it was also an event that typifies the role of visual technologies in shaping modern historicity.

To conclude, the approach I have taken to the revolutionary genre is an attempt to move beyond conventional readings that see national films strictly in terms of their alignment with official views and foreign films determined by derogatory stereotypes. Instead, I have considered cinema's alignment with the visual vernacular of Mexican modernity, that is, to the repertoire of nationalist images that were fashioned and circulated in the various visual and media practices before being reconstructed in the 1930s. The resilience of these historical modes of representing nation and identity has led me to examine multiple mediations at work in cinematic representations of the revolution. If cinema has recoded the visual themes and motifs of the archive, the meanings that emerge from their use are unstable and as such subject to competing interpretations and revisions.

Notes

CHAPTER 1

1. Guzmán wrote *The Eagle and the Serpent* during his second exile in Spain (1924–1935). Initially it was published in installments in *El Universal,* one of Mexico City's daily newspapers, as soon as each chapter was written. It appeared in book form in 1928, and the first English translation was printed in New York in 1930.

2. Considering the involvement of the Ministry of Defense, it is not surprising that military figures from the various factions who distinguished themselves in these battles are named, and at times appear, in the film.

3. As Miquel indicates, this documentary is an updated version of *La marcha del ejército constitucionalista por diversas poblaciones de la república y su entrada a Guadalajara y México y el viaje del señor Carranza a esta ciudad* (The March of the Constitutionalist Army through Different Cities of the Republic and Its Entrance to Mexico City and Guadalajara, and the Trip of Mr. Carranza until His Arrival to This City [Veracruz]) exhibited in Veracruz in December 1914 (2005, 17).

4. An unrelated scene that shows Obregón participating in a corn harvest breaks the continuity of the sequence. Although the effect is disruptive, the markings on the existing print indicate that this scene was placed there to facilitate reel changes during projection.

5. Further research may expand these attributions and identify footage presumed to have been shot by other contemporary filmmakers, such as Julio Lamadrid, Guillermo Becerril, José Cava, and Indalcio Noriega (De los Reyes, 1996, 15–16).

6. The foundation has also facilitated investigation into the work of Toscano, and lately Abítia, by providing access to its extensive visual and paper holdings. It has been involved in film restoration and has distributed valuable research materials. In 2003 it produced the CD-Rom *Un pionero del cine en México: Salvador Toscano y su colección de carteles* (Salvador Toscano: A Pioneer of Cinema in Mexico and His Collection of Placards and Handbills) (in association with the Autonomous National University of Mexico) and a video documentary, *La revolución maderista: Un triunfo mediático. Investigación sobre el contexto político de las imágenes filmadas por Salvador Toscano* (The Maderista Revolution: A Media Tri-

umph. Investigation of the Political Content of the Images Filmed by Salvador Toscano) (with credits to Alejandra Moreno Toscano, researcher and writer, and Silvia Manuel Signoret, researcher and coordinator).

7. In addition to segments discussed below, it is worth mentioning those relative to the meetings of revolutionary leaders, including Pancho Villa, Pascual Orozco, and Venustiano Carranza, with Francisco I. Madero at a makeshift camp on the Rio Grande in the outskirts of Ciudad Juarez (1911); the battle of Bachimba in the state of Chihuahua where the Federal Army commanded by Victoriano Huerta defeated the Orozco rebellion (1912); the U.S. invasion of Veracruz (1914); the Zapata revolution in Morelos (1911–1914); the advance of the Constitutionalist armies and their arrival in Mexico City (1914); the assassinations and burials of Zapata and Carranza (1919, 1920); the Adolfo de la Huerta rebellion and the military campaigns of Obregón (1919, 1920); Villa's rendition and murder (1920, 1923); and the 1821 Independence festivities presided over by Obregón (1921).

8. Comments on the film are based on the video rerelease of 1996, which opens with color views of the Toscano house and archive located in Ocoyoacac in the state of Mexico.

CHAPTER 2

1. The contract deposited in the Condumex Archives in Mexico City is fully reprinted in Delgadillo and Limongi, 2000, 163–173.

2. As Brownlow points out, this film was released under various titles, including *The Tragedy in the Career of General Villa* and *The Tragic Early Life of General Villa* (1979, 102).

3. The title of this section makes reference to the heading of the section on the Villa-Mutual deal in Terry Ramsaye's *A Million and One Nights: A History of the Motion Picture* (1964, 670). I have chosen this heading to point out the systematic denigrating and racist attitudes exhibited by early film historians in their accounts of this deal.

4. I use quotation marks to distinguish the film-within-the-film from the actual film produced by Mutual, which no longer exists.

5. Reproductions can be found in De los Reyes ([1985] 1992, illus. no. 31, 135) and Brownlow (1979, 88–89).

6. This first edition consists of a series of twenty-five broadsheet-sized magazines. The image appears twice in issue 7, printed correctly on the colored cover and reversed in the inside with the caption "Gen. Villa during his triumphant entry into the city of Torreón on October 2, 1913" (Casasola, 1940, 7:626).

7. In later scenes moral outrage and antipathy for class privilege, for instance, trigger the out-of-control cruelty against the Ojinaga priest (Fernando Becerril) accused of raping a young girl and hostility toward landowner Luis Terrazas (Pedro Armendáriz Jr.).

8. In his book *Con Villa en México: Testimonios de camarógrafos norteamericanos*

en la revolución 1911-1916 (With Villa in Mexico: Testimonies of North Americans in the Revolution, 1911-1916) (1985), De los Reyes has scrutinized in detail the self-aggrandizing claims in Walsh's autobiography as director and scriptwriter of *The Life of General Villa*, as well as the numerous inaccuracies that may be attributable to faulty recall or careless copyediting (22-25).

9. The disparaging comments in Mexico about a Spanish rather than a local actor playing Villa are a reminder of the long-standing animosity toward Hollywood's treatment of Mexican history. See "Nationalists scoff at Spanish actor portraying revolutionary hero," posted on Sunday, December 29, 2002, at www.redding.com/newsarchive/20021229world017.shtml.

10. Reed's reports from Mexico place him with the troops of General Tomás "El Tigre" Urbina in January and February 1914 when the first newsreels were produced. He joined Villa in mid-March 1914, and he notes only in passing the presence of U.S. journalists, photographers, and cameramen covering the march toward Torreón (Reed, 1969, 219-220, 242-243, 257). The single mention of taking pictures details the hostility of a photographer toward an Italian soldier of fortune, Captain Marinelli, whose attention-grabbing antics are dismissed by a cursory "Go to hell!" (1969, 219-220).

11. These materials are the following (in order of appearance): *Unidentified Seffens* (U.S. newsreel materials; Library of Congress, Washington, DC, and National Archives and Records Administration, Maryland); Mutual Film newsreel footage of Villa at Ojinaga from *Revolution or The Shadow of Pancho Villa* (Miguel Contreras Torres, México, 1930); *Historia de la revolución mexicana* (History of the Mexican Revolution) (compilation documentary, Julio Lamadrid, México, 1928; London); *Inauguración del tráfico internacional en el istmo de Tehuantepec* (Inauguration of International Traffic in the Tehuantepec Isthmus) (Salvador Toscano, México, 1907; gift to Lord Cowdray, London); *The Mexican Joan of Arc* (Kalem Films, London, 1911); *The Colonel's Escape* (Kalem Films, Amsterdam, 1912); *The Mexican Telegram* (Amsterdam, 1914); newsreel of the Federal army under Victoriano Huerta, Mexico, 1914 (attributed to Fritz Arno Wagner, BFI, London); documentary material of Villa's presumed assassin, Jesús Salas Barraza, competing in the 1926 Pan-American Games and Plutarco Díaz Calles (Columbia, South Carolina); newsreel footage of the Punitive Expedition, 1916-1917 (Dawson City, Yukon find; Image and Sound Archives of Canada and National Film Board, Ottawa); *The Long Arm of Law and Order* (animation, Paramount, 1916); *The Vengeance of Pancho Villa* (Félix and Edmundo Padilla, University of Texas, El Paso, library, ca. 1930). The latter includes materials from *Liberty, Daughter of the USA*, serial (Universal, Jacques Jaccard and Henry McRae, 1916) and a segment from *The Life of General Villa* (Mutual Film Company, 1914).

12. The voice belongs to one of the unnamed Mexican actors from Durango who responds to a casting call set up by Rocha when he tries to re-create scenes from *The Life of General Villa* because he has been unable to locate the film. It is worth noting that while this voice-over may be considered an appropriation,

it is used to support De los Reyes's hypothesis that the screenplay was based on autobiographical anecdotes told by Villa himself to journalists ([1985] 1992, 267). Walsh, who claims to have related the screenplay he wrote to Villa, gives a competing account (1974, 89–90).

13. As Miriam Hansen points out, early actuality films involving reenactments "were considered legitimate. Though occasional complaints were heard early on, the standard of authenticity by which all such films would be rejected as 'fake pictures' evolved with the classical paradigm and became one of the war cries in the campaign against primitive modes" (1991, 31).

14. In the film, an English-speaking voice reads the extensive passage from Leyda's book that describes this project.

15. Images and plot summaries of the individual films provided by Rocha earlier make it possible to identify the characters in the reconstructed film. The plot can be summarized as follows. A group of local *rurales* (militia members) arrests a man at the post office. A young woman on the street sees what has happened and rushes to the train station. She rescues her lover when the train is attacked by revolutionaries and follows them after they seize weapons and ammunition. A military unit stalks the revolutionary troops, now commanded by her, across a mountainous landscape. Price's men set out to fight the soldiers and confront them at an isolated house. As Price and Willem escape through a window, Willem's elderly father reads a telegram and cheers. At the camp, the female revolutionary leader orders that a captured officer be shot. Willem has been caught and pleads for his life. As a shot is fired, his elderly father collapses. The woman looks away when the officer is executed by a firing squad. When Willem arrives home safely and finds his elderly parents sleeping, he wakes them from their nightmare. Both groups of revolutionaries celebrate victory.

16. The film is based on the real-life story of a Mexican widow from the state of Sonora who assembled an army to avenge her husband, Severino Talamantes, and sons, Severino and Arnulfo, who were executed by order of local officials loyal to Porfirio Díaz. Garcia Riera has questioned claims that the film was shot in Mexico (1987b, 49).

17. Before going to Mexico in 1911, Caryl Rhys Price served in the British army and the Royal Canadian Mounted Police. He went to Mexico, where he led a company of Mexicans, American mercenaries, and Wobblies (Industrial Workers of the World) who fought with the Partido Liberal Mexicano (Mexican Liberal Party) of the anarcho-syndicalist leaders Ricardo and Enrique Flores Magón. He went to the United States in 1912 and acted in *The Colonel's Escape*. Nothing is known of him after he joined the Canadian army during World War I. A postcard showing him in full body holding a riding crop is the only existing picture of this character (Hardman, n.d., 6).

18. Except for what Rocha says about this film, I have not been able to locate any other information. It is worth pointing out that Willem's character is highly feminized. In a scene that shows him writing at a window, his longing for the far-

away home is signified simultaneously by his sorrowful glance at the landscape and an affectionate embrace of his horse.

19. This segment represents a little-known episode on Villa's relationship with U.S. citizens living in Mexico. Mormons originally from Utah had established prosperous colonies in various parts of the state of Chihuahua since the late nineteenth century. In 1914 Villa offered protection to settlers in the territories he controlled. What the film segment refers to as "bandits" were actually members of a radical Villa faction. As the historian Frederick Katz points out, they were commanded by Máximo Castillo, who was fighting on his own for the return of land to the peasantry. Unwilling to respect Villa's directives to respect foreign properties, he raided them, including those owned by Mormons (1998, 414).

CHAPTER 3

1. Another book by Pinchon appeared in 1941: *Zapata, the Unconquerable* (New York: Doubleday, Page). While I have not found evidence that these books were translated into Spanish, it is worth noting that the writer convinced MGM to purchase screen rights for a biography of Emiliano Zapata in 1938. With the outset of the war, this project was shelved. A decade later, the rights were sold to 20th Century Fox. The studio got John Steinbeck to write a new script, and Darryl F. Zanuck hired Elia Kazan to direct *Viva Zapata!* (1952). See the conclusion for additional comments on this film.

2. By signing the 1922 agreement, the MPPDA consented reluctantly to the practice of having Mexicans censor films during or after production. For the context and provisions of this agreement, see Delpar (1984, 34–51) and De los Reyes (1993, 178–205).

3. Carlos Novarro, the brother of Mexican-born actor Ramón Novarro, who had facilitated the approval of the screenplay to ensure exhibit approval in Mexico, was called again to help get Tracy released from prison and flown out of Mexico.

4. For details on the film's production, Howard Hawks's involvement and reception in Mexico, see Haver (1980, 132–134, 148–151); "Viva Villa!" (1993, 2340–2341); McCarthy (1997, 188–196); and García Riera (1987b, 212–220).

5. I am assuming a global audience not only because of Hollywood's dominant place in film markets around the world during the period in which this film was produced, but because I subscribe to the argument made by Rey Choy in "Film and Cultural Identity." She writes, "Film has always been, since its inception, a *transcultural* phenomenon, having as it does the capacity to transcend 'culture'—to create modes of fascination which are readily accessible and which engage audiences in ways independent of their linguistic and cultural specificities" (1998, 174).

6. On the two occasions I showed this sequence to students and scholars in Mexico, Beery's lack of clothes provoked more negative reactions than did Villa's agreement to go along with Sykes's manipulation because it was considered inappropriate and disrespectful. The image of a half-clad Villa was seen as a reflection

of Hollywood's systemic denigration of Villa because it undermines his historical identity as a military leader and his lifelong struggle for social and political validation.

7. See chapter 2 for comments on the re-creation of this fiction in *And Starring Pancho Villa as Himself*. Also see Bruce-Novoa (2005) for a valuable comparison of the Beresford and Conway films.

8. At a screening organized in Mexico City in April 1934, officials objected that not enough soldiers were being shown in this scene. With their assistance, the Mexican army provided more troops for reshooting ("Viva Villa!" 1993, 2341).

9. The documentary citations come from the extant footage of the celebrations welcoming Madero in 1911 and the pageant of the Villista and Zapatista armies in 1914, discussed in the first chapter of this book. Among the landmarks used as backdrop are the Cathedral in the Zócalo, the Juárez monument on the Alameda Central, the Paseo de la Reforma, and the Palace of Fine Arts inaugurated in 1934.

10. It is not clear whether these montage inserts were in the initial screenplay written by Oliver H. P. Garrett or created later when Selznick hired Ben Hecht to write the final script (King Hanson, 1993, 2341). Be that as it may, this was a standard device in Hollywood historical and biographical dramas of the 1930s.

11. Todd McCarthy contends that Howard Hawks and the cinematographer, James Wong Howe, shot some if not all the scenes in this insert (1997, 196).

12. This scene does not come from Pinchon's book and is based in part on the section of *The Eagle and the Serpent* titled "The Carnival of the Bullets," in which Guzmán recounts in gruesome detail how Fierro killed five hundred prisoners after the battle of Ciudad Juárez in 1913 (1965, 163–174).

13. In the 1930s Carrillo realized his dream of retrieving the Spanish traditions of California. He had a group of adobe houses built near Carlsbad known as the Rancho de Quiotes, or Ranch of the Spanish Daggers, named after the flowers of the yucca found there. This facet of Carrillo's identity is the antithesis of the actor's, who is best remembered for his role as Pancho in the 1940s *Cisco Kid* films. As stated by his acting partner, Duncan Renaldo, his reputation for playing negative stereotypes in the 1930s led to a warning by the Mexican government that "if he continued representing 'greasers,' he would be declared *persona non grata* in that country" (quoted in Hadley-Garcia, 1991, 108).

14. These shots, credited to associate director Charles Rosson, and title signal as well the improvement of U.S.-Mexico relations as they echo the enthusiasm expressed by U.S. Ambassador Josephus Daniels in Mexico for President-elect Lázaro Cárdenas, who would assume power at the end of 1934.

15. Writing about the version shown on Mexican television in 1982 that included an additional ten-minute segment, the film critic Jorge Ayala Blanco speculated that producers might have prepared up to three different versions (*La cultura en Mexico,* supplement of *Siempre!* September 22, 1982, reprinted in García Riera,

1984, 39). The DVD version of the film released in 2005 includes the alternative ending found in a print deposited at the Filmoteca of the Autonomous National University of Mexico. This ending is set in 1915 after the defeat of Villa's army in Celaya and shows Tiburcio at home but still yearning to fight alongside his leader. Yet his reencounter with Villa ends tragically. Even though Villa appears convinced that Tiburcio is needed at home, he kills the wife and daughter. The shocked rancher confronts the leader but is shot in the back by Fierro. Now orphaned, his young son Pedro (José del Río) agrees to leave with the Villistas. In the original screenplay, Tiburcio lowers the rifle and joins again, this time with his son.

16. In his social study of the literature of the revolution, Rutherford notes, "the temptation to exaggerate and over-emphasize was made stronger by the large amounts of money novelists could make by selling plots to the directors of the rising Mexican film industry" (1971, 69). Notwithstanding this claim, and as Eduardo de la Vega indicates, only three of the seventeen long features dealing with the revolution produced between 1930 and 1939 were literary adaptations. I have already mentioned two of these films: *El compadre Mendoza,* based on a short story by Mauricio Magdaleno, and *Let's Go with Pancho Villa!* The third is *Los de abajo* (1939) based on the homonymous novel by Manuel Azuela and directed by Chano Urueta (De la Vega, 2004, 69).

17. Although the literal translation of *la bola* is "guerrilla fighting," the term is used as well to convey the idea that the revolution was a disorderly revolt lacking ideological coherence and a unified sense of purpose.

18. Raúl de Anda was the son of a *charro* from the Los Altos region of the state of Jalisco whose family moved to Mexico City during the revolution and traded horses for a living. He performed regularly in Mexico and the United States. His expertise and reputation led to film contracts. His role as a fearless rancher in *Juan Pistolas* (Robert Curwood, 1935) earned him the nickname "black *charro*," which he retained throughout his prolific acting career.

19. In an interview published in *Cuadernos de la Cinemateca,* no. 3 (May 1976), the actor recounts that when the filming ended, the crew, actors, and extras rewarded him (like the character) with a collective round of applause (cited in García Riera, 1984, 34–35).

20. Miguel Torres Contreras and Alfredo B. Cuéllar interpreted the main characters, respectively. Both were active promoters of *charrería:* the first, as actor, director, and producer; the second, as a founding member of the National Association of Charros.

21. Ayala Blanco is referring to *La Cucaracha* (Ismael Rodríguez, 1958), the hugely popular super-production starring María Félix, Dolores del Río, Pedro Armendáriz, and Emilio Fernández that spawned innumerable imitations in the 1960s and 1970s and came to typify the most clichéd excessive and commodified treatment of the revolution in Mexican cinema.

CHAPTER 4

1. This chapter is an extended and modified version of my article "¿Usted sabe lo que es un *serape?*" Intercambios culturales y los debates entorno a lo mexicano en el proyecto incompleto de Eisenstein," *Takwá, Revista de Historia* 5:8 (otoño 2005): 137–153.

2. The main activities were the 1996 screening of the recently discovered *Desastre en Oaxaca* (Eisenstein, 1930), the launching of Eduardo de la Vega Alfaro's book *From the Wall to the Screen: S. M. Eisenstein and the Pictorial Mexican Art* (1997), the thematic section "Chabela and Eisenstein in Mexico" included in the 1997 exhibition of the work of Isabel Villaseñor in Guadalajara, and the 1998 Eisenstein retrospective at the Cineteca Nacional in Mexico City. Two films were produced: a four-part television documentary, *Eisenstein in Mexico: The Eternal Circle* (Alejandra Islas, 1995), and, later, *A Banquet at Tetlapayac* (Olivier Debroise, 2000), an experimental work that is in part re-creation of and reflection on Eisenstein's project.

3. Contained in the article is Eisenstein's account of the plight of thousands left homeless and terrified by the aftershocks and the difficulties of estimating accurately the number of dead and wounded buried under the debris. His remarks were categorized as "being those of a formidable observer who made the airplane in which he traveled to the city fly as low as possible to film some scenes that are picturesque, others frightful and horrible, and all, absolutely all, interesting" (quoted in De la Vega Alfaro, 2000, 349).

4. For complementary information on press coverage, see De los Reyes, 1994, 26–27.

5. For Eisenstein's description of the flight over the volcanoes, see Karetnikova, 1991, 12; and Eisenstein, 1965, 211.

6. The serape trope appears in the "Rough Outline of the Mexican Picture" that Eisenstein prepared for Sinclair. In spite of its innumerable inclusions in the Eisenstein literature, it is worth reproducing the full quote: "Do you know what a 'Serape' is? A Serape is the striped blanket that the Mexican indio, the Mexican charro—every Mexican wears. And the Serape could be the symbol of Mexico. So striped and violently contrasting are the cultures in Mexico running next to each other and at the same time being centuries away. No plot, no whole story could run through this Serape without being false or artificial. And we took the contrasting independent adjacence of its violent colors as the motif for constructing our film: six episodes following each other—different in character, different in people, different in animals, trees and flowers. And still held together by the unity of the weave—a rhythmic and musical construction and the unrolling of the Mexican spirit and character" (*Film Sense*, 1942, 251). The original document is in the Eisenstein Collection of the Museum of Modern Art Library.

7. For commentary on the artistic and personal affinities between Siqueiros and Eisenstein, see De la Vega Alfaro, 1997, 51–56.

8. While it is unclear whether the drawings were purchased from or donated to the Banco Cinematográfico by Fernández Ledesma, they were included in a show organized by the Cineteca Nacional de México in 1978 titled *S. M. Eisenstein: Dibujos inéditos*. Currently only the reproductions published in the exhibition catalogue and the copies kept at the Cineteca Nacional exist because the originals were destroyed in a 1982 fire that ravaged the facilities of the Cineteca. Consequently, these works are less known than the collections of drawings deposited at the Museum of Modern Art in New York and the Eisenstein archives in Moscow.

9. It is worth noting that Debroise's film *The Banquet at Tetlapayac* opens with a reenactment of this incident that is most likely based on *Hacienda*, the novella by the American writer Katherine Anne Porter, who visited Tetlapayac at that time. She uses parody to recount this and other events that took place during the filming of Eisenstein's project and to express her own disillusionment with the revolution.

10. For a general discussion of the elements of the *charrería* tradition, see the section on *Let's Go with Pancho Villa!* in chapter 3.

CHAPTER 5

1. I have opted here for the most commonly accepted time line for this period. For a discussion on the issue of periodization of the golden age and the various time lines suggested by Mexican film historians, see Noble 2005, 14–15.

2. Admittedly these influences were so evident that a noted film reviewer for *El Universal Gráfico* who signed his column with the pseudonym "El Duende Filmo" cited these titles. (See García Riera, 1987a, 66–67.)

3. For a detailed examination of the events and their portrayal in *The Grey Automobile*, see De los Reyes, 1996, 175–191. In a conversation, De los Reyes mentioned *Las tribulaciones de una familia decente* (1918) as an additional source. This novel, by Mariano Azuela, deals with the travails of a middle-class family forced to move to the city during the revolution and offers a compelling portrait of urban life during the presidency of Venustiano Carranza.

4. The *sala comedor* figures prominently in the subcategory of family melodrama. It is the primary setting in which the breaks and negotiations of modernity are enacted and gender roles, socials norms, and values are reaffirmed.

5. Armendáriz's characterization in this film anticipates his role in *Woman in Love* (1946). In this now-canonical film he appears as General Juan José, a revolutionary whose love for Beatriz (María Félix) drives him to spare the town he brutally occupied by withdrawing his troops. For an extensive commentary on this film, see Tierney, 2003.

CHAPTER 6

1. Some of these paintings are posted on the official Web site, www.maria felix.com.mx/, along with other visual materials, including the actor's famed collections of porcelains and furniture. Yet, like many official sites, the information value is minimal.

2. As a version of *The Hidden Woman* was being prepared for a screening at the Cannes film festival in 1956, Taibo I. reports, rumors began to circulate about a romance between then–seventy-nine-year-old Diego Rivera and Félix (1985, 190–191). The same year, Félix married Swiss-born industrialist Alexander Berger and began splitting her residence between Paris and Mexico City, living six months of the year in each city. After the death of her husband in 1974, she spent more time in Mexico and returned there permanently in 1991. For comments about the actor's spectacular homecoming in the 1990s, see Dever 2003, 62–70.

3. These two images are the subject of an anecdote that Figueroa liked to tell when asked about the influence of painters on his work. During a preview screening of *Wildflower* organized by Dolores del Río, Orozco was sitting next to him. "When [the scene] came on the screen," the cinematographer recounted, "he leaned forward in his chair recognizing his work. So I grabbed his leg and said, 'Maestro, I am an honorable thief: that is from you.' To which he replied, 'But you have a perspective that I wasn't able to achieve. You must invite me to watch you work'" (Dey, 1992, 35).

4. See a detailed discussion of this image in chapter 4.

5. When Armendáriz was hired by Galvadón to play Felipe in *The Hidden Woman*, he had already been working in France, Italy, and Hollywood since 1951. He interpreted a variety of roles in films by Henri Decoin (*Les amants de Tolède*, 1952), Christian Jacque (*Lucrèce Borgia*, 1953), Bernard Broderie (*Fortune Carrée*, 1954), Giuseppe de Santis (*Uomini e Lupi*, 1955), and George Sherman (*Border River*, 1953). In the late 1940s, he had also appeared in films by John Ford (*The Fugitive*, 1947; *Fort Apache* and *Three Godfathers*, both 1948) and John Huston (*We Are Strangers*, 1949).

6. This postcard has been reproduced in *The Graphic History of the Mexican Revolution* published by the Casasola Archive. The 1940 edition that I consulted in Mexico includes it in a chapter titled "The End of the Northern Division," which deals with the 1916 campaign against the remnants of Villa's army. The caption identifies the image as follows: "An execution in Agua Prieta, Sonora" (Casasola 1940, 3:12, 999).

7. The most comprehensive account of the film's history can be found in David Weddle's extensive biography of Sam Peckinpah's life and career (1995, 307–377). See also *The Wild Bunch: An Album in Montage* (1995), a 37-minute documentary produced by Nick Redman and directed and written by Paul Seydor. It is included in the DVD versions of the film.

8. As Seydor notes, the review that appeared in *Time* magazine in the June 20, 1969, issue included a comment on the detrimental effect of the train attack scene

on the film's continuity (1994a, 51-52). The review, titled "New Movies—Man and Myth," is reprinted in Prince, 1999, 201-203.

9. As a matter of expediency, I am using the title headings in the chapter selection menu of the DVD versions of *The Wild Bunch*.

10. Also in this collection were photographs of U.S. soldiers of fortune, including some of Sam Drebben, which according to Weddle served as inspiration both for the film's story about a group of men with nothing to lose who cross the border into Mexico and the production stills that were later used to market *The Wild Bunch* (1994, 297).

11. Seydor uses these quotes in the voice-over narration of *The Wild Bunch: An Album in Montage*. The second precedes Peckinpah's explanation about why he decided to add the farewell scene.

12. In his detailed study of the screenplay, Seydor notes that Peckinpah added this scene. The original document of the final version contains the following handwritten notation: "Four men in line and the air of impending violence is so STRONG around them that as they pass through the celebrating soldiers, the song and laughter begin to die" (Seydor, 1999, 39).

CHAPTER 7

1. See Reed, 1969, pt. 2, "Francisco Villa," 113-146; and the chapter titled "First Blood" (187-191).

2. See Reed, 1969, "Duello a la Frigada" (153-161) and "The Fall of Gómez Palacio" (253-258).

3. Yet the book that cemented Reed's reputation, *Ten Days That Shook the World* (1919), was the starting point for *October* (Sergei M. Eisenstein, 1928), and the journalist's trajectory from Greenwich Village bohemia to the Soviet Union was the topic of *Reds* (Warren Beatty, 1981). *Red Bells* (Sergei Bondarchuk, USSR, 1982) is the only film that offers a comprehensive treatment of Reed's biography by incorporating Mexico and the Soviet revolution. (See Rosenstone, 2006, 101-103.)

4. As the remarks in chapter 4 make clear, cultural practices proposed different—even competing—views about what was then understood as being authentically Mexican. Which explains why even in 1928, two years after Weston's departure, the First Show of National Photographic Art exhibited the work of the renowned pictorialists Hugo Brehme (whose *Picturesque Mexico* appeared in 1923) and Antonio Garduño alongside that of emerging photographers Modotti and Manuel Álvarez Bravo, who represented a new generation, more radical and attuned to the cosmopolitan vanguard (Albiñana and Fernández, 1998, 56).

5. See chapter 2 for comments on how these anecdotes are represented in *And Starring Pancho Villa as Himself* (Bruce Beresford, 2003).

6. For these sequences, Leduc adapted incidents described in the chapters titled "The Lion of Durango at Home" and "La Tropa on the March." See Reed, 1969, 21-27, 33-40.

7. See Reed, 1969, pt. I, chap. 12, "Elizabetta," 99–109.

8. For this fictional segment, screenwriter Juan Tovar, collaborator Emilio Carballido, and Paul Leduc selected statements from the chapters in Reed's book that offer a compelling portrait of Villa. See Reed, 1969, 113–146.

9. For Reed's account of this battle and its aftermath, see "The Coming of the Colorados" and "Meester's Flight," in Reed, 1969, 80–99.

10. While no mention is made in Reed's *Insurgent Mexico* of Reed taking a picture of the old man, the portrait session with Urbina is recounted at the end of chap. 2, "The Lion of Durango at Home," 27.

11. Between November 1995 and September 1996, participants in a workshop on the history of photography in Mexico, held at the Centro de la Imagen, undertook to reconstruct this exhibition. For the result of their research, including period documents and reproductions of the Modotti photographs identified as having been shown, see Nieto Sotelo and Lozano Alvarez.

12. The film omits Modotti's activities as an underground liaison agent for the International Red Aid, an agency funded by the Soviet Union to assist Communist militants and organizers. Between 1930 and 1935, she traveled from Moscow to France, Germany, and other countries before being sent to Spain. She worked there from 1936 to 1939 in a variety of capacities and, like other Communist militants who supported the Republican forces, was forced to flee to France at the end of the Civil War.

13. Allegra Fulton is an award-winning Canadian stage actor who is best known for her leading role in *Frida K.*, a play especially written for her by Gloria Montero that was first staged in Toronto in 1994 and has since been performed in Canada and abroad. The production was revived and staged in Ottawa by its original director, Peter Hinton, in 2007 as part of the activities commemorating the centenary of Frida Kahlo's birth.

14. This passing mention of the Hayek-Taymor film is meant as a reminder. Already in 1983, and on the occasion of the *Frida Kahlo and Tina Modotti* exhibition held at the Whitechapel Gallery in London, Laura Mulvey and Peter Wollen explored the affinities between the two artists. The last statement in the catalogue article is revealing of the British cultural theorists' intention: "In many ways their work may be more relevant than the central traditions of modernity, at a time when, in the light of feminism, the history of art is being revalued and remade" (Mulvey and Wollen, 1998, 105).

15. These photographs have been reprinted in books and still circulate widely in the form of postcards. *Tina Modotti y el muralismo mexicano* (1999) is a compilation of the 115 photographs in the collection of the Photographic Archive of the Instituto de Investigaciones Estéticas of the National Autonomous University of Mexico. In her introduction, the curator, Maricela González Cruz Manjarrez, indicates that the photographer "succeeded in documenting and highlighting the expressivity of the murals through photography, using framing to create a different perception of them, for instance, with particular angles, approaches, or by emphasizing certain details" (1999, 12). Also see the account in Albers, 1999, 219.

Bibliography

Ades, Dawn. 1989. *Art in Latin America: The Modern Era, 1820-1980*. New Haven: Yale University Press.
Albers, Patricia. 1999. *Shadows, Fire, Snow: The Life of Tina Modotti*. New York: Clarkson Potters.
Albiñana, Salvador, and Horacio Fernández. 1998. "Tina Modotti." In *Mexicana: Fotografía moderna en México, 1923-1940*, 41-60; English trans., 247-251. Valencia: IVAM Centre Julio González.
Anderson, Mark Cronlund. 2000. *Pancho Villa's Revolution by Headlines*. Norman: University of Oklahoma Press.
Aragón Leiva, Agustín. 1932. "Mexico y la tragedia de Eisenstein." *El Nacional*, México City: September 11, n.p.
Ayala Blanco, Jorge. 1985. *La aventura del cine mexicano*. Mexico: Editorial Posada.
———. 1986. *La búsqueda del cine mexicano (1968-1972)*. México: Editorial Posada.
Benjamin, Thomas. 2000. *La Revolución: Mexico's Great Revolution as Memory, Myth, and History*. Austin: University of Texas Press.
Blanco, José Joaquín. 1996. "Memorias de un mexicano." *La Jornada*, October 2: n.p.
Brenner, Anita. 1929. *Idols behind Altars*. New York: Harcourt, Brace.
Britton, John A. 1995. *Revolution and Ideology: Images of the Mexican Revolution in the United States*. Lexington: University Press of Kentucky.
Brownlow, Kevin. 1968. *The Parade's Gone By . . . .* New York: Ballantine Books.
———. 1979. *The War, the West and the Wilderness*. New York: Alfred A. Knopf.
Bruce-Novoa, Juan. 2005. "Pancho Villa: Post-Colonial Colonialism, or the Return of the Americano." *Kritikos: An International and Interdisciplinary Journal of Postmodern Sound, Text, and Image* 2 (March). Online ed. http://garnet.acns.fsu.edu/~nr03/Pancho%20Villa.htm. Accessed February 8, 2006.
Buffington, Robert M., and William E. French. 2000. "The Culture of Modernity." In *The Oxford History of Mexico*, ed. Michael C. Meyer and William H. Beezley, 397-434. Oxford: Oxford University Press.
Bush, W. Stephen. 1914. "Mexican War Pictures. About Two Reels. The Mutual. Films." *Motion Picture World* 657 (February). [Spanish version in Aurelio de los Reyes, *Con Villa en México*, 122.]

Bustamante Fernández, Adolfo. 1931. "Eisenstein orientador." *El Universal Ilustrado,* Mexico City, July 16: n.p.

Carrera, Magali M. 2005. "From Royal Subject to Citizen: The Territory of the Body in Eighteenth- and Nineteenth-Century Mexican Visual Practices." In *Images of Power: Iconography, Culture and State in Latin America,* ed. Jens Andermann and William Rowe, 17–35. New York: Berghahn Books.

Carroll, Noël. 1998. "The Professional Western: South of the Border." In *Back in the Saddle Again: New Essays on the Western,* ed. Edward Buscombe and Roberta E. Pearson, 45–62. London: British Film Institute.

Casasola, Gustavo. 1940. *Historia gráfica de la revolución: 1900–1940.* Mexico City.

Choy, Rey. 1998. "Film and Cultural Identity." In *The Oxford Guide to Film Studies,* ed. John Hill and Pamela Church Gibson, 169–175. New York: Oxford University Press.

Cordero Reiman, Karen. 1993. "La construcción de un arte mexicano moderno, 1910–1940 / Constructing a Modern Mexican Art, 1910–1940." In *South of the Border: Mexico in the American Imagination, 1914–1947 / México en la imaginación norteamericana,* by James Oles, 11–47. Washington, DC: Smithsonian Institution Press.

Debroise, Olivier. 2001. *Mexican Suite: A History of Photography in Mexico.* Trans. and rev., in collaboration with the author, Stella Sá Rego. Austin: University of Texas Press.

De la Colina, José. 1972. "Crea un Nuevo Cine: 'Reed, Mexico Insurgente.'" *El Universal,* March 29: n.p.

De la Luna, Andrés. 1984. *La batalla y la sombra (La Revolución en el cine mexicano).* México: Universidad Autónoma Metropolitana-Xochimilco.

———. 1995. "The Labyrinths of History." In *Mexican Cinema,* ed. Paulo Antonio Paranaguá, 171–177. London: British Film Institute, in association with IMCINE, Mexico.

De la Mora, Sergio. 2006. *Cinemachismo: Masculinity and Sexuality in Mexican Film.* Austin: University of Texas Press.

De la Vega Alfaro, Eduardo. 1993. "Una visita a Tetlapayac." *El Acordéon* 9: 40–48.

———. 1997. *Del muro a la pantalla: S. M. Eisenstein y el arte pictórico mexicano.* Guadalajara and Mexico City: Universidad de Guadalajara, Instituto Mexiquense de la Cultura e Instituto Mexicano de la Cinematografía.

———. 1998. *La aventura de Eisenstein en México.* Cuadernos de la Cineteca Nacional, Nueva Época no. 6. México: Cineteca Nacional.

———. 1999a. "Chabela Villaseñor o La Santa Camaleoncita de Tetlapayac." In *Chabela Villaseñor: Perfil de una época.* Mexico City: Museo de la Secretaría de Hacienda y Créditos Público, Antiguo Museo del Arzobispado.

———. 1999b. "The Decline of the Golden Age and the Making of a Crisis." In *Mexico's Cinema: A Century of Films and Filmmakers,* ed. Joanne Hershfield and David R. Maciel, 165–191. Wilmington, DE: Scholarly Resources.

———. 2000. "Visiones eisensteinianas de Oaxaca." In *Microhistorias del cine mexicano*. Guadalajara and Mexico City: Universidad de Guadalajara, Universidad Nacional Autónoma de Mexico, Instituto Mexicano de Cinematografía, Cineteca Nacional, Instituto Mora.

———. 2004. "Del texto literario al texto audiovisual: Literatura y cine de la Revolución (1930-1979)." In *Fotografía, cine y literatura de la Revolución mexicana*, by Ángel Miquel, Zuzana M. Pick, and Eduardo de la Vega Alfaro, 49-69. Cuernavaca: Universidad Autonóma del Estado de Morelos, Facultad de Artes.

Delgadillo, Willibando, and Maribel Limongi. 2000. *La mirada desenterrada: Juárez y El Paso vistos por el cine (1896-1916)*. Ciudad Juárez: Cuadro X Cuadro, Miguel Ángel Berumen Campos, Edición e Investigación Iconográfica.

De los Reyes, Aurelio. 1977. "El cine en México, 1896-1930." In *80 años de cine mexicano*, ed. Aurelio de los Reyes, David Ramón, María Luisa Amador, and Rodolfo Rivera, 9-92. Mexico City: Universidad Autonóma de México, Difusión Cultural.

———. 1996. *Cine y sociedad en México: Vivir de sueños*. Vol. 1, *1896-1920*. Rev. ed. Mexico City: Universidad Nacional Autónoma de México/ Cineteca Nacional.

———. [1985] 1992. *Con Villa en México: Testimonios de camarógrafos norteamericanos en la revolución 1911-1916*. Mexico City: Universidad Autónoma de México.

———. [1987] 1997. *Medio siglo de cine mexicano*. Mexico City: Editorial Trillas.

———. 1993. *Cine y sociedad en México 1896-1930: Bajo el cielo de México*. Vol. 2, *1920-1924*. Mexico City: Instituto de Investigaciones Estéticas, Universidad Nacional Autónoma de México.

———. 1994. "Una película de Eisenstein en la ciudad de Oaxaca." *El Acordéon* 12 (July-October): 26-27.

———. 1996. "El gobierno mexicano y las películas denigrantes 1920-1931." In *México-Estados Unidos: Encuentros y desencuentros en el cine*, ed. Ignacio Durán, Iván Trujillo, and Mónica Verea, 23-35. Mexico City: Filmoteca UNAM, IMCINE, CISAN.

———. 2001a. "El nacimiento de *¡Qué Viva México!* de Sergei Eisenstein: Conjeturas." *Anales del Instituto de Investigaciones Estéticas* 23 (Spring): 78, 149-173.

———. 2001b. "Francisco Villa: The Use and Abuse of Colonialist Cinema." *Journal of Film Preservation* 63 (October): 36-40.

———. 2002. "Eisenstein y Orozco: Una relación de mutual admiración." *Anales del Instituto de Investigaciones Estéticas* 24 (Spring): 80, 129-146.

———. 2006. *El nacimiento de "Qué Viva México!"* Mexico City: Instituto de Investigaciones Estéticas.

De Orellana, Margarita. 1990. "The Voice of the Present over Images of the Past: Historical Narration in *Memories of a Mexican*." In *The Social Documentary in Latin America*, ed. Julianne Burton. Pittsburgh: University of Pittsburgh Press.

———. 1993. "The Circular Look: The Incursion of North American Fictional

Cinema, 1911–1917, into the Mexican Revolution." In *Mediating Two Worlds: Cinematic Encounters in the Americas,* ed. John King, Ana M. López, and Manuel Alvarado, 3–14. London: British Film Institute.

———. 1999. *La mirada circular: El cine norteamericano de la revolución mexicana, 1911–1917.* Mexico City: Artes de México.

Delpar, Helen. 1984. "Goodbye to the 'Greaser': Mexico, the MPPSA, and Derogatory Films, 1922–1926." *Journal of Popular Film and Televisión* 12:1 (Spring): 34–41.

———. 1992. *The Enormous Vogue of Things Mexican: Cultural Relations between the United States and Mexico, 1920–1935.* Tuscaloosa: University of Alabama Press.

Dever, Susan. 2003. *Celluloid Nationalism and Other Melodramas: From Post-Revolutionary Mexico to "Fin de Siglo" Mexamérica.* Albany: State University of New York Press.

Dey, Tom. 1992. "Gabriel Figueroa: Mexico's Master Cinematographer." *American Cinematographer* 73:2 (March): 34–40.

Doanne, Mary Ann. 2002. *The Emergence of Cinematic Time: Modernity, Contingency, the Archive.* Cambridge, MA: Harvard University Press.

Doñán, Juan José. 2000. "Fictional Ties. Jorge Negrete Shall Speak for My People." Trans. Richard Moszka. *Charrería, Artes de México* 50: 93–94.

Dyer, Richard. 1991. "*A Star Is Born* and the Construction of Authenticity." In *Stardom: Industry of Desire,* ed. Christine Glendhill, 132–140. London: Routledge.

Eisenstein, Sergei M. [1931] 1942. "Rough Outline of the Mexican Picture." In *Film Sense,* ed. and trans. Jay Leyda, 251–255. New York: Harcourt, Brace.

Eisenstein, Sergei. 1965. *Immoral Memories: An Autobiography.* Trans. Herbert Marshall. London: Dennis Dobson.

———. 1982. "The Prometheus of Mexican Painting" (1935). In *Film Essays and a Lecture,* ed. Jay Leyda, 222–231. Princeton: Princeton University Press.

Eisenstein, Sergei, and G. V. Alexandroff [sic]. 1992. "¡Qué viva México! Original Scenario." In *Celluloid Power: Social Criticism from "Birth of a Nation" to "Judgement in Nuremberg,"* ed. David Platt, 197–219. Metuchen, NJ: Scarecrow Press.

Figueroa, Judith Alanís. 1998. *Chabela Villaseñor: Exposición retrospectiva.* Guadalajara: Instituto Cultural Cabañas.

Fox, Claire F. 1999. *The Fence and the River: Culture and Politics at the U.S.-Mexico Border.* Minneapolis: University of Minnesota Press.

García, Gustavo, and Rafael Aviña. 1997. *Época de oro del cine mexicano.* Mexico City: Editorial Clío Libros y Videos.

García Riera, Emilio. 1984. *Fernando de Fuentes (1894–1958).* Mexico City: Cineteca Nacional.

———. 1987a. *Emilio Fernández (1904–1986).* Guadalajara: Universidad de Guadalajara/CIEC.

———. 1987b. *México visto por el cine extranjero.* Vol. 1, 1894/1940. Mexico City and Guadalajara: Ediciones Era and Universidad de Guadalajara, Centro de Investigaciones y Enseñanzas Cinematográficas.

———. 1988. *México visto por el cine extranjero*. Vol. 3, *1941-1969*. Mexico City and Guadalajara: Ediciones Era and Universidad de Guadalajara, Centro de Investigaciones y Enseñanzas Cinematográficas.

———. 1994a. *Historia documental del cine mexicano*. Vol. 1, *1929-1937*. Guadalajara: Universidad de Guadalajara.

———. 1994b. *Historia documental del cine mexicano*. Vol. 5, *1949-1950*. Guadalajara: Universidad de Guadalajara.

———. 1994c. *La Historia documental del cine mexicano*. Vol. 8, *1955-1956*. Guadalajara: Universidad de Guadalajara.

———. 1994d. *La Historia documental del cine mexicano*. Vol. 11, *1961-1963*. Guadalajara: Universidad de Guadalajara.

———. 1994e. *La Historia documental del cine mexicano*. Vol. 15, *1970-1971*. Guadalajara: Universidad de Guadalajara.

García-Romeu, Emilia. 1998. "Sergei Eisenstein. *¡Qué Viva México!*" In *Mexicana: Fotografía moderna en México, 1923-1940*, ed. María Casanova, 91-100. Valencia: IVAM Institut Valencià d'Art Modern.

Geduld, Harry M., and Ronald Gottesman, eds. 1970. *Sergei Eisenstein and Upton Sinclair: The Making and Unmaking of "Que Viva México!"* Bloomington: Indiana University Press.

Gilbert, Mathew. 2003. "'Villa' Presents a Revolutionary Use of Spin." *Boston Globe*, September 6. http://www.boston.com/ae/tvarticle/villa_presents_a_revolutionary_use_of_spin/mode-P. Accessed October 24, 2003.

Gilly, Adolfo, 1983. *The Mexican Revolution*. Trans. Patrick Camiller. London: Verso Editions and New Left Books.

Gómez, Carmen Elisa. 2003. "*Reed: México Insurgente*, Reed: Insurgent Mexico. Paul Leduc, Mexico 1971." In *The Cinema of Latin America*, ed. Alberto Elena and Marina Díaz López, 131-139. London: Wallflower Press.

González Cruz Manjarrez, Maricela. 1999. *Tina Modotti y el muralismo mexicano*. Mexico City: UNAM.

González, Rita. 2003. "*Los rollos perdidos de Pancho Villa / The Lost Reels of Pancho Villa*. Dir. Gregorio Rocha, SubCine (www.subcine.com)." *Moving Image* 6:1: 145-148. Online ed. http://muse.uq.edu.au.proxy.library.carleton.ca/journals/the_moving_image/v006/6.1.gonzalez.pdf. Accessed March 8, 2007.

Goodwin, Michael. 1974. "Paul Leduc's *Reed: Insurgent Mexico*." *Take One* 4 (December): 7, 31.

Güemes, César. "Montaje televisivo, el segundo día de homenaje a la Félix en Bellas Artes." http://www.jornada.unam.mx/2002/abr02/020410/07an1wsp.php?printver=1. Accessed April 12, 2005.

Gutiérrez Ruvacalba, Ignacio. 1996. "A Fresh Look at the Casasola Archive." *History of Photography* 20:3 (Autumn): 191-195.

Guzmán, Martín Luis. 1965. "The Film of the Revolution." In *The Eagle and the*

Serpent, trans. Harriet de Onís, introd. Federico de Onís, 285–291. Garden City, NY: Dolphin Books, Doubleday.

"HBO Online Interview with Antonio Banderas." http://hbo.com/films/pancho villa/. Accessed April 12, 2004.

Hadley-Garcia, George. 1991. *Hollywood Hispano: Los Latinos en el mundo del cine.* New York: Carol Publishing Group.

Hansen, Miriam. 1991. *Babel and Babylon: Spectatorship in American Silent Film.* Cambridge, MA: Harvard University Press.

Hardman, John. n.d. "*Soldiers of Fortune*" in the Mexican Revolution. [Postcards of the Mexican Revolution.] http://www.netdotcom/revmexpc/fortune.num. Accessed March 5, 2001.

Harmetz, Aljean. 1994. "Man Was a Killer Long before He Served a God." In *Doing It Right: The Best Criticism on Sam Peckinpah's "The Wild Bunch,"* ed. Michael Bliss, 169–174. Carbondale: Southern Illinois University Press.

Haver, Ronald. 1980. *David O. Selznick's Hollywood.* Design Thomas Ingalls. New York: Alfred A. Knopf.

Hershfield, Joanne. 1996. *Mexican Cinema / Mexican Woman, 1940–1950.* Tucson: University of Arizona Press.

———. 2000. *The Invention of Dolores del Río.* Minneapolis: University of Minnesota Press.

Hess, Judith, and John Hess. 1974. "*Reed: Insurgent Mexico:* Between History and Homage." *Jump Cut* 1 (May–June): 7–8.

Indych, Anna. Fall 2001. "Made for the USA: Orozco's *Horrores de la Revolución.*" *Anales del Instituto de Investigaciones Estéticas* 23 (Fall): 79, 153–164.

Katz, Frederick. 1998. *The Life and Times of Pancho Villa.* Stanford: Stanford University Press.

Karetnikova, Inga, in coll. with Leon Steinmetz. 1991. *Mexico according to Eisenstein.* Albuquerque: University of New Mexico Press.

Kitses, Jim. 2004. *Horizons West: Directing the Western from John Ford to Clint Eastwood.* New ed. London: British Film Institute.

Leal, Juan Felipe, and Mario Huacuja Roundtree. 1982. *Economía y sistema de haciendas en México: La hacienda pulquera en el cambio. Siglos XVIII, XIX y XX.* Mexico City: Ediciones Era.

Leduc, Renato. 1968. "Preface to the New Edition," trans. Tana de Gámez. In *Insurgent Mexico,* by John Reed. New York: International.

Leyda, Jay. 1971. *Films Beget Films: A Study of the Compilation Film.* New York: Hill and Wang.

López, Ana M. 1990. "At the Limits of Documentary: Hypertextual Transformation and the New Latin American Cinema." In *The Social Documentary of Latin America,* ed. Julianne Burton, 403–432. Pittsburgh: University of Pittsburgh Press.

———. 1999. "Hollywood-México: Dolores del Río, una estrella transnacional." *Archivos de la Filmoteca* 31 (February): 14–35.

Maciel, David R. 1999. "Cinema and the State in Contemporary Mexico." In *Mexico's Cinema: A Century of Film and Filmmakers*, ed. Joanne Hershfield and David R. Maciel, 197–232. Wilmington, DE: Scholarly Resources.
Martín-Barbero, Jesús. 1993. *Communication, Culture and Hegemony: From Media to Mediations*. Trans. Elizabeth Fox and Robert A. White. London: Sage.
McCarthy, Todd. 1997. *Howard Hawks: The Grey Fox of Hollywood*. New York: Grove Press.
McKinney, Devin. 1999. "*The Wild Bunch:* Innovation and Retreat." In *Sam Peckinpah's "The Wild Bunch,"* ed. Stephen Prince, 175–199. Cambridge: Cambridge University Press.
Miller, Michael Nelson. 1998. *Red, White and Green: The Maturing of Mexicanidad, 1940–1946*. Austin: University of Texas Press.
Miquel, Ángel, 1997. *Salvador Toscano*. Mexico City and Veracruz: Universidad de Guadalajara and Universidad Veracruzana.
———. 2002. "El revolucionario que construía violines." *Luna Córnea* 24: 114–125.
———. 2004. "El registro de Jesús H. Abitía en las campañas constitutionalistas." In *Fotografía, cine y literatura de la Revolución Mexicana*, by Ángel Miquel, Zuzana M. Pick, and Eduardo de la Vega Alfaro, 7–30. Cuernavaca: Universidad Autonóma del Estado de Morelos, Facultad de Artes.
Mistron, Deborah E. 1983. "The Role of Pancho Villa in the Mexican and American Cinema." *Studies in Latin American Popular Culture* 2: 1–13.
Monsiváis, Carlos. 1977. "Agustín Lara: El harem ilusorio (Notas a partir de la memorización de la letra de 'Farolito"). In *Amor Perdido*, 61–97. Mexico City: Ediciones Era.
———. 1984. "A Continuity of Images: Notes Inspired by the Casasola Archive," trans. Andrea Morales. In *The World of Agustín Víctor Casasola. Mexico: 1900–1938*. Catalogue of an exhibition curated by Rebecca Kelly Crumlish. Washington, DC: Fondo del Sol Visual Arts and Media Center.
———. 1993. *Rostros del cine mexicano*. Milán: Americo Arte Editores.
———. 1995. "Mythologies." In *Mexican Cinema*, ed. Paulo Antonio Paranaguá, 117–127. London: British Film Institute.
———. 1997. "Dolores del Río: The Face as Institution." In *Mexican Postcards*, ed., trans., and introd. John Kraniauskas, 71–87. London: Verso.
———. 2004. "Laughing through One's Tears: Popular Culture in Mexico." In *Literary Cultures of Latin America: A Comparative History*. Vol. 1, *Configurations of Literary Culture*, ed. Mario J. Valdés and Djelal Kadir, 576–597. New York: Oxford University Press.
Mraz, John. 1997a. "How Real Is Reel? Fernando de Fuentes's Revolutionary Trilogy." In *Framing Latin American Cinema: Contemporary Critical Perspectives*, ed. Ann Marie Stock, 93–119. Minneapolis: University of Minnesota Press.
———. 1997b. "Photography." In *Encyclopedia of Mexico: History, Society and Culture*, vol. 2, ed. Michael S. Werner, 1085–1090. Chicago: Fitzroy Dearborn.

———. n.d. "Envisioning Mexico: Photography and National Identity." Working Paper no. 32. Duke UNC Program in Latin American Studies. Typescript.

Mulvey, Laura, with Peter Wollen. 1988. "Frida Kahlo and Tina Modotti." In *Visual and Other Pleasures*, 81–107. Bloomington: Indiana University Press.

"Nationalists Scoff at Spanish Actor Portraying Revolutionary Hero." 2002, December 29. http://www.redding.com/newsarchive/20021229world017.shtml. Accessed October 24, 2003.

Nicholson, Irene. 1953. "An Historical Film: *Memoirs of a Mexican.*" *Sight and Sound* 23:1 (July–September): 13–15.

Nieto Sotelo, Jesús, and Elisa Lozano Alvarez. 2000. *Tina Modotti. Una nueva Mirada, 1929 / A New Vision, 1929*. Mexico City: CNCA / Centro de la Imagen y Universidad Autónoma del Estado de Morelos.

Noble, Andrea. 2000. *Tina Modotti: Image, Texture, Photography*. Albuquerque: University of New Mexico Press.

———. 2005. *Mexican National Cinema*. London: Routledge.

———. 2006. "Seeing through *¡Que Viva Mexico!* Eisenstein's Travels in Mexico." *Journal of Iberian and Latin American Studies* 12:2–3: 173–187.

Obregón, Álvaro. 1959. *Ocho mil kilómetros de campaña*. Con "Estudios Preliminares" a cargo de Francisco L. Urquizo y Francisco J. Grajales y material gráfico proveniente del archivo de Jesús H. Abitía. Mexico City: Fondo de Cultura Económica.

Oles, James. 1993. "South of the Border: American Artists in Mexico, 1914–1947." In *South of the Border: Mexico in the American Imagination, 1914–1947: México en la imaginación norteamericana*. Washington, DC: Smithsonian Institution Press.

O'Malley, Ilene V. 1986. *The Myth of the Revolution: Hero Cults and Institutionalization of the Mexican State, 1920–1940*. New York: Greenwood Press.

Palomar Verea, Cristina. 2004. *En cada charro, un hermano: La charrería en el estado de Jalisco*. Guadalajara: Secretaría de Cultura, Gobierno del Estado de Jalisco.

Paranaguá, Paulo Antonio. 2003. *Tradición y modernidad en el cine de América Latina*. Madrid: Fondo de Cultura Económica de España.

Peredo Castro, Francisco Martín. 2000. "Cine e historia: Discurso histórico y producción cinematográfica (1940–1952)." Ph.D. diss., Facultad de Filosofía y Letras, Universidad Nacional Autónoma de México.

Pérez Montfort, Ricardo. 1994a. *Estampas del nacionalismo popular mexicano: Ensayos sobre cultura popular y nacionalismo*. Mexico City: Centro de Investigaciones y Estudios Superiores en Antropología Social (Ciesas).

———. 1994b. "Indigenismo, hispanismo y panamericanismo en la cultura popular mexicana de 1920 a 1940." In *Cultura e Identidad Nacional*, comp. Roberto Blancarte, 343–383. Mexico City: Consejo Nacional para la Cultura y las Artes, Fondo de Cultura Económica.

———. 1997. "El México de charros y chinas poblanas / The México of Charros

and Chinas Poblanas." *Luna Córnea* 13 (September–December): 43–47, 146–149.
Pérez Turrent, Tomás. 1973. "Pasar de la contemplación a la actividad." *El Universal*, January 29, n.p.
Pettit, Arthur G. 1980. *Images of the Mexican American in Fiction and Film*. College Station: Texas A&M University Press.
Pick, Zuzana M. Fall 2000. "A Romance with Mexico: The Epic Spectacle of the Revolution. The Martin Walsh Memorial Lecture (2000)." *Canadian Journal of Film Studies / Revue canadienne d'Études cinématographiques* 9:2: 3–22.
———. otoño 2005. "'¿Usted sabe lo que es un serape?' Intercambios culturales y los debates en torno a lo mexicano en el proyecto inconcluso de Eisenstein." *Takwá, Revista de Historia* 5:8: 137–153.
Pinchon, Edgcumb, with Odo B. Stade. 1933. *Viva Villa! A Recovery of the Real Pancho Villa: Peon . . . Bandit . . . Soldier . . . Patriot*. New York: Harcourt, Brace.
Poniatowska, Elena. 1995. *Tinisima*. Trans. Katherine Silver. New York: Penguin Books.
Prince, Stephen. 1999. "Introduction: Sam Peckinpah, Savage Poet of American Cinema." in *Sam Peckinpah's "The Wild Bunch,"* 1–36. Cambridge: Cambridge University Press.
Ramírez Berg, Charles. 1994. "The Cinematic Invention of Mexico: The Poetics and Politics of the Fernandez-Figueroa Style." In *The Mexican Cinema Project*, ed. Chon Noriega and Steven Ricci, 13–24. Los Angeles: UCLA Film and Television Archive. Reprinted from *Spectator* 13:1 (1992): 24–41.
———. 2002. *Latino Images in Film: Stereotypes, Subversion, Resistance*. Austin: University of Texas Press.
Ramírez, Fausto. 1999. "Los saldos de la modernidad y de la revolución." In *Pintura y vida cotidiana en México, 1650–1950*, by Gustavo Curiel, Fausto Ramírez, Antonio Rubial and Angélica Velásquez. Mexico City: Fomento Cultural Banamex.
Ramsaye, Terry. 1964. "Panchito Villa Sells a War." In *A Million and One Nights: A History of the Motion Picture*, 670–673. London: Frank Coss.
Reed, John. 1969. *Insurgent Mexico*, with new preface by Renato Leduc. Trans. Tana de Gámez. New York: Greenwood Press.
Renaud, Tristan. Mai 1974. "John Reed (*Mexico Insurgente*): L'oeil de la camera." *Cinéma 73* 174: 121–123.
Reyes Nevares, Beatriz. 1973. "El cine como reportaje." *Siempre* (Mexico), September 19, 42–43.
Robé, Chris. Winter 2006. "Revolting Women: The Role of Gender in Sergei Eisenstein's *Que Viva Mexico!* and U.S. Depression-Era Left Film Criticism." *Jump Cut* (Winter): 48. http://www.ejumpcut.or/currentissue/QueVivaMexico/text.html. Accessed October 2, 2006.
Rocha, Gregorio. 2002. "*La venganza de Pancho Villa (The Vengeance of Pancho*

Villa): A Lost and Found Border Film." *Journal of Film Preservation* 65 (December): 24–29.
Rochfort, Desmond. 1991. *Mexican Muralists: Orozco, Rivera, Siqueiros*. San Francisco: Chronicle Books.
Rodríguez Álvarez, Gabriel. 2002. "La sociedad de los cinéfilos." *Luna Córnea* 24: 74–78, 279–283.
Rosenstone, Robert A. 1975. *Romantic Revolutionary: A Biography of John Reed*. New York: Alfred A. Knopf.
———. 2006. "Telling Lives." In *History on Film / Film on History*, 89–110. Harlow, U.K.: Pearson Longman.
Rutherford, John. 1971. *Mexican Society during the Revolution: A Literary Approach*. Oxford: Clarendon Press.
S. M. Eisenstein: Dibujos inéditos. Con nota introductoria de Salvador Elizondo. Mexico City: Cineteca Nacional, 1978.
Schrader, Paul. 1994. "Sam Peckinpah Going to Mexico." In *Doing It Right: The Best Criticism on Sam Peckinpah's "The Wild Bunch,"* ed. Michael Bliss, 17–30. Carbondale: Southern Illinois University Press.
Segre, Erica. 2007. *Intersected Identities: Strategies of Visualization in Nineteenth- and Twentieth-Century Mexican Culture*. New York: Berghahn Books.
Seton, Marie. 1978. *Sergei Eisenstein*. Rev. ed. London: Dennis Dobson.
Seydor, Paul, 1994a. "The Versions of *The Wild Bunch*." In *Doing It Right: The Best Criticism on Sam Peckinpah's "The Wild Bunch,"* ed. Michael Bliss, 46–73. Carbondale: Southern Illinois University Press.
———. 1994b. "*The Wild Bunch* as Epic." In *Doing It Right: The Best Criticism on Sam Peckinpah's "The Wild Bunch,"* ed. Michael Bliss, 113–157. Carbondale: Southern Illinois University Press.
———. 1999. "*The Wild Bunch*: The Screenplay." In *Sam Peckinpah's "The Wild Bunch,"* ed. Stephen Prince, 37–78. Cambridge: Cambridge University Press.
Sharrett, Christopher. 1999. "Peckinpah the Radical: The Politics of *The Wild Bunch*." In *Sam Peckinpah's "The Wild Bunch,"* ed. Stephen Prince, 79–104. Cambridge: Cambridge University Press.
Sierra, Javier. 1976. Archivo de la Palabra (formerly known as Programa de Historia Oral), Instituto Nacional de Antropología e Historia (INAH), Mexico. PHO2/11, 153–155.
Sontag, Susan. 1977. *On Photography*. New York: Picador, Farrar, Straus, and Giroux.
Taibo I., Paco Ignacio. 1985. *María Félix: 47 pasos por el cine*. Mexico City: Joaquín Mortiz / Planeta.
Tenorio, Mauricio. 1995. "El indigenista." In *Mitos mexicanos*, ed. Enrique Florescano, 257–266. Mexico City: Nuevo Siglo Aguilar.
Thord-Gray, Ivar. 1983. Excerpt of *Gringo Rebel (Mexico, 1913–1914)*. In *Fragments of the Mexican Revolution: Personal Accounts from the Border*, ed. Oscar J. Martínez, 53–59. Albuquerque: University of New Mexico Press.

Tuñón, Julia. 1996. "La trilogía de Fernando de Fuentes." *Revista de Cultura Acordeón* 17 (May–August): 51–58.

———. 1997. "Félix Güareña, María de los Angeles." In *Encyclopedia of Mexico: History, Society, and Culture*, vol. 1, ed. Michael S. Werner, 479–480. Chicago: Fitzroy Dearborn.

———. 1998. *Mujeres de luz y sombra en el cine mexicano: La construcción de una imagen (1939–1952)*. Mexico City: El Colegio de México e Instituto Mexicano de Cinematografía.

———. 2000. *Los Rostros de un Mito: Personajes Femeninos en las Películas de Emilio "El Indio" Fernández*. Mexico City: Conaculta, Series Imcine Arte e Imagen.

Turner, Timothy G. 1935. *Bullets, Battles and Gardenias*. Dallas: South-West Press.

"Una curiosidad cinematográfica: Una super-producción no industrial." 1971. *Esto* (Mexico), March 3: n.p.

Vanderwood, Paul J., and Frank N. Samponaro. 1988. *Border Fury: A Picture Postcard Record of Mexico's Revolution and U.S. War Preparedness, 1910–1917*. Albuquerque: University of New Mexico Press.

Velázquez Guadarrama, Angélica. 1999. "Pervivencias novohispanas y tránsito a la modernidad." In *Pintura y vida cotidiana en México, 1650–1950*, ed. Gustavo Gustavo, Fausto Ramírez, Antonio Rubial, and Angélica Velásquez, 155–241. Mexico City: Fomento Cultural Banamex.

"Villa at the Front: 'Movies' Sign Him Up." 1914. *New York Times*, January 7: 1–2. [Spanish-language version in Reyes, *Con Villa en México*, 104–106.]

"Viva Villa!" 1993. In *The American Film Institute Catalogue of Motion Pictures Produced in the United States: Feature Films, 1931–1940*, exec. ed. Patricia King-Hanson, assoc. ed. Alan Gevinson, 2340–41, film entries M–Z. Berkeley: University of California Press.

"Viva Villa!" 1934. *Time* 23 (April 16): 45.

Vassey, Ruth. 1997. *The World according to Hollywood*. Madison: University of Wisconsin Press.

Walker, Ronald G. 1978. *Infernal Paradise: Mexico and the Modern English Novel*. Berkeley: University of California Press.

"Wallace Beery en 'Viva Villa' visto por el caricaturista Matías Santoyo." 1934. *Excelsior*, September 4: n.p.

Walsh, Raoul. 1974. *Each Man in His Time*. New York: Farrar, Straus and Giroux.

Weddle, David. 1994. *"If They Move . . . Kill 'Em": The Life and Times of Sam Peckinpah*. New York: Grove Press.

Weston, Edward. [1961] 1973. *The Daybooks of Edward Weston*. Vol. 1, *Mexico*, ed. Nancy Newhall. New York: Aperture.

Wilson, Christopher P. 1993. "Plotting the Border: John Reed, Pancho Villa and *Insurgent Mexico*." In *Cultures of United States Imperialism*, ed. Amy Kaplan and Donald E. Pease, 338–361. Durham, NC: Duke University Press.

"With Villa in Mexico." 1914. *Reel Life: Magazine of Moving Pictures* (Mutual Film Company, New York) 4 (May 9): 8, 10–11. [Spanish-language version in Reyes, *Con Villa en México*, 228–232.]

Zolov, Eric. 2001. "Discovering a Land 'Mysterious and Obvious': The Renarrativizing of Postrevolutionary Mexico." In *Fragments of a Golden Age: The Politics and Culture of Mexico since 1940,* ed. Gilbert Joseph, Anne Rubenstein, and Eric Zolov, 234–272. Durham, NC: Duke University Press.

Zúñiga, Ariel, 1995. "Roberto Galvadón." In *Mexican Cinema,* ed. Paulo Antonio Paranaguá, 193–201. London: British Film Institute.

Index

Note: Page numbers referring to images appear in *italics*.

Abandoned Women, 8, 126, 127–144; and the *cabaretera* film, 143, 144; and celebrity, 128, 137–140, 144; and Dolores Del Río, 137–141, 144, 153, 228n3; gender in, 8, 128, 129, 134–137, 140, 141–144; images from, *128, 132, 135, 136, 138, 139*; and melodrama, 8, 127, 128, 129, 131, 144; plot of, 130–131; prostitute in, 127, 128–129, 134–136, 142–144; urban locations in, 127, 128, 131–133, 144, 216

Abitía, Jesús H., 2, 6, 11, 89, 193; and *Epics of the Revolution*, 14, 16–25; and *Memories of a Mexican*, 25; and postcards, 16, 18–21, 21, 25, 90; and relationship with Obregón and Carranza, 21

Adelita, La, 3

Ades, Dawn, 109

Aitken, Harry E., 39

Alba, Luz, 74

Albers, Patricia, 202–203

Alexandrov, Grigori, 97, 98, 114

Allá en el rancho grande, 84, 96

Alva, Carlos. *See* Alva brothers

Alva, Eduardo. *See* Alva brothers

Alva, Guillermo. *See* Alva brothers

Alva, Salvador. *See* Alva brothers

Alva brothers, 11; and *Díaz-Taft Interview*, 29; and material in *Epics of the Revolution*, 14, 17, 23, 25; and material in *The Life Of General Villa*, 65; and material in *Memories of a Mexican*, 25

Álvarez Bravo, Lola, 104

Álvarez Bravo, Manuel, 102, 104, 112, 114, 229n4

Anderson, Mark Cronlund, 53, 176

And Starring Pancho Villa as Himself, 3, 6, 40–57, 68; images from, *43, 53*; plot of, 41–42; and political manipulation of images, 56–57; and postcards, 45–46; and the role of vision in negotiating identity, 42, 46–50; and spectatorship, 6, 41, 42, 45, 52–53, 54–56, 68; translation of cultural difference in, 54–57; Villa's identity in, 48–50, 51, 220n7

Aragón, Alejandro, 73

Aragón Leiva, Agustín, 112, 117

Arango, Doroteo. *See* Villa, Pancho

Armendáriz, Pedro: in *Abandoned Women*, 8, 127, 128, 129, 130, 139, 140, 225n21; in *The Hidden Woman*, 146, 152, 158, 159–160, 228n5; in *Woman in Love*, 152, 227n5

artists in Mexico, 178–180, 204, 209, 212. *See also* individual artists

automóvil gris, El, 129

avant-garde in Mexico. *See* Eisenstein: and the Mexican vanguard; *and under individual artists*
Ayala Blanco, Jorge, 95, 194, 217, 224n15, 225n21
Azuela, Manuel, 111, 225n16, 227n3

Banderas, Antonio, 41, 49, 52–54, 68, 221n9
bandida, La, 151
Banquet at Tetlapayac, The, 226n2, 227n9
Becerril, Guillermo, 11, 219n5
Beery, Wallace, 52; as Villa, 72, 76, 81–84, 96, 223n6
belle Otéro, La, 154
Bellmore, Stephen, 58
Benjamin, Thomas, 209
Beresford, Bruce, 41, 57. See also *And Starring Pancho Villa as Himself*
Best Maugard, Adolfo, 103, 115
Birth of a Nation, 72
Black Crown, The, 154
Blanco, José Joaquin, 26
bola, la, 87, 225n17
Brehme, Hugo, 43, 89, 119, 158, 229n4
Brenner, Anita, 8, 99, 104–106, 120, 201, 204. See also *Idols behind Altars*
Britton, John A., 39, 176, 178, 204
Brownlow, Kevin, 57, 58, 60–61
Bruce-Novoa, Juan, 52
Buffington, Robert M., 30

Cabagne Ibarra, Tania, 196
Call for Independence or The Grito of Dolores, The, 30–32
cameramen. *See* Mexican Revolution
campaña constitutionalista, La, 16
Caporal, El, 92
Cárdenas, Lázaro, 84, 224n14
Carmen Toscano Foundation, 26, 219n6

Carranza, Venustiano, 1, 12–13, 23, 76, 78, 181; in *Epics of the Revolution,* 14, 16, 20, 22–23
Carrera, Magali M., 109
Carrillo, Leo, 72, 74, 78, 81, 224n13
Carroll, Noël, 147–148
Casasola, Agustín Víctor, 48, 89, 192, 212
Casasola, Gustavo, 48, 192
Casasola Archive, 48, 228n6; images from, *12*; photographs in, 29, 164, 165, 170, 193, 210, 217
Cava, José, 11, 219n5
celebrity. *See* Mexican cinema
chacal del Nahueltoro, El, 189
Charlot, Jean, 103, 112, 204
charrería. See Let's Go with Pancho Villa!; "Maguey" episode
charro, 8, 71, 90–92, 121, 214. *See also* "Maguey" episode; Mexican cinema; *Viva Villa!*
charro attire, 84, 94, 110, 111, 122; and Emiliano Zapata, 43; in *Let's Go with Pancho Villa!,* 74, 76, 82, 83, 88; in *Viva Villa!,* 74, 81–83
Cherchi-Usai, Paolo, 58
Choy, Rey, 223n5
cinema. *See* Mexican cinema; Mexican Revolution in film
cita de amor, Una, 126–127
CLASA studios, 14, 86, 129, 133
Colonel's Escape, The, 64, 222n17
comedia ranchera, 84, 96
comedy. *See Viva Villa!*
compadre Mendoza, El, 3, 85, 210, 214
compilation films, 2, 6, 11–38, 59, 65. See also *Epics of the Mexican Revolution; Memories of a Mexican*
Complete History of the Revolution from 1910 to 1912, The, 13
Complete History of the Revolution from 1910 to 1915, The, 13
Conesa, Maria, 101

Constitutionalist Campaign, The, 16
Conway, Jack, 3, 73, 81
Cordero Reiman, Karen, 179
corona negra, La, 154
corridos, 4, 114, 214; about Pancho Villa, 69–70
costumbrista painting, 32, 214
Cucaracha, La, 150, 151, 188, 217, 225n21

Dean, Herbert M., 51
De Anda, Raúl, 85, 92, 225nn18–19
Debroise, Olivier, 30, 42, 227n9
De Fuentes, Fernando, 3, 151; and *Let's Go with Pancho Villa!*, 70, 84, 86, 88, 89, 90, 96. See also *El compadre Mendoza*; *Let's Go with Pancho Villa!*
De la Colina, José, 181, 184
De la Luna, Andrés, 71
De la Mora, Sergio, 140
De la Vega Alfaro, Eduardo, 97–98, 114, 122, 225n16, 226n2; on *Disaster in Oaxaca*, 101–102, 103
De los Reyes, Aurelio, 11, 37, 71, 220n8, 227n3; on aristocracy and film, 29; on cameramen covering the revolution, 2, 11; on Eisenstein, 97–98, 103, 104, 124; on *Epics of the Revolution*, 14; on *The Life of General Villa*, 221n12; on U.S.-produced documentary footage, 62; on Villa, 56, 71; on the Villa-Mutual deal, 50
Delpar, Helen, 70, 178, 212
Del Río, Dolores: in *Abandoned Women*, 8, 127, 128, 129, 130, 225n21; as a celebrity, 137–141, *138*
De Orellana, Margarita, 27, 50, 57, 61, 63, 66
Desastre en Oaxaca. See *Disaster in Oaxaca*
Dever, Susan, 150

Díaz, Porfirio, 1, 29, 33, 122; regime of, 98, 152, 154. See also *Memories of a Mexican*; Mexican cinema
Díaz-Taft Interview, 29
diosa arrodillada, La, 153
Disaster in Oaxaca, 8, 98, 100–103, 226n2
Distinto amanecer, 140
documentary films. See compilation films
Doña Bárbara, 151
Doñán, Juan José, 91
Dorados, 67, 77, 85, 94, 164, 211
Dormundo, Baltasar, 195
Dr. Alt, 132
Drebben, Sam, 48, 54, 229n10
Dyer, Richard, 154

Each Man in His Time: The Life Story of a Director, 49–50, 220n8
Eagle and the Serpent, The, 12–13, 69, 219n1, 224n12
Echániz Brust, Enrique, 11, 13, 25
8 mil kilómetros de campaña, 14
8,000-Kilometer Campaign, 14
Eisenstein, Sergei M., 3, 97–124, 132, 180, 226n2; and debates on Mexicanness, 99, 118; and the earthquake in Oaxaca, 100–103, 226n3; influence of *Idols behind Altars* on, 104–105; and Isabel Villaseñor, 112–117, *115*, 227n8; and José Clemente Orozco, 99, 111, 112, 124, 147; Mexican enthusiasm toward, 100, *101*; and the Mexican image, 104, 117–118; and the Mexican vanguard, 8, 99, 102, 103–104, 109–117, 120; and the serape trope, 105, 226n6. See also *Disaster in Oaxaca*; *Que Viva Mexico!*; "Maguey" episode; Mexican cinema: and Eisenstein; *Thunder over Mexico*

Enamorada. See *Woman in Love*
Entrevista Díaz-Taft, 29
Epics of the Mexican Revolution, 2, 6, 14, 16–25, 210, 219nn1–5; and Abitía's postcards, 18–21; images from, *19*, *20*; military parades in, 22–24, *23*; viewer responses to, 37–38
escondida, La. See *The Hidden Woman*
experimental films. See *Reed: Insurgent Mexico*; *Tina in Mexico*

faked footage, 222n13. See also *The Lost Reels of Pancho Villa*; Villa-Mutual deal
Fall of Ciudad Juárez and Trip of the Revolutionary Hero Francisco I. Madero, The, 11, 26, 33, 34
Félix, María, 132, 145, *150*, 153, *155*, 188, 228nn1–2; as a celebrity, 148–151; as the *devoradora*, 151; femininity associated with, 154; and glamour, 9, 146, 149, 155–156, 160, 225n21; as the *machorra*, 151; and Mexican authenticity, 155–156, 160; in *Woman in Love*, 149, 151, 152, 154–156, 160, 227n5. See also *The Hidden Woman*
Fernández, Emilio "El Indio," 3–4, 126, 143, 144, 25n21; films by, 151; repetition in the films of, 152–153; in *The Wild Bunch*, 148, 166, *166*, 171; in *Wildflower*, 166, *166*. See also *Abandoned Women*; *cita de amor, Una*; Fernández-Figueroa; *Hidden River*; *Wildflower*; *Woman in Love*
Fernández-Figueroa, 126, 129, 139, 170, 216. See also *Abandoned Women*; *cita de amor, Una*; *Hidden River*; *Wildflower*; *Woman in Love*
Fernández Ledesma, Gabriel, 104, 110, 112, *113*, 114, 116, 227n8

Festivities of the Centenary of Independence, 26, 29–32
Fierro, Rodolfo, 79, 224n12
Figueroa, Gabriel, 4, 126, 145–146, 147, 149, 212, 214; influence of painters on, 228n3. See also *Abandoned Women*; *cita de amor, Una*; Fernández-Figueroa; *Hidden River*; *Wildflower*; *Woman in Love*
Figueroa, Judith Alanís, 114
film. See Mexican cinema; Mexican Revolution in film
Florescano, Enrique, 1–2
Flor silvestre. See *Wildflower*
Ford, John, 215
Fox, Claire F., 45
French, William E., 30
French Can-Can, 154
Frida, 196, 230n14
Fugitive, The, 215
Fulton, Allegra, 196, 198, 230n13
Funeral of Zapata, The, 17

Galán, Mario, 88
Galvadón, Roberto, 9, 145, 152–153. See also *The Hidden Woman*
García Riera, Emilio, 190; on *Abandoned Women*, 131; on *Epics of the Revolution*, 17; on *The Hidden Woman*, 156; on *Let's Go with Pancho Villa!*, 85, 89; on *Memories of a Mexican*, 27; on *The Wild Bunch*, 171
García-Romeu, Emilia, 118
generala, La, 151
Gilly, Adolfo, 18, 24
Gonzalez, Rita, 67
Goodwin, Michael, 189
Graphic History of the Revolution 1900–1940, The, 48, 192–193, 220n6, 228n6
"greaser," 3, 43, 81, 82, 213, 224n13; Villa as, 72

Grey Automobile, The, 129
Güemes, César, 148
Gutiérrez Ruvacalba, Ignacio, 193
Guzmán, Martín Luis, 12–13, 37, 38, 69, 219n1, 224n12

Hansen, Miriam, 64, 222n13
Hawks, Howard, 73, 81, 223n4, 224n11
Hecht, Ben, 76, 224n10
Heros and Sinners, 154
Héros sont fatigues, Les, 154
Hershfield, Joanne, 129, 143
Hess, John, 183
Hess, Judith, 183
Hidden River, 126, 127, 132, 151
Hidden Woman, The, 9, 145–147, 148–160, 175; citation in, 156–160; citations of Diego Rivera in, 145, 146, 158; citations of the "Maguey" episode in, 145, 158–159; disregard for José Clemente Orozco in, 146–147; and the hacienda, 157–158; images from, *151*, *155*, *157*; and muralism, 146–147; nationalism in, 146, 152–159; plot of, 153–154; and stardom, 152, 154–155. See also Armendáriz, Pedro; Félix, María
Historia completa de la revolución mexicana de 1910 a 1912, La, 13
Historia completa de la revolución mexicana de 1910 a 1915, La, 13
History of the Revolution, 25
Hoffman, D. W., photographs by, 44, 45
Hollywood: authentic "Mexico" in the films of, 212–213; inability to overcome historical attitudes, 7, 72, 84, 96; influence on Mexican cinema, 127, 129, 227n2; Mexican anxieties about, 174; relations with Mexico in the 1930s, 73. See also *And Starring Pancho Villa as Himself*;

Fugitive, The; *Life of General Villa, The*; *Viva Villa!*; *Viva Zapata!*; *Wild Bunch, The*
Horne, Walter H., 79, 160–161. See also Triple Execution
Horrors of the Revolution, The. See Orozco, José Clemente
Huacuja Roundtree, Mario, 121
Huerta, Victoriano, 1, 62, 71, 188, 220n7; media censorship under, 22; and stereotype, 148, 166

Idols behind Altars, 8, 99, 104, 119. See also Eisenstein, Sergei M.; "Maguey" episode; Modotti, Tina; *Que Viva Mexico!*; Weston, Edward
Inauguration of International Traffic in the Tehuantepec Isthmus, The, 33
indigenismo, 8, 99, 108–111
Indych, Anna, 120
Insurgent Mexico, 55, 103, 176, 177; and Reed: *Insurgent Mexico*, 180, 184, 186, 190, 229n3, 230n8
inundados, Los, 189
Izquierdo, María, 112

Jackal of Nahueltoro, The, 189
Jiménez, Agustín, 102, 112
Juana Gallo, 151

Kahlo, Frida, 196, 197, 230n14
Katz, Frederick, 40, 70, 223n19
Kazan, Elia, 212, 223n1. See also *Viva Zapata!*
Kitses, Jim, 148
Kneeling Goddess, The, 153

Lamadrid, Julio, 11, 219n5
Leal, Fernando, 104
Leal, Juan Felipe, 121
Leduc, Paul, 9, 177–194 passim
Leduc, Renato, 184, 189
Let's Go with Pancho Villa!, 3, 7, 70,

71, 120, 210; archival influences on, 89–90; bravery in, 84, 85, 95, 96; and *charrería*, 7, 71, 85, 89–96, 214, 225n18; death in, 84, 85, 94–96; different versions of, 224n15; images from, 87, 92, 93; and José Clemente Orozco, 96; the Leones in, 86–88, 94–95; plot of, 85–86; public response to, 84–85, 86, 89, 96; role of the revolver in, 94–95; Villa legend in, 86–89

Leyda, Jay, 59, 63–64, 222n14

Liberty, Daughter of the United States, 65–67

Life of General Villa, The, 6, 40, 60, 220nn2,8; in *The Lost Reels of Pancho Villa,* 58, 59, 65, 67, 221n11; Mormons in, 65, 67. See also *And Starring Pancho Villa as Himself; Lost Reels of Pancho Villa, The*

Like Water for Chocolate, 217

Lira, Migue Nicolás, 152

literary adaptations, 4, 86, 225n16. See also *compadre Mendoza, El; Hidden Woman, The; Let's Go with Pancho Villa!*

Longfellow, Brenda, 9, 178–207 passim

López, Ana, 189–190

Los de abajo, 4, 225n16

Lost Reels of Pancho Villa, The, 3, 6–7, 41, 57–68, 217; and faked footage, 61, 67; images from, *58, 63*; materials included in, 59, 221n11; montage in, 64–65, 222n15; plot of, 57–58; and period imagery, 61–65; reclamation in, 57, 64; and spectacle, 63; and U.S.-produced representations of Mexico, 62–63; and *The Vengeance of Pancho Villa,* 65, 67; Villa as a character in, 59, 221n12

Love Parade, 77

Maciel, Daniel, 182

Maclovia, 151

Madam X, 129

Maderista Revolution: A Media Triumph, The, 33, 219n6

Madero, Francisco I. See *Memories of a Mexican; Mexican cinema; Viva Villa!*

Magdaleno, Mauricio, 129

"Maguey" episode, 8, 112, 145, 214; and *charrería,* 122–123; and the *charro,* 99, 117–124; gender in, 110–111; and the hacienda, 99, 107, 117–124; images from, *106, 108, 111, 119, 123*; influence of *Idols behind Altars* on, 104–105; and Mexican peasants, 105–108; plot of, 98–99; racialized representations in, 108–111. See also Eisenstein, Sergei M.; *Que Viva Mexico!*

Major Dundee, 147

María Candelaria, 129, 140, 141

Martín-Barbero, Jesús, 126, 131, 141

McCarthy, Todd, 76, 81, 224n11

McKinney, Devin, 171

Mella, Julio Antonio, 196, 201

Memorias del subdesarrollo, 189

Memories of a Mexican, 2, 6, 25–38, 79, 164, 210; and apotheosis, 34–35; images from, *31, 34, 35, 37, 80*; and the Madero years, 32–38; making of, 14–15; meta-archival component of, 27–28; and the Porfirian decade, 28–32; rereleases of, 25–26, 220n8; and scenes from *The Call for Independence or The Grito of Dolores,* 30–32; and scenes from *The Fall of Ciudad Juárez and the Trip of the Hero of the Revolution D. Francisco I. Madero,* 26, 33, 34; and scenes from *Festivities of the Centenary of Independence,* 26, 29–32; and scenes from *The Inaugu-*

ration of *International Traffic in the Tehuantepec Isthmus*, 33; and scenes from *Ten Tragic Days in Mexico*, 26, 35–36; as a silent film, 25–26; and spectatorship, 34–35; train imagery in, 33; viewer responses to, 37–38
Memories of Underdevelopment, 189
Mérida, Carlos, 112
Merry Widow, The, 77
mestizo identity, 108–109, 121, 140, 213
Metro-Goldwyn-Mayer studios, 70, 72, 78, 82, 223n1
Mexican cinema: under Adolfo Ruíz Cortines, 152–153; and celebrity, 125–144; *charros* and *charreadas* in, 92–93; and Eisenstein, 97–98, 100; golden age of, 3–4, 8, 125, 145, 146, 160, 227n1; during the Madero years, 32–38; and nationalism, 8, 9, 107, 125, 128, 145–147; during the Porfirian decade, 28–32; during the post-1950 period, 145; *Reed: Insurgent Mexico* as a turning point in, 181, 182–183; revival of the revolution in, 126; and stars, 125, 145. *See also individual films*
mexicanidad, 5, 125, 127, 153; and charro attire, 94; and Isabel Villaseñor, 114; and *Tina in Mexico*, 198, 202–204
Mexican Joan of Arc, The, 64, 222n16
Mexican Revolution, 1–2, 209–210; access of photographers and cameramen into, 11, 12, 39; and photography, 42–45, 47, 210, 211; in postcards, 23, 45–46, 45, 46, 90, 161
Mexican Revolution in film: death as a theme of, 171–175; made during the Revolution, 11–38; and overlap with western genre, 168, 211; overview of, 2–10

Mexican stereotypes. *See* stereotypes
Mexican Telegram, The, 64, 222n18
Mexican vanguard. *See* Eisenstein: and the Mexican vanguard; *and under individual artists*
Mexican War Photo Postcard Company. *See* Horne, Walter H.
MGM studios. *See* Metro-Goldwyn-Mayer studios
Miller, Michael Nelson, 125
Miquel, Ángel, 13–14, 18, 25–26, 32, 36, 219n3
mirada circular, La, 66
Mistron, Deborah E., 95
Modotti, Tina, 102, 178–180, 204, 212, 229n4, 230nn12,14; canonization of, 197; and her exhibit in Mexico, 195, 230n11; and *Idols behind Altars*, 104; as a Mexican photographer, 195, 208; and photographs of Rivera and Orozco's murals, 201, 230n15; and *The Worker's Parade*, 24. *See also Tina in Mexico*
Monsiváis, Carlos, 142, 145, 165, 216; on audience expectations, 126; on the bourgeoisie, 29; on Dolores del Río, 137; on María Félix, 149; on Pedro Armendáriz, 159; on photographs, 210
Montenegro, Roberto, 112
Mraz, John, 85, 88, 90, 203
mujer sin alma, La, 151
Muñoz, Rafael Felipe, 70, 86
Murillo, Gerardo, 132
Mutual Film Company. *See* Villa-Mutual deal

nationalism. *See Hidden Woman, The*; Mexican cinema; *Wild Bunch, The*
negra Angustias, La, 4, 216
New Morning, A, 140
Nicholson, Irene, 15

Noble, Andrea, 3, 38; on the *charro* hat, 82; on de Fuentes's trilogy, 85; on Eisenstein, 117; on *Memories of a Mexican*, 27, 28; on new imagery during the revolution, 33; on race, 108; on the revolution and Mexico's image abroad, 93; on Tina Modotti, 24, 196, 197-198, 201
Noriega, Indalcio, 11, 219n5

Obregón, Alvaro, 1, 14, 16, 93, 178; in *Epics of the Revolution*, 18-21, 219n4
Obregón, Claudio, 9, 181, 182, 184
Obregón, José, 109
Ocañas, Antonio, 11, 13, 25; collaborations with Toscano, 26, 29-30, 33
October, 103, 229n3
O'Higgins, Pablo, 104, 118
Oles, James, 39, 104, 106
Olvera, Félix, 121-122, 227n9
O'Malley, Irene, 86, 89
Orozco, José Clemente, 96, 120, 146-147, 158, 228n3; and Eisenstein, 99, 111, 112, 124, 147, 214; *The Horrors of the Revolution* by, 96, 120, 147, 172; and *The Wild Bunch*, 9, 147, 148
Osorio, Rubén, 58, 61, 62
Other, The, 153
Otra, La, 153
Over There on the Big Ranch, 84, 96

Padilla, Félix and Edmundo, 7, 41, 58, 65-67. See also *Vengeance of Pancho Villa, The*
Palomar Verea, Cristina, 91
Pancho Villa Returns, 4
Pancho Villa vuelve, 4
Peckinpah, Sam, 9, 147, 148, 163-174 passim. See also *Wild Bunch, The*

Pérez Monfort, Ricardo, 108, 121
Pérez Turrent, Tomás, 183
Pettit, Arthur G., 148, 169, 172
photography, and the Mexican public, 43-45. See also Mexican revolution; Villa, Pancho; *and under individual photographers*
Picturesque Mexico, 119, 158, 229n4
Pinchon, Edgcumb, 47, 70, 82, 223n1
Poniatowska, Elena, 201, 202, 203
Porter, Katherine Anne, 146, 227n9
Posada, José Guadalupe, 112, 116
postcards, 2, 6, 45-46. See also Abitía, Jesús H.: and postcards; *And Starring Pancho Villa as Himself*: and postcards; Horne, Walter H.; Mexican Revolution: in postcards; Triple Execution
Prince, Stephen, 162
prisionero trece, El, 3, 85
Prisoner 13, The, 3, 85
Pryor, Charles, 60-61

Que Viva Mexico!, 3, 97-124, 214; imagery of, 118-124; influence of *Idols behind Altars* on, 104-105; and postrevolution Mexico, 98; and the "Sandunga" episode, 102, 112. See also Eisenstein, Sergei M.; "Maguey" episode

Ramírez, Fausto, 110
Ramírez Berg, Charles, 52, 126-127, 132
Ramsaye, Terry, 47
recycling footage, 65-67. See also compilation films
Red Bells, 229n3
Reds, 229n3
Reed: Insurgent Mexico, 9, 177-178, 180-195, 208, 217, 290n10; critical response to, 182-183; and depictions of war, 189-191, 195; filming

of, 181; identification between Reed and Mexico in, 184–188, 195; images from, *185, 191, 192, 194*; and Mexicanization of Reed, 184–185; and period imagery, 191–193, 195, 230n10; plot of, 181; and Villa legend, 188–189
Reed, John, 9, 39, 91–92, 212, 221n10, 229n3; in *And Starring Pancho Villa as Himself*, 42, 46, 54–56; and coverage of the Mexican Revolution, 176–177, 180; and Villa, 176–177, 188–189, 230n8
Reiss, Winold, 106–107
Renaud, Tristan, 183
Rendezvous with Love, 126–127
Revolución o La sombra de Pancho Villa, 211
revolution. *See* Mexican Revolution; Mexican Revolution in film
Reyes Nevares, Berta, 32
Rhys Price, Carl, 64, 222n17
Río Escondido. *See Hidden River*
Rivera, Diego, 149, 179, 201, 204, 206, 216, 228n2; and Eisenstein, 103, 112, 147; and *The Hidden Woman*, 145, 146, 158; Indian themes in the work of, 109; and the murals at the Secretariat of Public Education, 109, 145, 158, 179; and *The Wild Bunch*, 9
Robé, Chris, 106, 111
Roberts, John W., 76
Rocha, Gregorio, 41, 57–67 passim. See also *Lost Reels of Pancho Villa, The*
Rosario's Wedding, 92
Rosas, Enrique, 11, 26, 129, 227n3
Rosenda, 4
Rosenstone, Robert A., 177–178, 181, 186
Rosher, Charles, 58, 60–61
Rutherford, John, 69, 225n16

Samponaro, Frank N., 161
Santa, 15
Schrader, Paul, 147
Seffens material, 57, 61, 62, 221n11
Segre, Erica, 30, 131–132, 133, 213, 214, 216
Selznick, David O., 70, 224n10
Seton, Maria, 99, 122
Seydor, Paul, 164, 168, 228n8, 229nn11–12
Sharrett, Christopher, 173–174
Sinclair, Upton, 97, 212
Sins of Madeleine Bodet, The, 129
Siqueiros, David Alfaro, 9, 103, 110, 112, 195
soldadera, La, 216
Soler, Domingo, 86, 88–89, 153
Sontag, Susan, 198
spectatorship, 2, 5, 6, 61. See also *And Starring Pancho Villa as Himself*; *Memories of a Mexican*; *The Wild Bunch*
Stade, Odo B., 70, 104
Steinbeck, John, 212, 223n1
Stella Dallas, 129
stereotypes, 43, 71, 106, 107, 121, 145, 213; of femininity, 128, 155–156, 216–217; of masculinity, 52, 128, 140, 186–187; and *The Wild Bunch*, 166, 174. *See also* "greaser"
Strand, Paul, 107

Taibo I., Paco Ignacio, 149, 151, 154, 228n2
Tenorio, Mauricio, 109
Ten Tragic Days in Mexico, 26, 35–36
Territorio de Quintana Roo, 28
Territory of Quintana Roo, 28
tesoro de Pancho Villa, El, 3
¡30-30! Group, 112, 116
Thord-Grey, Ivar, 49
Thunder over Mexico, 72, 117–118
Tina in Mexico, 9, 178, 180, 195–208,

217; and exhibit in Mexico, 198, 205–206; and feminism, 201, 206–207, 208; images from, *197, 199, 200, 207*; and *mexicanidad*, 198, 202–204; and nude photographs by Weston, 198–201, 204; party sequence in, 204–205; plot of, 195–196; and Tina as an artist, 199–203
Tinisima, 201–202
Tissé, Eduard, 97, 100, 121
Toscano, Salvador, 2, 11, 89, 193; collaborations with Ocañas, 26, 29–30, 33; as a collector, 25; and compilation films, 13–14. See also *Memories of a Mexican*
Toscano de Moreno Sánchez, Carmen, 14–15, 25–26, 32
Toscano Historical Cinematographic Archive. *See* Carmen Toscano Foundation
Tracy, Lee, 73, 223n3
Treasure of Pancho Villa, The, 3
Triple Execution, 160–161, *161*, 162, 172–173, 228n6
Trueba, Alfonso, 15
Tuñón, Julia, 85, 143, 149, 155
Turner, John Kenneth, 39
Turner, Timothy G., 43, 45

Underdogs, The, 4, 225n16
United States: media and the Mexican Revolution, 2, 62, 63; and the public's views of Mexico, 7, 39–40; and the public's views of the revolution, 47; and responses to Villa, 7. *See also* Hollywood
Urueta, Chano, 4, 162, 225n16

valentina, La, 151
¡Vámonos con Pancho Villa! (book), 70, 95

¡Vámonos con Pancho Villa! (film). *See Let's Go with Pancho Villa!*
Vanderwood, Paul J., 161
vanguard in Mexico. *See* Eisenstein, Sergei M.: and the Mexican vanguard; *and under individual artists*
Vasconcelos, José, 109
Vassey, Ruth, 78
Velázquez Guadarrama, Angélica, 32
Vengeance of Pancho Villa, The, 7, 41, 58–59, 65–67, *66*
Victims of Sin, 143
Villa, Pancho: as archetypal Mexican bandit, 7, 41, 50, 59, 71; as cinematic hero, 7, 40, 41, 52, 53, 56, 67; as comic bandit, 82; disparate responses to, 7, 70; in *Epics of the Revolution*, 24; and legend, 7, 69–96; and the media, 39–68, 176; and Mormons, 65, 223n19; and photography, 44, 47–48, *48*, 220n6; as a ubiquitous theme, 210–211; U.S. views of, 50–51, 71–72. *See also And Starring Pancho Villa as Himself; Let's Go with Pancho Villa; Life of General Villa, The; Lost Reels of Pancho Villa, The; Vengeance of Pancho Villa, The*; Villa-Mutual deal; *Viva Villa!; Wild Bunch, The*
Villa-Mutual deal, 6, 39–41, 47, 72, 213, 220n1; and faked footage, 51, negative ramifications of, 40; U.S. views of, 50–51. *See also And Starring Pancho Villa as Himself*
Villa Rides!, 164
Villaseñor, Chabela. *See* Villaseñor, Isabel
Villaseñor, Isabel, 8, 98, 99, 104, 112–117, 226n2, 227n8; images of, *111, 113, 115*
Villaurrutia, Xavier, 70, 86
Vino el remolino y nos alevantó, 4

Viva Villa!, 3, 7, 70, 71, 96; and the *charro*, 81–84; comedy in, 72, 74–77, 81–84; and comic portrayal of Villa, 81–84; crowd shots in, 78, 224n9; epic spectacle in, 72, 74–77, 83; images from, *75, 80, 81, 83;* Madero in, 72–73, 78, 82; melodrama in, 72; Mexican reception of, 73; montage inserts in, 78–79, 224n10–11; notoriety of, 73–74; plot of, 72–73; Sierra in, 72, 77, 79; and Villa legend, 71–84, 96
Viva Villa! A Recovery of the Real Pancho Villa. Peon . . . Bandit . . . Soldier . . . Patriot, 47, 70, 104
Viva Zapata!, 72, 211–212, 223n1

Walker, Ronald, 215
Walsh, Raoul, 49–50, 51, 67, 220n8, 221n12
Weston, Edward, 102, 179, 204, 229n4; and *Idols behind Altars*, 104, 119; in *Tina in Mexico*, 195–196, 198–201, 204
Whirlwind Came and Swept Us Away, The, 4
Wild Bunch, The, 9, 147–148, 160–175; "battle of bloody porch" in, 161, 171–175; in contrast to nationalism, 172; death in, 162, 171–175; iconography in, 169–171; images from, *165, 166, 168, 173;* and José Clemente Orozco, 9, 120, 172, 174, 179, 201; and "Mapache under attack," 163–166; Mexican reactions to the film, 170–171; and murals of Diego Rivera and David Alfaro Siqueiros, 9; and period imagery, 160–161, *161*, 162, 164, 168, 170, 172–173, 229n10; plot of, 162–163; settings in, 169–171; spectatorship in, 162, 163–168, 174–175; and Villa, 164–165, 211
Wild Bunch, The: An Album in Montage, 168, 228n7, 229n11
Wildflower, 4, 126, 129, 140, 158, 166, 228n3; images from, *159, 166*
Wilson, Christopher P., 176–177
Woman in Love, 126, 149, 151, 152, 160, 227n5
Woman without a Soul, The, 151

Zapata, Emiliano, 1, 17, 223n1; in *Epics of the Revolution*, 23–24; as photographed by Hugo Brehme, 43, 82. See also *Viva Zapata!*
Zolov, Eric, 145

www.ingramcontent.com/pod-product-compliance
Lightning Source LLC
Chambersburg PA
CBHW022055160426
43198CB00008B/240